The Flute and The Lotus

The Flute and the Lotus

Romantic Moments
in Indian Poetry & Painting

Harsha Dehejia

Mapin Publishing, Ahmedabad

Author's Note:

Grateful thanks to Dr. B. N. Goswamy for insights and inspiration and to Shridhar Andhare, Aditya Behl, Usha Bhatia, Naval Krishna and Ellen Smart for help and guidance.

Diacritical marks have not been used. Unattributed poetry is by the author. Attributed poetry is a free rendering by the author from the primary or secondary text.

Captions:
Front jacket: Kangara, late 18th century
Back jacket: Jaipur, 19th century
Full title page: Bikaner, mid 17th century
Page 4: Deccan, 18th century
Page 5: Jaipur, late 18th century
Page 108: Mewar, c. 1640
all from the author's collection

First published in the United States of America in 2002 by
Grantha Corporation
80 Cliffedgeway, Middletown, NJ 07701
in association with
Mapin Publishing Pvt. Ltd.
31, Somnath Road
Usmanpura, Ahmedabad 380013 India
Tel: 79-755 1833 / 755 1793 • Fax: 79-755 0955
email: mapin@icenet.net • www.mapinpub.com

Text © Harsha Dehejia
Photographs © as listed
Photographs of author's paintings by
Richard Garner, Ottawa, ON, Canada

Distributed in North America by
Antique Collectors' Club
Market Street Industrial Park
Wappingers' Falls, NY 12590
Tel: 800-252 5321 • Fax: 845-297 0068
email: info@antiquecc.com • www.antiquecc.com

Distributed in the United Kingdom, Europe and the Middle East by
Art Books International
Unit 14, Groves Business Centre, Shipton Road
Milton-under-Wychwood, Chipping Norton
Oxon. OX7 6JP
Tel: 01993-830000 • Fax: 01993-830007
email: sales@art-bks.com
www.artbooksinternational.co.uk

Distributed in Asia by
Hemisphere Publication Services
240 MacPherson Road
#08-01 Pines Industrial Building, Singapore
Tel: 65-6741 5166 • Fax: 65-6742 9356
email: info@hemisphere.com.sg

ISBN: 1-890206-32-6 (Grantha)
ISBN: 81-85822-89-1 (Mapin)
LC: 2001090905

Design: Supriya Saran / Mapin Design Studio
Separations & Printing:
Ajanta Offset, New Delhi

When melody longs for lyric
and lyrics wrap around that melody
when a vriksha sings through its blossoms
and a lata tenderly winds around that vriksha
when the chataka waits for a drop of rain
and rain comes down like a blessing from the sky
when the chakravaka calls for its mate
on the banks of the Ganga
and the mate responds and longs for union
when purusha and prakriti seek each other
and finding themselves, rejoice
these are moments of romance

CONTENTS

कृष्ण श्रृंगार

109
Krishna Shringar
Krishna of Love

प्रेम रस

126
Prem Rasa
Sufi Stories of Love

श्रृंगार काव्य

132
Shringar Kavya
The Poems of Love

शणगार एवं श्रृंगार

151
Shangar and *Shringar*
Adornment and Love

A*nuraga:*
The First Glance

This is a book about romantic moments, heart-throbbing moments, soul-stirring moments, enchanted moments that have inspired our poets and have been celebrated by our artists, patronised by the *raja* and indulged in by the *praja*, moments that have enlivened courts and enriched *havelis*, moments alive with passion and radiant with emotion, sensual moments that were born with the first glance and grew with the first touch, nurtured by the first embrace, moments of amorous pleasure and of heart-rending pathos. Such moments are a very special part of romantic love between a man and a woman. But then, what exactly is romance? While no simple definition of this beautiful state exists, even attempting to define romance would be to destroy the many hues and nuances of this exalted part of love. Would you tear a flower apart to see from where its fragrance came? Could you capture the colours of a rainbow or the song of a bird in your hands? For romance is the pleasure of belonging and the pathos of longing, the thrill of a touch, the excitement of exchanging glances, it is the celebration of a specially charmed moment and the remembrance of such moments long after they have passed, it is the messages of love written in the sky and feelings that lie so deep that they can only be expressed by petals and not by words, it is an attitude that can convert a moment into eternity and the ability to live that eternity within that beautiful moment. Romance is all this but much more. It is the flute of Krishna and the footsteps of the *gopis*, it is the blossoms of the enchanted Vrindavana and the counting of lotus petals by the *ragini* who waits for the beloved, it is the courage of the *abhisarika nayika* and the pangs of a *manini nayika*. But this is not all. Romance is at once sensual and spiritual, playful and sombre, erotic and serene, coy and demanding. And yet there is more. In the midst of uncertainties romance is the certitude of love, in a world of commercial relationships bound by ethical and social norms romance is that silken thread that binds two people together. To one heart questing for love of the other romance is an assurance that this feeling will defy circumstance and surpass rationality and in so doing become a rich and beautiful state of living and being. Romance defines love but yet goes beyond it, romance is the joyousness of love but even more it is the chastening of the heart, romance is the fire of love but even more the light of the mind that glows at the mere thought of one's beloved. Having said all this, romance is ultimately the joyous dance of *purusha* with *prakriti*, of primal subject with primordial matter.

Detail, **Radha and Krishna in a grove**

see page 118

After the fashion of the oft-repeated dialogue between a king and a *rishi* we could conceive of a similar dialogue between a would be *rasika* and a *rishi*.

A *rasika* desirous of learning what is romance approached a *rishi* and asked

Rasika: Sir, pray teach me what is romance.

Rishi: To learn about romance first read *Amarushataka* and Bharatrhari's *Shatakatrayi*.

The *rasika* read these ancient poetic works and returned in a year.

Rasika: Sir, I have read Amaru and Bharatrhari, now pray teach me what is romance.

Rishi: Very well, but you cannot know what is romance until you have read Tamil *aham* poetry. Read these and come back.

The *rasika* obeyed his instructions and returned.

Rasika: Sir I have read Tamil poetry, pray teach me what is romance.

Rishi: You are not yet ready son. You must read the *dashama skanda* of the *Bhagavata Purana* and then Jayadeva's *Gita Govinda*.

The *rasika* read these two texts and returned in a year.

Rasika: I have read the *Bhagavata* and the *Gita Govinda*, now am I ready to learn what is romance?

Rishi: Not yet my son. Read Vidyapati, Keshavdas, Bihari, Bhanudatta, Ghanananda and Chandidas and then come back.

The *rasika* read all this love poetry in the *bhashas* and returned.

Rasika: Sir I have done as you asked. Now can you teach me all about romance?

Rishi: Not so soon. Have you read all the Sufi romances? Go to a *madarsa* and learn about Sufi stories of love.

The *rasika* did as he was told and returned.

Rasika: Sir I have read *Laur Chanda, Mrigavat, Padmavat* and *Raj Kunwar*. Please teach me about romance.

Rishi: You are not yet ready. Study all the Rajput miniature paintings and once you have done that we can study romance.

The *rasika* saw and studied the miniature paintings from Rajasthan and the hill states of Punjab and returned to the *rishi*.

Rishi: Now that you have studied everything I have asked you to, do you now understand the mind of Radha?

Rasika: Yes sir, I do understand the beautiful mind of Radha.

Rishi: Once you have known Radha's mind you have understood what is romance.

If the secret of coming to an understanding of what is romance lies in probing the mind of Radha, the meaning of love is in the flute of Krishna. Radha and Krishna are one, yet different, *bheda abheda*. In the mellifluous

Detail, **Radha pines for Krishna**

see page 110

sounds of Krishna's flute is the breath of love, for love is a beautiful feeling that is beyond words, and in its sweet melody is a call to eternity, for Krishna's love is timeless. As Chandidas says:

> *How can I describe his relentless flute*
> *which pulls virtuous women from their homes*
> *and drags them by their hair to Shyam*
> *as thirst and hunger pull the doe to the snare?*
> *Chaste ladies forget their lords*
> *wise men forget their wisdom*
> *and clinging vines shake loose from their trees*
> *hearing that music.*
> *Then how shall a simple dairymaid withstand its call?*

It is for this reason that in the *shringara* traditions of India, whether it be *rasa* or *bhakti*, that Krishna is so central. Krishna is at once divine and human, child-like in his pranks and sophisticated in his love games, worldly in his demands and yet hinting that to be with him one has to transcend the bonds of *samsara* and the limitations of one's *ahamkara*, boldly sensuous and ultimately spiritual, *saulabhya* or easily available and yet hidden, everpresent in our minds but yet driving us to seek him in Vrindavana so that we who love him are driven to ask, in Vidyapati's words

> *as a mirror to my hand*
> *so you to me*
> *tell me*
> *Madhava beloved*
> *who are you*
> *who are you really?*

Krishna dominates not only love poetry but equally miniature painting and when Krishna is the subject of artistic creation it is difficult to say where art ends and spirituality begins. When one is rapt in his amorous sports, at one moment one is a *rasika* and at another moment a *bhakta*, and when one is engrossed in worshipping him our prayers become love songs and our rituals are transformed into love sport. Such is the beauty of Krishna and the enchantment of his love.

In the countless taxonomies of love that are created by our poets a fundamental division is that of *svakiya* and *parakiya*. Understood rather naively as love of one's own wife and the love of another's wife, or love that is sanctioned by society and adulterous love, the true meaning of *svakiya* and *parakiya* is much more profound. *Svakiya* love is played out within the rules and dictates, norms and sanctions of society, determined by social and political factors. Governed by *dharma* and underpinned by *karma*, it has rights and responsibilities and is subordinated to the larger aims and goals of life. In many ways *svakiya* love is narcissistic, it is in the end love of one's own self and possessions, love that is as much a commercial transaction as it is an affair of the heart. *Parakiya* love on the other hand, commonly regarded as adulterous love, is outside the norms and structures of society, a love that does not have the security of the four walls of the home but thrives under the vast canopy of the sky and sheltering branches of trees, a love that does not have manicured paths but treads on thorny pathways, a romance that is clandestine for the world of humankind but open to the gods of love, a love that defies logic and reason, morality and religiosity and, above all, it is a love that endures pain, undertakes penance, suffers adversity, faces heart-rending separation, and in accepting unfulfilled longing transcends the ego in its eventual fulfillment. *Parakiya* love as exemplified by Radha *virahini* in the Hindu tradition and the romantic hero of the Sufi tradition who destroys himself in reaching for his ultimate love, takes on another hue, a different meaning. While the Sufi poets clothe this *parakiya* love with the hues of Islamic metaphor, Hindu poets have us understand *parakiya* love in the language of *bhakti*. Radha *virahini* is not only a *nayika* but a *bhakta*. *Parakiya* love is a love not of the immediate but of the ultimate, not just sensual but equally spiritual, a love that transcends the limited personal ego and reaches out to the vast and unfettered consciousness, a love whose only reward is to burn in its own fire, a love that does not have the pleasure of the oneness of *mithuna* but the joy of the *advaita* of the heart. *Parakiya* love understood in this light is no longer an illicit and adulterous romance but a higher love, a valiant *yoga* of two pulsating hearts who wish to be one. *Parakiya* love is that joyous dance of *purusha* and *prakriti*.

Romantic Moments
in Poetry

Detail, **Raas Panchadhyayi**
see page 119

yriad are the manifestations of love, endless its expressions, varied its impact on civilisation, diverse the ways in which it is understood and countless the manners in which it is glorified and celebrated. So central is love to the human condition that it touches the *raja* and the *praja*, the *bhakta* and the *rasika*, the poet and the potter; its songs are sung in the streets and its hymns are chanted in temples, its messengers walk in the corridors of a *haveli* and fly in the boundless sky, at times it is heard in the rhythm of the dancer's bells and at others in the whisper of the wind, for the *apsara* it is an elixir and for the *ganika* an intoxicant, some loves survive in the glory of monuments while others in the plaintive cry of the *chakravaka* bird that calls for its mate, for some, love is the fulfillment of a cherished dream while for others it is a culmination of a political conquest. For us in the Indian tradition *shringara rasa*, the word deriving from the root *shringa* or peak, is *rajarasa*, the king of *rasas*, the peak of human experiences, the supreme human emotion, the quintessence of what it is to be human and a celebration of that love is to extol the splendour and exult in the many nuances of that beautiful emotion.

Love is an overarching term and denotes affection and attraction between two individuals and thus incorporates a variety of relationships. *Rati* or love between a man and a woman, among the various loves of mankind, takes on different shades and hues, nuances and experiences, and within this love between man and woman one can differentiate at least three distinct strands. There is the romantic, the erotic and the settled *dampatya* love within marriage. We separate the three strands while fully recognising that they are three parts of a larger whole, one reinforcing, even anticipating the other. However, these three aspects of *rati* have their own aesthetic dynamics and equally their very special artistic expressions and therefore we feel justified in exploring only one aspect of love, namely the romantic. Fleeting but intense passion whether of union or longing, the thrill of an amorous moment and the excitement of a charged sensuality are the hallmarks of romantic love and this kind of love is best expressed in the brevity of *khandakavya* or *muktaka*, fragmented poetry and the beautiful and sensual space of a miniature painting. It does not take an epic or a mural to depict the thrill of the exchange of glances, the hushed joy of a clandestine

Detail, **A Prince at a Well**
see page 169

meeting, the expectation and anticipation of a tryst or the pathos of longing, for this can be done even with a few well-sculpted words of a poet or deft strokes of a miniature painter. Romantic love is all about that beautiful, charged, amorous, intense, albeit transient moment, it is not an elaborate love story. By their very nature romantic moments are evanescent, spontaneous, unexpected and unrehearsed and it is only the skilled poet or the consummate artist who is able to capture that heart-throbbing moment and convert it to a moment of beauty in an artistic creation. These evanescent romantic moments are complete in themselves, for what they lack in their narrative content they more than make up in their emotional surcharge, for in that momentary and intense romantic happening there is not only the outpouring of the heart but in that poetic moment is the fulfillment of one's very being. The beauty of that moment can only be captured poetically, whether it be through the lyrics of the poet or the brush of the artist. That poetic moment is alive and throbbing, moving and sensuous, a whole universe of feeling, it is a still moment within orbits of amorous movements and activities. It is sheer romantic beauty, be it of longing or rejoicing, of belonging or expectant waiting, of bubbling joy or heart-rending remorse, of anger or jealousy, of the many seasons and faces of romance, all of that and more, fully alive and present in that brief but beautiful poetic moment. It is this moment which we shall explore on this journey. Our tradition of *smriti, purana, mahakavya* and *natya*, grand epics, mythic lore, epic poetry and drama, are rich with the treasure of love stories where romantic moments are a small part of a larger narrative. Romantic moments in these art forms are subservient to the unfolding of cosmic and human drama, the expression of religious and metaphysical truths, as well as the dynamics of storytelling and therefore, will not form a part of our study.

Like any other human activity, *shringara rasa* or the artistic expression of the romantic emotion in the Indian tradition can elicit a sociological analysis and can lead to ethical questions. It is true that the people and places, the heroes and heroines, the ethos and the ambience depicted in romantic poetry and painting are those of the upper and leisured class, the royalty and the nobility. It is equally true that romantic love is idealised through the arts and is not a historical or photographic representation of love. What is also true is that the model of the romantic couple that is most often used is that of *parakiya shringara* or illicit love. This however in no way diminishes the aesthetic beauty and artistic splendour of that emotion, for *shringara rasa* is indeed a testament and document of the creative imagination of the poet and the painter and equally the re-creation of that emotion by the *rasika*. Some would argue that *shringara rasa* both in poetry and painting was meant merely as a solace for the repressed desires and passions of women in harems, and even if this is partly true it should not detract from the sheer refinement and exquisite grace that romantic poetry and painting exude. Romantic poetry and painting should be considered and celebrated on their aesthetic merits. Aesthetic truth need not subordinate itself to any sociological or ethical norms and standards and indeed, has never done so in the Indian tradition. And finally, in the Indian tradition we can never separate romantic love from the beautiful relationship of Radha and Krishna, for they are the prototypical romantic couple. In their love, sensuality merges imperceptibly into spirituality, *shringara rasa* blends into *shringara bhakti* where romantic longing breaks out of ethical norms and is no different from the human quest for bliss and ecstasy.

The Indian tradition is quintessentially oral and in that pristine bubble of air was created, preserved and transmitted our sacred hymns and our religious chants, our many songs and our countless stories. The origins of the romantic emotion are to be found in poetry, which in its primeval form was oral and from that primal art form many new art forms were to emerge. For when poetry was recited with a certain metre and melody a song was created. When that poetry was turned into a *bandish* it lent a certain emotional content or *khayal* to a *raga*. And when *ragas* were converted to *ragamala* paintings the inspiration for it arose from a poetic imagination of a *raga*. And when a song was performed on stage with gesture and movement we had *natya* or dance drama. And when that oral poetry was given a spatial dimension it became *shilpa* or sculpture. And when that very poetry inspired artists to create a painting it led to *chitra* which was visual poetry. So it was the spoken or the chanted romantic and poetic word that led to so many different art forms, each with its special aesthetic, ambience and audience. The poet was therefore not just a writer but a performer. The charmed atmosphere of hearing poetry whether it was heard by caravan traders or by royalty or nobility in a court, gave a certain life to that poetry. It touched the sensitive listeners in the innermost recesses of their minds. Monks and merchants alike heard, repeated, remembered and transmitted this poetry, as it was taken along the ancient trade routes of our country. For these trade routes were alive not only with people and products, carts and caravans, but equally with poetic idioms and images which travelled great distances on these routes. Romantic poetry for these travellers was perhaps at one level mere entertainment, but at another it was more than that, it was for them the living expression of a way of life, a world view, and above all a certain aesthetic truth. Thus, while the basic emotion of love remains the same, it is interesting that the aesthetic experience it creates changes significantly as it is transformed into varied art forms, each art form with its unique formal and structural characteristics and the ambience in which it is enjoyed.

The Sanskrit word *shringara* captures within it the many meanings of love. *Shringara* (*shangar* in the *bhashas*) is adornment of the expectant *nayika*, it is equally the sensual thrill of romance, the sentimental pathos of longing and the joy and exhilaration of union, and finally it is also *bhakti* or a love divine, of the human for the ultimate. The exploration of this romantic poetic word and its manifold meanings will take us on a journey where we will encounter the beauty of poetry, the charm of miniature paintings and finally the hushed world of the devotee and his loving devotion to his chosen deity. This will be our journey, our celebration. On this journey we will pass monuments and mausoleums which are glorious testaments to love, we will peer into the pages of the book of history which has recorded the loves and lives of our royalty and nobility and their political and social intrigue in the pursuit of romantic love, we will see footsteps of ordinary men and women who built no grand monuments but whose love stories are no less magnificent and touching, but we will leave all these behind as we pursue the aesthetics of romance in poetry and painting.

To seek a historical beginning of the emotion of love in the Indian tradition would be to try and attempt to catch the first breath of our civilisation. Historicity, in the Western sense, has never been a strong pre-occupation with us, as a historical approach brings with it concepts of linearity and causality, while for us the ideas of *anitya* and *brahat,* eternal and vast, *apaurusheya* and *svayambhu*, untouched by humans and spontaneous, best describe our world view. The Indian tradition is pluralistic and not monolithic, inclusive rather than exclusive, joyous and celebratory and it is no different when it comes to the human manifestation and the artistic expression of the emotion of love. Even so, within these qualifications the emotion of love has been variously understood and diversely expressed and there is some justification in tracing the various streams within the tradition through both history and geography.

The well-springs of Indian civilisation are in its oral traditions and this is true of its philosophic discourse as it is equally of its romantic creations. The beginnings of the romantic emotion must be searched in poetry. There are at least three major streams in the Indian river of the poetic celebration of love that we must recognise, each contributing its own unique flavour and enriching the vast literary treasure of love poetry. There is the ancient Prakrit stream, understood variously as autochthonous or earthy or folk, which expresses best the romantic side of love. Then there is the equally ancient Tamil stream which shares many features with Prakrit literature but stands self-assuredly alone and is a tribute to the creative genius of the Tamil psyche. And, finally, there is the Sanskrit stream, sometimes also called the courtly or the classical, which is the repository of mature court poetry and portrays best the settled and conjugal love between man and woman set in the framework of *dharma*. The three streams arise from different sources, follow different paths, course through different terrains and therefore must be studied separately, but since they ultimately mingle in the same river of love they must be considered parts of the same whole. The Prakrit, the Tamil and the Sanskrit streams of the Indian tradition constitute the *purnatva*, the wholeness of the aesthetics of the emotion of love for us in India.

Detail, **Rasikapriya**
see page 144

The Indian romantic tradition is largely, though not totally Hindu, as within the tradition there are the many hues of Islam, especially Sufi, as well as the variegated colors of Jain and Buddhist thought. Each of the other religions has contributed its own unique facet of the understanding of love and has expressed it variously but the overall ethos of the aesthetics of love in India remains Hindu. It is not accidental that the Sanskrit word *shringara* has within it the nuances of not only the connotation of romantic love but also that of *shangar* or adornment and equally that of *bhakti* or religious devotion. For the Hindu mind the three are a continuum, one merges imperceptibly into another, defying distinctions such as profane and sacred, denying any hierarchy, for to adorn is to beautify and prepare with anticipation and excitement for the meeting with the beloved and to love is to elevate the mind to heights of joyous ecstasy so that it reflects the cosmic *lila*, at which point love and devotion become indistinguishable. Understood through the many layers of meanings of *shringara* the three streams of love in the Indian tradition provide the bedrock upon which the magnificent artistic edifice of love in all its diverse manifestations is built.

The Indian tradition, whether religious or artistic, is quintessentially oral and the prototypical artform of this tradition is *kavya* or poetry. Poetry in ancient India was never to be silently read but chanted, sung, performed and celebrated in the company of others. Literary and performing arts were not fragmented, as they seem to be today, and it is not an aberration that the first major work on Indian aesthetics, compiled in the first century BC, was Bharata's *Natyashastra*. *Natya* combined equally dance, poetry and music, an early reminder that the various arts in India were integrally and organically related. There were no silent spectators in our artistic activity but enlightened and sensitive participants, not just an inner, solitary and exclusive enjoyment of art, but a festive and public celebration, whether it was in a *haveli* or a court or a temple. A high level of aesthetic sensitivity prevailed at that time, a sensitivity that was charged with imagination and sensuality, a world view in which life was a celebration, an outlook where sensual indulgence was a merit, when emotional gratification was raised to a fine art form, where a relationship between a man and a woman was treated with artistic finesse and every nuance of the romantic emotion was tastefully expressed and gracefully experienced. The many and diverse artistic expressions of the romantic emotion attest to this ethos of the Indian tradition, an ambience that led not only to the creation of art objects of unsurpassed excellence and beauty, but equally its enjoyment by refined connoisseurs. Ancient Prakrit poetry was enjoyed not only in *havelis* and homes but equally in village squares where people would gather, at caravan-serais where travellers would meet and caravans would take shelter for the night. Tamil poetry was part of the life-affirming ambience of the Tamil country where the chieftain and noble, poet and aesthete would share the pleasures of the arts, where romantic poetry was matched by the spirit of adventure and the joy of living, a sense of good cheer with admiration for the heroic virtues of generosity and valour. Sanskrit poetry, on the other hand, was a connoisseurship of the sensitive *nagariaka*, the urban elite and that of the cultured nobility and patronising royalty. Conforming to strict rules of grammar and rhetoric, Sanskrit poetry was created at a time of unhurried delectation of the arts, where every word was savoured not only for its meaning but equally for its sound, where creative imagination was allowed to soar to heights of perfection and each poetic image was relished and in turn led the aesthete to heights of rapture. Sanskrit poetry flourished in an era of urban sophistication, where the cultivation of a refined taste was as important as the trappings of power and prestige, when poetry flowed, conversation was sophisticated, the ambience was aristocratic and the mood was one of exaltation of *kavi* and *rasika*. It was a time when poets vied with each other to present their choicest offerings and this they did with the utmost deference and respect to their audience. There was in that era a special bond between the artist and the art lover, that of the creator and the *sahradaya*.

While scholars debate whether Prakrit borrowed from Tamil or the other way around, none would disagree that both of these ancient poetic traditions were later appropriated by Sanskrit. There always was a certain inhibition and distancing by the classical Aryans from the pre-Aryan indigenous tradition whether it was in philosophic thought or artistic creations. While, for example, the pre-Aryans were indulgent image makers the Aryans were aniconic, while the pre-Aryans celebrated the *saguna brahman*, ultimate reality rich with ratiocinative and emotional concepts, the Aryans affirmed the beauty of the *nirguna brahman*, ultimate reality devoid of thought constructs. The world of romantic poetry was no different. The Prakrit and the Tamil poets were prolific in their romantic creations while early Sanskrit poets felt that their language, *devbhasha*, which was the language of the gods, should be reserved only for philosophic discourse and religious ritual and not be used on romantic literature. The pejorative view that Sanskritists had for Prakrit is seen best in Sanskrit drama where Prakrit is spoken by women and people of a lower social order and Sanskrit uttered by men and the nobility. However, Sanskrit poets could not resist the flood of Prakrit and Tamil poetry and eventually gave in and started creating Sanskrit romantic poetry in their fashion. While Ashvaghosha who wrote the *Buddhacharita* is credited with being the first classical Sanskrit poet, Kalidasa, Bharatrhari and Amaru are three early Sanskrit poets who composed romantic poetry. The process of Sanskritisation involved a rich and free transfer of the idioms and metaphors of Prakrit and Tamil poetry into Sanskrit. The ancient poetic motifs and situations were stylised and refined and rendered in Sanskrit. What poetry in Sanskrit gained in refinement it lost in spontaneity, its excellence in style through grammar and diction meant the loss of the earthiness and a certain freshness of Prakrit. Sanskrit poets could never shake off a certain restraint in their language, there was a definite constraint in their imagery lest they give into hedonism and vulgarity, romance in their hands unfolded within a certain structure of *dharma*. While Prakrit and Tamil poetry excelled in depicting a free, sensually charged and heart-throbbing romance, Sanskrit poetry captured the settled, demure and dignified grace of courtly romance and conjugal love.

Detail, **Adorning her feet**
see page 158

Early love poetry in all three languages took the form of short or miniature lyrics that captured in a few lines the idyllic world of romance and love, the joys of togetherness and the pain of separation, of the truant lover who is abroad on account of commerce or duty to his family or clan, of romantic trysts in the forest or by the village well, of bangles that slip from the hands of a lovelorn *nayika* suggesting the emaciation of the lonely heroine, of rain clouds that excite passion and peacocks that comfort the lover, of the traveller who knocks on the door and is met by the coy maiden and as she serves him water their gazes meet, of love messengers that arrange clandestine meetings or are a vital part of a joyous rendezvous, of parrots who give away secrets or *chakravaka* birds that cry for their mates on the banks of the Ganga, and many other romantic situations and motifs. This they achieved not only through apt and pithy metaphors but equally through the use of *dhvani* or extended metaphors which aroused suggested meanings in the minds of the prepared aesthetes. In this way these miniature poems could express more than what they said on the surface, they conveyed so much more in suggested meanings than in their surface meanings, meanings that resonated in the charmed spaces where sensitive *rasikas* would gather.

Our knowledge of the social and literary traditions of the ancient Tamil country is derived from a large corpus of literature called the Sangam literature. Dated variously, a conservative estimate places the period of Sangam literature at about 800 years from the 3rd century BC to the 5th century AD. It must be noted that anthologising of Sangam poetry was late and took place in the first few centuries of the first millennium, but despite this it would be fair to say that this genre of romantic literature takes pride of place as being the oldest in the Indian tradition. A good number of Sangam poems are contemporaneous with the Maurya period and many belong to the Buddhist missionary period of the 1st century BC to the 1st century AD. Considered the high point of Tamil literature, the predominant Sangam poetry, consisting of about 3500 poems, was romantic in nature, called *aham* or *ahattinai* meaning inner or household, but it also contained heroic poetry called *puram* or *attruppadai* meaning outer or public. *Aham* poetry resembled the miniature Prakrit verses in format and imagery and had two important features: it was spoken in the first person by the beloved, the friend or the mother and thereby created an ambience where the poetic persona was given a clear voice without any inhibition, meant to be heard not only by us the audience but also by the other characters in the romantic situation, akin to the speech in a play. Secondly, *aham* poetry was always depersonalised and therefore became universalised as no names were mentioned. The landscapes in which the romance was set were of generic types rather than particular places and were strictly codified. The land was divided into five types—*kurinji* (hill), *mullai* (forest), *marudham* (pastoral), *neithal* (coast) and *palai* (desert)—and each area was associated with a specific deity, a particular flower and a certain mood of love. The landscape in Tamil poetry is thus both a place and a mood, and speaking of one evokes the other. The poetic conventions extended to other aspects of the landscape as well, such as flowers, rivers and clouds. Thus lovers' union is associated with *kurinji*, separation with *palai*, patient waiting with *mullai*, anxious waiting with *neithal* and infidelity with *marudham*. The words and images of *aham* poetry create a certain movement from the outer world of romantic dalliance to the inner space of romantic emotion, and the poetic moment mostly unfolds at the threshold of the two, for it is here that outer realities meet the inner sensibilities. In keeping both dramatis personae and the landscape generic rather than specific the *aham* poems become archetypal rather than historical. An interesting and apocryphal story is told of the origin of love poetry in the Tamil country. When the Pandyan kingdom was devastated by famine for 12 years the king asked his men to disperse from the kingdom and return only when the famine ended. When the drought was over and men returned the king was disappointed to find that there were only grammarians in his kingdom for he felt that the real relish of language came from poetry. Shiva responded to the king's lamentation and wrote 60 love *sutras* on copper-plates and concealed them in the sanctum of the temple at Madurai, and only a five year old mute boy who could interpret these *sutras* to the King. *Aham* poetry celebrates love in all its aspects—clandestine, forbidden, permissive, formal and domestic—and within this poetic ambience, the four principal characters, namely the romantic hero, the romantic heroine, the courtesan and the love messenger emerge, a foursome that defined the entire romantic genre in the literary and the visual arts for many centuries to come.

Detail, **Madanika Darpana**
see page 155

The romantic hero of *aham* poetry is one who comes from a high stratum of society and is possessed of good masculine looks enhanced by appropriate ornaments such as necklaces, flowers in his hair or garlands around his neck. A picture of a handsome, well groomed youth of the *aham* poetry emerges in this poem in *Kurincipattu*:

> *A youth appeared*
> *His curly hair was well oiled*
> *and smeared with the cool scented paste*
> *of sandalwood*
> *He drew his fingers through his hair*
> *to help it dry sooner*
> *In his hair, made fragrant*
> *with the smoke of black aloewood*
> *dark and glossy like sapphires*
> *and attracting beautiful, striped bees*

he wore a cool fragrant chaplet of various hues
strung from choice blossoms.
Behind one ear he tucked
the pretty shoots of the acoku
that blooms bright red like fire.
On his high and broad chest
smeared with sandal paste
and where strength resides
he wore a fragrant garland
In his long arms with well built wrists
he held a painted, well strung bow
with chosen arrows.
He wore an ornate belt round his waist.
When he moved
his bright golden anklets
tinkled around his faultless legs.

This unnamed handsome hero of *aham* poetry is as strong as he is heroic, well-versed in the arts and possessed of compassion and generosity and is often compared to Murugan and is therefore praised and venerated in his community. *Aham* poets maintain a strongly secular and an amoral ethos and therefore do not speak of the hero's religious feelings and beliefs and neither do they refer to his caste.

The romantic heroine of *aham* poetry, like the hero, is also young and beautiful and from the upper stratum of society. She is well-versed in the arts, especially singing. In one poem the heroine sings a tune so sweetly that the elephant in the field is overcome by the melody. Another heroine guarding a millet field sings, while she keeps a watch, for the song is useful in keeping the parrots away. And there are songs sung by the heroine which are meant to be heard by the hero who may be in a far off place so that he may return soon. An important attribute of the heroine is her chastity which is seen as fit to be revered and extolled like the northern star or the jasmine flower which she wears. The Tamil heroine is modest; her desires are seen only in her gestures, they are not spoken explicitly and her maidenly inhibition is dearer than life itself. Such a woman who worships not god but her husband and lover, possesses extraordinary powers such that she can bring down the rains at her wish. The ancient Tamils believed that failure to observe chastity could bring harm not only to the family but also to the village. *Aham* poetry speaks of elopement particularly when there is a strict mother who might thwart a marriage. The beauty of the Tamil heroine is described by a third person, usually the hero and not the poet, and rather than a detailed description, an account of her beauty is restricted to some parts of the body, leaving the rest to be inferred. Another way of describing the beauty of the heroine is by comparing her to birds and flowers as in:

The dancing peacock was like you
The guileless deer looked like you
The jasmine bloom smelt of you
Thus it was I came rushing here my dear
Faster than the cloud with rain.

Tamil poets also celebrate the courtesan although her position is distinctly secondary to that of the wife. The wife is the primary woman, the mother and the mistress of the house although the courtesan does influence the hero in many different ways. She stands at the entrance to her home or visits festivals where she can display her attractiveness. The wife's reaction to her husband's infidelity is obviously one of hurt and jealousy as is seen in:

Let him come here.
I shall seize his garland and his upper garment
and tie him down to me
with my long tresses.

Infidelity leaves its tell-tale marks on the hero and creates its own romantic dynamics both for him and the women in his life. Courtesans are as various as the heroines. There are courtesans who are abandoned and those who are sheltered and protected, those who ignore the hero's family and those who treat the hero's children as their own and give them ornaments. Often they are compared to birds that go in search of trees laden with fruits or bees that suck honey from fresh flowers while discarding the old ones.

While *aham* poets in the Tamil country set the standard in romantic literature and were to influence the entire romantic genre for centuries to come, the court of King Hala of the Shatvahana dynasty was humming with poetic activity. The Shatvahanas were leaders of caravan traders and their capital was Pratisthana or Paithan in present-day Maharashtra. Pratisthana was on an important north south trade route, and the Shatvahanas held sway over a large area of the Andhra empire from Ujjain in the north to Cuddalore in the south. The 17th leader of this dynasty was King Hala who was an accomplished poet and who during his short reign of four years from AD 20 to 24 gathered around him in his court other poets who excelled in celebrating the romantic emotion through miniature poems called *gathas*, seven hundred of which were gathered, out of several thousand, in an anthology called the *Gathasaptasati*. While recognising the primacy of the Tamil poets *Gathasaptasati* also occupies a uniquely important place in the history of Indian romantic literature. Not only is it the first extant collection of Prakrit poetry but through its miniature and lyrical compositions it exudes a sensuous charm and a pulsating earthiness, covers every aspect of romantic love, captures the many and varied delicate nuances of romance, and evokes a certain aesthetic sensibility which lingers and is copied even today.

The *gathas* were sung, perhaps even performed, and the full delight of these beautiful miniature compositions came through as much in the suggested meanings of their metaphors as in their sounds that were heard in the aesthetically charged ambience of the court in which they were sung. There is in these *gathas* a disarming openness and a passionate sensuality, a robust earthiness and a vibrant spontaneity, the many hues of romance and the variegated textures of love as they celebrate love and romance in a variety of situations. Stridently secular and amoral, Hala and his poets delight in sensitively presenting every colour and emotion, every gesture and mood of romantic love. The music and meanings inherent in the language of Prakrit are used to their fullest in these *gathas*. Hala had a penchant for Prakrit and since it was the language of the people the romantic *gathas* centered around common people like the farmer and the hunter, the traveller and the merchant. There is none of the courtly elegance or regal splendour in these *gathas* but the thrill and excitement of lovers' glances and hints of amorous adventures, the pangs of separation and the pathos of longing, the humming of bees and the chatter at village wells.

Clandestine meetings at a lonely spot are suggested thus:

> *look, the heron sits*
> *on a lotus leaf, still*
> *and motionless*
> *it shines like a conch*
> *on an emerald plate.*

Or a meeting at sunset is spoken thus:

> *when can we meet alone? (he asked)*
> *She couldn't answer*
> *with so many around*
> *but looked at him and*
> *closed the petals of the lotus in her hand.*

Intimate moments are presented thus:

> *with some effort*
> *he was able to release himself from my arms*
> *which firmly held him*
> *and I gently drew my breasts away*
> *so deeply dug into his chest.*

And the naughty parrot is tricked thus:

> *what the couple spoke at night*
> *the parrot heard and the next day*
> *began to say it all aloud*
> *in the presence of elders*

the bride blushing in shame
put into the parrot's beak
a ruby out of her earring
as if it were a pomegranate seed
hoping to silence it.

When a weary traveller knocks at the door and asks for water:
eyes aloft, the traveller
drinks the water, letting it spill
through his fingers wide, to tarry long
the girl at the door alike
makes the flow thinner and thinner.

Through 700 and more verses we are led into an enchanted world of romance and love, where neither affairs of the home nor of the court intrude into the sheer pleasure of the creation and enjoyment of romantic poetry, where there are no priests or kings to stand in judgement on affairs of the heart, where the commerce of the world can stand still while lovers exchange glances, where the pathos of longing is more important than the suffering of mankind, where there is no guilt and no penance, where the humming of bees takes pride of place rather than the chanting of scriptures, for here love rules supreme. Simple but not banal, it is a tribute to the creative genius of the poet and the beauty of Prakrit that these little gems were brought into the elegance and grace of the court of Hala. Little did they know that these *gathas* would be read and enjoyed almost 2000 years later and that they would become the aesthetic prototypes of the romantic emotion, not only in literature, but in the visual and performing arts as well. Remaining close to the soil from where it emerged the stream of Prakrit poetry remained vibrant and undiminished, even though it was to be dominated by Sanskrit for centuries. It made a second major reappearance in the post-Jayadeva outpouring of poets such as Vidyapati and Keshavdas who chose the *bhashas* once again to express a warm and pulsating romantic sentiment.

Detail, **A Nayika in a Jarokha**
see page 159

To understand the tenor and the mood of classical Sanskrit love poetry one should start with the *Vedas* where one finds hints of later classical thought and art. The *Vedas* are the seminal repository of much of the classical or the *nigamic* stream and there is in the Vedic ambience an unmistakable sacerdotal and hierarchical stamp. The *Vedas* recognise *kama*, understood as desire, to be the first seed of the mind and therefore its main driving force. It is this *kama* that leads to an awakening and an initial feeling of isolation, which gives rise to a desire to know the other which in turn leads to the awareness of *amo 'ham asmi sa tvam*, I am he, you are she. In this assertion of gender identity there is a hint of romance. However, the mind for the Vedic *rishis* is a god-searching, truth questing mind and *kama* for this radiant mind is the desire for the realisation of ultimate reality which transcends the gratification of the romantic emotion. The desire to know the other is not a mere emotional experience but has to be consummated in a conjugal relationship so that *dharma* or the moral order of the universe is safeguarded and enhanced. What is immediate for the *Vedas* is not unimportant but what is ultimate is fundamental. In this spirit Vedic *kama* does not exclude romantic love but neither does it dwell on it or emphasise it. The microcosm in the *Vedas* is a replica of the macrocosm, every action a re-creation of the primal act of creation, every movement a step in the cosmic dance of the universe. The broad and catholic vision of the *Vedas* envisages humankind as a part of the *brhat rta* or the vast cosmic order of which we are a part and which we must subserve. The Vedic, and later *Upanishadic, rishis* are preoccupied with moving away from the immediate to the ultimate, from appearances to reality and from death to immortality, and this thereby creates an epistemic duality between the here and the beyond, between life affirmation and ultimate realisation, a duality that persists right through the classical tradition. The romantic emotion for the *Vedas* is to be a prelude to conjugal love and the sacred bond between a man and a woman was to be a noble sacrament in the cosmic harmony. The Vedic *rishi* states that the goddess of speech reveals the inner beauty and deeper meaning of words only to the learned, like a wife who reveals all her bodily charms only to her husband. The Vedic ideal for humankind was the *yajamana*, the one who performs at a Vedic sacrifice, surrounded by the elders and his family, presided over by priests and in the company of the community and to whose welfare the *yajna* was dedicated. When the Vedic *yajna* was replaced by the *Upanishadic tapas*, the ideal person in ancient brahminical thought was the philosopher king, like Janaka, who was steeped in philosophic discourse even while presiding over the affairs of the state. A spiritual realisation of one's ultimate self is the preoccupation of the Upanishads, for the *Brahadaranyaka Upanishada* clearly states, *atmanastu kamaya sarva priyam bhavati*, it is love for one self that is exhibited as love for others. While elevating love to a noblesse oblige the *Vedas* and *Vedanta* have little or no room for extolling the romantic or dwelling on the erotic, they do not explore the many nuances and shades of the romantic emotion of which the human mind is capable, and do not celebrate the many pleasures of sheer sensuality. Sensuality in early classical thought was to be questioned, rejected or subordinated to religious rituals and spiritual endeavours. There was thus for the Vedic Indian a deliberate and definite distancing from the autochthonous *agamic* stream of Indian civilisation. For the *agamic* world-view the immediate, the sensual and the romantic were not to be negated or overlooked but to be joyously affirmed and enjoyed even while striving for a higher state of being. This fundamental difference between the two streams of Indian thought and art, the *agamic* or the autochthonous and the *nigamic* or the classical, can be seen even today, millenia later.

The strongly contemplative and discursive ambience of classical Indian thought was further enhanced by the linguistics of Sanskrit. Sanskrit was a language of the courts and of priests, of the nobility and the cultured but not of the common person, of the peasant or the potter. Sanskrit was *devbhasha*, the language of the gods, and in maintaining its aloofness from matters plebeian and issues pedestrian it was to distance itself from matters of the heart for almost 2000 years. Even Ashvaghosa's *Buddhacharita*, the first poem in classical Sanskrit, written in the 1st century BC, while describing the sensuous charm of women, denies the pleasures of sensual indulgence. For the son of Shakya, not yet the Buddha, when exhorted by his friend Udayin to submit to the charms of women, tells his friend "even though the beauty of women were to remain perpetual, still delight in the pleasure of desires would not be worthy of the wise man." (4.87) Perhaps contemporaneous with Ashvaghosha was Bharata whose *Natyashastra* was to become the foundational work for the performing arts. Bharata in his taxonomy of emotions recognises *shringara* as a primary emotion and goes on to offer a very detailed classification of the various stages and types of romantic love and lovers and their depiction on the stage through *natya*. It would be a safe assumption that the many autochthonous streams and folk nuances of romantic love were well known to Bharata and it was left to him to appropriate and assimilate, codify and classify the romantic emotion for its expression on the stage through *natya*. However, Bharata wrote a *shastra*—a treatise and a compendium—not a *kavya* or poem, and in this lies the strength and the weakness of the *Natyashastra*. The fact that the *Natyashastra* was elevated to the status of the fifth *Veda* is a testament to the authority it wielded not only in the performing arts of its day but equally, through its ethos of elegant and stylised emotions, in the lives and minds of the cultivated aesthete, and continues to do so even today, two millennia later. However, Bharata in enclosing the romantic emotion within the exalted but rigid space of a *shastra* and giving it an ordered and structured *vyakarana*, grammar, deprived the artistic expression of the romantic emotion of its spontaneity and uninhibited expression. In giving the romantic emotion a structure the *Natyashastra* took away its freedom, in raising it to a classical art form it confined it to a certain prescribed structure. Like the four *Vedas* that preceded it, the *Natyashastra* left its stamp on all classical art and thought and remains even today a foundational treatise, but like the *Vedas*, it placed certain constraints, regulated the expression and articulation of the romantic emotion and therefore it could not prevent a protest through an evolution of the concepts and expressions of the romantic emotion. The *Natyashastra* did to classical Sanskrit what the *Tolkapiyam* did to ancient Tamil, namely, it became a banyan tree which covered and protected creativity, and thereby gave it sanctity, but under which new and renegade growth was discouraged. Within 500 years of the first millennium, both in the north and south, there was both an artistic and a political exhaustion; romantic idioms were becoming stale and worn out and the political and cultural will

Detail, **Sat Sai**
see page 148

Detail, **Bhagavata Purana**
see page 101

to conquer and assimilate the entire country was equally weak. Creativity in the two classical languages was at a low ebb, the ritualistic Vedic literature was overpowering, the Puranas entrenched in myth, Buddhism and Jainism too austere and ascetic. This was to lead to the emergence of a cult of sensuality and pleasure seeking in the north and it was this that contributed to the emergence of romantic literature in Sanskrit. In the Tamil country, similar conditions led to the transformation of the romantic idioms of *aham* poetry to those of *bhakti* and the development of the *shringara bhakti* cult in the south. Both these movements were of singular importance to the evolution of the romantic emotion in the Indian tradition as they took the romantic idiom in two different directions, and were responsible for a significant growth in romantic art, both visual and oral. Before we look at these two movements it is important to take stock of what was happening in the early classical period of Sanskrit literature in the north.

Despite the hierarchical attitude of Sanskrit and everything it espoused, the constraining effects of the *Vedas* and the *Natyashastra* which went beyond just the performing arts, and the ascetic ambience of Buddhism and Jainism, Sanskrit literature could not remain untouched by the effervescent and vibrant romantic ethos of Prakrit and Tamil romantic poetry and so embraced sensuality and romanticism, albeit in a subdued fashion. The Gupta period and the next several centuries, described as the golden period for the arts, saw the emergence of romantic *mahakavya* (epic court poetry), *natya* (drama), *muktaka* (miniature poetry) and *khandakavya* (lyrical poetry). The names of Kalidasa, Bharatrhari and Amaru, among many others, are written in letters of gold in the genre of romantic literature of early classical Sanskrit. The canvas of epic court poetry was so large that romantic love was only one out of a multitude of human emotions and endeavours that concerned the poet. The depiction of romance in classical Sanskrit was as elegant as it was graceful, courtly and dignified, never far removed from mythology and *dharma*, with ornamented descriptions and well structured plots. The general ethos of early classical Sanskrit literature and art was to integrate sensual delight with spiritual realisation, the joy of the material with the serenity of the metaphysical, beauty with introspection, the *sundari* with the *yogi*. One has only to turn to Kalidasa, the celebrated poet of this period to be reminded that sensuality must be tempered with spirituality when he says: *rupam papavrittaye na*, beauty is never intended for sin (*Kumarasambhava*, v.36) and *priyesu saubhagya phala hi charuta*, the charm of beauty is intended for the delight of the husband (*Kumarasambhava*, v.1). Another feature of early classical Sanskrit poetry, like other classical arts of that period, was that it was intricately linked with the politics and patronage of royalty and nobility, and it arose from and in turn supported a certain elite class structure. This was its strength and its weakness. Sanskrit romantic poetry lacked the earthiness and effervescence of Prakrit and Tamil poetry and therefore did not reach or reflect the ethos of the proletariat. Romance in the hands of these Sanskrit poets was never an end in itself, in its expressions it was subdued, in its gestures restrained, in its ends it remained subordinated to *dharma*, understood both as religion and metaphysics.

The *Shatakatrayi*, the anthology of 300 verses of Bharatrhari, is one of the earliest contributions of early classical Sanskrit to romantic literature. Although the anthology was compiled around the 4th century AD Bharatrhari probably lived in an earlier century of the Christian era, which was also the time frame of Bharata of the *Natyashastra*. Bharatrhari in his poetic creations gives equal space to ethics, romance and renunciation. *Shringarashataka*, which is part of the *Shatakatrayi*, the 100 romantic verses, bear some resemblance to *Gathasaptasati* and does raise the obvious question of how much Bharatrhari was influenced by the idioms and metaphors of Prakrit love poetry. Notice how he talks about the joy of being with one's *priyatama* or beloved, lines which are reminiscent of the *Gathasaptasati*:

> white jasmine about to bloom in her hair
> sandal paste mixed with saffron on her body
> my beloved languorous in her intoxicating youth
> resting on my chest
> this is nothing but heaven paying me a visit.

Bharatrhari's *shringara* has an unmistakable undercurrent of *vairagya* or renunciation and this becomes the hallmark of *shringara rasa kavya* in early classical Sanskrit. Even when Bharatrhari speaks of the pleasures of the moon and the beloved's face he says *sarvam ramyam anityam upagate citte ne kinchit punah*, once the mind has sensed impermanence nothing at all is the same. In another *muktaka* he reminds his listeners that if one is surrounded by songs, accomplished poets and the sound of jingling bracelets of fanning maids one may as well enjoy the delights of the world, but if this is not the case then one must plunge at once into a state of meditation. Bharatrhari is never far even in his romantic verses from the dialectic of *shringara* and *vairagya*, romantic rejoicing and ascetic renunciation. At one moment Bharatrhari is rapturous about the exalted state of a loving couple when he compares perfect love to the *ardhanari* where there is no duality and no space between the lover and the loved; at the very next moment he cautions us that if such is not the case then one must be an ascetic like Shiva. In another verse the choice for a man is to rest between the breasts of a maid whose necklace snares the mind or on the shores of Ganga whose waters ward off sin. Bharatrhari's romance is always tempered with a caveat and this in many ways is the tenor and mood of early romantic Sanskrit poetry. He maintains a tension between sensuality and spirituality, between joyously embracing this world and renouncing it. It was not until the Tamil poets created the idioms of *bhakti shringara* that this tension was to be resolved. However, before we examine their contributions we must take stock of at least two other major romantic Sanskrit poets, namely Amaru and Kalidasa both of whom contributed significantly to early classical romantic poetry.

Amaru, also called Amaruka, is believed to have lived in the 7th century, and wrote a number of *muktakas* or miniature romantic verses which were later compiled under the title *Amarushataka* or the centenary of Amaru. Biographical details of Amaru are sketchy and one legend equates him with the spirit of Adi Shankara who, to win a debate with the noted philosopher Mandanamishra, animated the body of king Amaru of Kashmir and experienced love with hundred women of his harem, and returned to win the debate. As with other ancient anthologies there are many recessions and interpolations of the *Shataka*, as well as many commentaries, and the number of verses seem to vary from 96 to 115. Of the many commentaries two are especially to be noted namely, the *Shringara Dipika* of Vema Bhupala and the *Rasika Sanjivini* of Arjunavarmadeva. The benedictory verse of *Amarushataka* captures the essence and ethos of Amaru's centenary, for it invokes the blessings of Ambika whose sidelong glances are as beautiful as the bees that hover over the blossoming twigs that adorn her ear and resplendent as the nails of her hand held in the *khatakamukha* gesture. Amaru prepares for us a feast both for the eyes and the ears, for the *muktakas* create an emotionally charged world where every nuance of romantic love is explored, where the pangs and pleasures, pathos and poignancy of amorous dalliances are sensitively portrayed, where neither the restraint of *dharma* nor the restriction of society is allowed to interfere with a glorious celebration of love, for he clearly says:

May the face of the fair lady, her languid eyes, the slightly fluttering hairlocks,
the moving earrings and her tilaka partially effaced by
tiny drops of perspiration protect you.
Gods like Shiva and Skanda serve no purpose.

In Amaru's gems, and incidentally some have suggested that Amaru was a goldsmith by profession, love is not measured but experienced, it is not evaluated but felt in the deepest recesses of the mind and heart. Unlike Bharatrhari, Amaru is committed to the primacy of love. He paints the varied moods and nuances of love with words that evoke vivid colours and lines that are sonorous with music.

Give up your sulking for your beloved waits outside drawing lines on the ground,
your friends who weep ceaselessly have swollen eyes and have gone without food, the
parrots in their cages laugh or speak no more.

Amarushataka basks in a sunlit space, fragrant with the aroma of love, brilliant with the hues of a throbbing heart and within the minute compass of a verse we are privy to a universe of romance. Amaru's lovers are driven by desire, devoid of guilt, finding their fulfillment in a passionate embrace or a loving gaze. Amaru taps into traditional Prakrit romantic idioms of the anguish of separated lovers such as the rumbling of rain clouds, the fragrance of blooming jasmine flowers, bangles that slip from an emaciated arm and bodies weakened by the anxiety of long separation.

Amaru's *nayikas* have languid eyes, fluttering hair, moving earrings, eyes that betray longing and tear-filled eyes that speak of the pangs of separation. In his verses we are privy to passionate embraces and coquetry that undermines the desire for an embrace. Amaru's world of romance is inhabited by mischievous parrots that threaten to reveal intimate conversations and lamps that are extinguished by flower garlands to create spaces of intimacy, of mango blossoms and summer winds, of jingling anklets that destroy the

Detail, **Theft of the Flute**
see page 122

secrecy of clandestine meetings. In his imitable style Amaru laments the gods who churned the oceans to obtain the ambrosia of immortality when, he says, a passionate kiss would have yielded sweeter nectar.

We are not sure about the audience that Amaru's sparkling gems would have had in his day, but it is fair to assume that it was made up of cultivated aesthetes and poets. Like other ancient poetry it was probably recited and sung and even performed and not read inwardly and silently. We are not aware of any depictions of Amaru's verses in painting in his own time, but within a few centuries his verses were sculpted, making the *Amarushataka* the first romantic poetry to be represented three dimensionally. An illustration of one of Amaru's verses is found on the frieze of the stupa at Nagarjunakonda.

Khandakavya or romantic lyrical love poetry in classical Sanskrit comes into its own with Kalidasa and of these the two most important by him are *Ritusamharam* and *Meghadutam* and these set the tone for those that are to follow in the tradition. Kalidasa's evocation of the romantic emotion through his well-chosen words depict a graceful sensuality and restrained passion. The colours and the music of romantic love between man and woman resonate with the world of blossoms and birds, the moods of his *nayaka* and *nayika* are shared by the trees and the sky. It is a world where trees long for the touch of a woman as much as a man longs for her embrace, in the hushed silence of the forest there is an unspoken understanding between the song of the peacock and the lament of the separated lover, messages are conveyed through clouds and the changing seasons are understood as the changing colours of love. Kalidasa's *nayika* turns to the *kalpavriksha* or the wish-fulfilling tree to adorn herself, for it is from the tree that she gets her garments, from its sap she obtains wine that facilitate graceful movements of her eyes, its blossoms and sprouts become her ornaments and the red dye from it decorates her lotus-like feet (*Ritusamharam* 2.12). In choosing to adorn herself with various flowers, a *padma* in her hands, *kunda* blossoms in her hair, the pollen of *lodhra* flowers on her face, the fresh *kurbaka* flowers in her braid, the lovely *sirisha* flowers on her ears and the *nipa* flowers that bloom in the parting of her hair as she approaches the plant, Kalidasa is not describing just beauty but is suggesting a vital link between a woman's sensuality and the living sap of nature (2.2). The nocturnal path of the lovelorn *abhisarika nayika* is revealed in Kalidasa's words at dawn by the *mandara* flowers that have fallen from her hair and the golden lotuses that have slipped off her ears (2.11). Kalidasa's depictions are not merely adorned words but metaphors of shared sensuality between a woman and a tree, for a passionate woman for Kalidasa is not a mere mortal but a *yakshi*, the very life and spirit of a tree, and by the same token the tree is the mirror of her exuberant and overflowing passion. Although this homology between humans and nature in the expressions and reflections of romantic love was not unknown to the Tamil poets, classical Sanskrit poetry raises and refines this to a fine art form, and in so doing asserts the Upanishadic dictum *raso vai sah*, he is *rasa*, in its own unique way, which is poetic rather than metaphysical. The sap that informs and energises the plants and the trees, that makes it blossom and grow, is no different from the *rasa* of *shringara* that throbs and pulsates through the romantic pleasures and pangs of the lover and the beloved. Kalidasa continues the Prakrit and Tamil traditions of impersonality of romantic characters thereby creating a universal ambience rather than a historical setting.

Detail, **Patralekha, A Love Letter**
see page 210

Kalidasa's *virahini*, a *nayika* separated from her lover, who dominates the *Meghadutam* is a chaste, lovelorn woman, who lives in a home shorn of its beauty, like a lotus deprived of the sun (*Meghadutam* 2.20), like a solitary *Chakravaka* bird isolated from her mate, looking like a lotus withered by winter (2.23), sitting with her head resting in her hands, her hair covering her face as clouds cover the moon (2.24), painting the likeness of her beloved and talking to the *Sarika* bird (2.25), singing a song that contains his name (2.26), counting the days of her separation by placing flowers on the threshold (2.27), lying alone on her side in her bed (2.29) and with ornaments cast off (2.33). There is dignity in her poignancy, a certain grace in her sorrow, the colours of her pathos are borrowed from the wilted flower and her movements, whether of her eyes or limbs, speak of her pain even when words do not.

If the *Meghadutam* is the epitome of the *virahini* in early Sanskrit poetry Kalidasa's *Ritusamharam* is poetic testimony of how intimately the moods of the human mind are tied up with the colours and sounds of the seasons in classical Sanskrit thought and art. Of all the seasons *vasanta* or spring is specially important to those in love, for the blossoms of spring are like the arrows of Kama. Red is the colour of the spring season everywhere and it is when:

> *The mango tree bent with clusters of red sprouts kindle ardent desire in*
> *women's hearts*
> *The ashoka tree that bears blossoms red like coral makes the hearts of*
> *women sorrowful*
> *The atimukta creepers whose blossoms are sucked by intoxicated bees*
> *excite the minds of lovers*
> *The kurbaka tree whose blossoms are lovely as the faces of women pain*
> *the hearts of sensitive men*
> *The kimsuka grove bent with blossoms, waved by winds, appears like a*
> *bride with red garments.*
> *Ritusamharam* (15–20)

Vasanta is also the season when cuckoos sing in indistinct notes and bees hum intoxicating sweet sounds and travellers separated from their lovers lament. Spring, according to Kalidasa, is the perfect companion to Kama the god of love and the two together wage a war, as it were, on those in love. Kama fashions his arrow from the mango blossom, his bow from the *kimsuka* flower, the bowstring from a row of bees, his parasol is the moon, he wafts the gentle breeze from the Malaya mountain whose bards are the cuckoos (*Ritusamharam* 28).

While not much is known about Prakrit love poetry after the *Gathasaptasati* there is hardly any doubt that love poetry in this genre must have flourished orally, in homes and village squares if not in courts and theatres. Prakrit was the natural language, the language at the ground level, and despite the elevated status of Sanskrit poetry and everything it stood for, Prakrit continued to be the heart throb of the people. Sanskritists on the other hand continued to enrich the treasure house of romantic poetry through their poetic creations both in *kavya* and *natya*. This poetic activity was mainly in the north although Sanskrit had come to occupy an important place in the Tamil country as well. Romantic idioms were well established and Sanskrit poets used them with a flourish.

Bana describes *anuraga* or the blossoming of love:

> *His gesture of cupped hands is from afar*
> *and not for drinking water;*
> *he shakes his head at wonder at her beauty*
> *not from satisfying his thirst;*
> *the bristling of his flesh derives from pleasure*
> *not from water's coolness.*
> *The traveller takes to strange behavior*
> *when he sees the girl who tends the well.*

Sonnoka relates the plight of offended lovers:

The youthful lovers play no sportive game
A secret grievance lies in either heart,
with both too proud for armistice.
Each looks to other for the first apology
and while the symptoms of their love foretell
forgiveness at the end, they meanwhile waste the night.

Rajashekhara depicts the separated lover thus:

If the moon by melting might become a pool of nectar
and its mark might be therein a pool of waterlilies
by bathing there I might so cool my limbs
as to escape the torture of these flames of love.

Dimboka portrays a *sakhi* or a love messenger who says to a *nayaka*:

To dispel her pain of fever
your mistress painted you upon her canvas
although with lines that shook from trembling of her hands
Then to deceive her friends who saw her tears
she offered mango sprays and bowed her head
implying that the portrait was of the god love.

Sanskrit romantic poetry, despite a tentative start flourished in the ambience of courtly culture and within the framework of *dharma*. It established itself and was responsible for making *shringara rasa* the dominant emotion of the various arts. The romantic emotion in this classical period is expressed mainly in the literary and the performing arts, namely *kavya* and *natya*, not so much in the visual arts. The idiom of the visual arts in this period was sculpture which flourished in temples. While temple sculpture featured *mithuna* or loving couples and even erotic and copulating couples, Indian *shilpa* or sculpture laid more emphasis on fertility and sensuality rather than exploring the tender nuances of the romantic emotion. A woman was closely associated with the *yakshi*, the tree spirit, who was the source and spirit of fecundity. As the clinging *salabhanjika* on the *toranas* of the stupa at Sanchi she is the life of the mango tree, as a *yakshi* on a railing pillar at Bharhut she is sensuous and enticing, as an *apsara* she is a celestial nymph that allures even the gods, as a *surasundari* wringing her hair after her bath with a *hamsa* at her feet she invites our sensual adoration, and as a *madanika* looking at herself in a mirror she is the epitome of self-assured beauty. Fertility was important to the ancient Indians, as to other ancient civilisations, for obvious social and economic reasons. However, the importance of sons, who could not only inherit the family property and lineage, but also ensure through the correct performance of ancestral rituals the after-life of their ancestors, was a unique feature of and integral to the Hindu religious traditions. It was not until the advent of miniature paintings that the delicate and graceful expression of the romantic emotion was to find expression in the visual arts. Miniature paintings were to become visual poetry but the tradition had to wait several centuries for this to happen.

While Sanskrit poetry with the strong undercurrent of Prakrit poetry ensured the prominence of the romantic idiom in the arts in the north of the country, momentous changes were taking place in the Tamil country, changes that were to further enhance the artistic expression of the romantic emotion and take it in a different direction altogether[1]. By about the 6th century AD *Aham* poetry had reached its zenith and Tamil creativity had plateaued. Added to this there was a certain political exhaustion in the Tamil country as a result of the failure of imperial conquests to unify India. This along with the Kalabra conquest of the Tamil country and the austere asceticism that was fostered by the Jain rulers went counter to the Tamil ideas of joyous celebration and life-affirmation. The stage was set for a new ecstatic way of life that could only come from an outpouring of love towards an intimate and a personal god. Tamil singer-saints transmuted the romantic idioms of *Aham* poetry into *bhakti* songs and went from temple to temple singing these songs. So strong was the impact of these Tamil *bhakti* saints, the Alvars and the Nayanmars, that there was a mass *bhakti* movement in the Tamil country which touched prince and peasant alike. These *bhakti* poets freely used romantic idioms and conventions from the *Aham* genre to convey their love of their chosen god. The Tamil poet assumed the persona of the heroine and addressed God as she would a lover.

Notice how Andal sings of her love for Krishna as Venkateshvara:

> *My complexion, my bangles, my mind and my sleep*
> *They have all life been with me, me poor and alone*
> *I sing of him Govinda, of the cool waterfalls of Venkatam*
> *And I wait and wait, O clouds rich with water.*

> *O clouds bearing lightning within your heart*
> *Tell him who bears the goddess of wealth on His chest*
> *How my young breasts yearn deeply everyday*
> *To clasp his golden chest in tight embrace.*

Clouds, peacock, rain and lightning which were the standard idioms of *Aham* poetry are richly transmuted into *bhakti* poetry. The major *Aham* convention of speaking in the first person singular about one's feelings is strictly followed by the Tamil *bhakti* poets and all the subsidiary rules about the appropriate landscape and flowers to harmonise with the mood are also meticulously observed. The one convention that is of course deliberately

---

1. I am indebted to Prof. V. Subramanian of Carleton University, Ottawa, Canada for leading me through the nuances of *bhakti shringara*.

Detail, **Cheer Harana**
see page 114

violated is mentioning the name of the lover, who for the Alvars is Krishna. Another Alvar poet Kulashekhara writes as a jilted *gopi* when he addresses Krishna:

> You asked me to come
> To the bower of jasmine
> And you slept with another there
> And seeing me, you became apologetic
> Pretended to be scared, and you slipped away
> Holding your golden cloth by your hand
> But if you do come within my reach, someday
> I shall settle my scores with you, O Lord.

Thus it was that *Aham* romanticism was used to express a passionate love for God and this was a turning point in the course of romantic poetry in the Indian tradition, for not only did it create a higher level of *bhakti* than mere prayer and praise, but equally it took the romantic emotion to greater heights. This was particularly true of Krishna *bhakti*. The Alvars in their devotional songs were responsible for making Krishna the prototypical romantic hero. Romantic poetry from now on would never be the same for *shringara* and *bhakti* were fused into one as Krishna became the divine lover. *Bhaktishringara* arose in the Tamil country from a bed rock of romantic poetry on the one hand and a joyous life-affirming view on the other, and when this confronted Aryan sacerdotalism and ritualism along with the strong northern Puranic tradition, it led to the creation of the *Bhagavata Purana*. There is enough evidence to state that the *Bhagavata Purana* was composed in Tamil country perhaps in Pandya country, and that it attained the status of a major *Purana* very quickly. The popularity of this *Purana* not only in the south but all across the continent is due in no small measure to the richly romantic ambience that pervades it, especially the 10th chapter. Once the *Bhagavata Purana* was exported to the east and the north of India, the *bhakti* movement changed substantially, and in different ways in the north and the south, leading to very different developments in the two parts of India. However, we must return to our central concern which is the romantic emotion.

While the *Bhagavata Purana* portrays the entire story of Krishna, as a *Purana* was enjoined to do, the central event in the *Purana* of significance to the study of the romantic emotion, is the *raas lila* of Krishna and the *gopis* in the 10th chapter, a poetic creation which was to change the aesthetics of not only the romantic emotion but equally of the dynamics and epistemology of *bhakti*:

> The young *gopis* who had fallen in love with Krishna beseeched
> the goddess Katyayani with a prayer to make Krishna their
> husband. On a full moon night in autumn when the earth was

bathed in serene moonlight and the trees had blossomed Krishna began to play on his flute. Enraptured by its beautiful sounds the *gopis* left their homes to find their beloved Krishna in the enchanted forest of Vrindavana. Those who could not get away made love to Krishna through devoted contemplation. Krishna admonished those *gopis* who came but when they pleaded with him not to send them back, Krishna relented and sported and dallied with them on the idyllic banks of the Yamuna, where black bees swarmed in the gentle breeze charged with the fragrance of jasmine and *Mandara* flowers. Krishna multiplied himself and stood between every two women and by embracing, touching, casting loving glances, making amorous gestures and laughing heartily sported with the *gopis*. Finding that the *gopis* were conceited Krishna abandoned them and left Vrindavana never to return.

The enchanted forest of Vrindavana is where the love of Radha and the *gopis* unfolds, it is under the *kadamba* tree that Krishna waits, it is in the waters of the Yamuna that the *gopis* sport, it is here that his flute is heard, the birds sing, the peacock dances and trees blossom, in this lyrical space the *gopis* carry pots of milk and Krishna waits to extract his toll, it is in this sensuous space that amorous glances are exchanged and passionate embraces take place, it is here that their beautiful love comes alive. Vrindavana is not only sensually charged but aesthetically nuanced and religiously meaningful.

It is in this charmed space that the *raas lila* takes place. This is the essence of the *raas lila* of the *Bhagavata Purana*, a poetic creation and a mythic event that was to change both *shringara rasa* and Krishna *bhakti* for ever in the Indian tradition. Krishna from now on became the prototypical romantic hero of all love poetry, whether or not he was mentioned by name, and a whole new genre of romantic poetry was to emerge from this. For several centuries after the *Bhagavata Purana*, for *kavis* and *rasikas* alike, Krishna was *raseshvara*, the embodiment and fulfillment of *shringara rasa*. The *Bhagavata Purana* makes it clear that the *gopis* were ignorant of Krishna's divinity, for them Krishna was only a lover and not god, they were unaware that Krishna had descended from the mythic *goloka* to the material *gokul* entirely for their sake, and their only desire was to love Krishna passionately. However, both for the *kavi* and the *rasika*, for whom Krishna lived in artistic creations and aesthetic re-creations, Krishna was both god and lover at once, and this ambiguity between the two personae of Krishna, contributed to a heightened tension within the framework of the aesthetics of the romantic emotion. The ethical ambiguity of Krishna having an adulterous relationship with the *gopis* in the enchanted forest of Vrindavana, for the *gopis* were after all *parakiya* or married women, led to a variety of explanations being offered, the chief of which was that the dalliance of Krishna and the *gopis* was to be understood as an allegory of the

Facing page
Detail, **Baisakhi**
see page 178

relationship of *jivatman* with *parmatman*, the human soul with the divine, the microcosm with the macrocosm. It was further argued that Krishna created the entire *lila* out of his *maya*. To the ethically minded this may provide a solution to the puzzle of the sport of Krishna with the *gopis* in the *Bhagavata*, but to the aesthetically inclined there need not be any ethical considerations within a *rasa* experience. Krishna as *raseshvara* should be celebrated solely for the beauty and the charm of the *shringara rasa* that he engages in. The *rasa* doctrine of Bharata which is reaffirmed through the amorous sports of Krishna in the *Bhagavata* can stand on its own aesthetic merit without recourse to the *dharmashastras*, and *rasananda* or the bliss in the fruition of aesthetic experience can be derived purely from the aesthetic and not the ethical attributes of the work of art. Vallabhacharya in his *Subodhini* establishes the primacy of *kama* or desire, which according to him, comes first and later follows *samkalpa* or intention in matters of love, and rightly does he call that primal desire *kamapitamaha*, the grandfather of love. Ecstatic desire from which arises passionate longing for Krishna is affirmed, not rejected, by the *Bhagavata* and becomes seminal in the epistemology of the *Bhagavata*, in sharp contrast to the *bhakti* epistemology of the Gita and the *jnana* epistemology of the *Upanishadas*. The *Bhagavata* establishes the primacy of emotion in *bhakti* epistemology. The *Vedas* and *Vedanta* and the heterodox philosophies of Buddhism and Jainism that followed did not give pride of place to the recognition and celebration of emotion. The *Bhagavata* marks a turning point in making *ananda* or bliss dependent upon exultation of human emotion. *Ananda* in the *Bhagavata* is not just an exalted state of being, nor is it the serene and inward termination of *yoga*, but is emotion transformed into the rejoicing and ecstasy of bliss. In the dynamics of romantic emotion the *Bhagavata Purana* exalts the *virahini nayika*, the lovelorn heroine, and builds the entire edifice of romantic love on the foundation of passionate longing rather than the ecstatic fulfillment of love. The credo of the *Bhagavata* is that while to be able to see the beloved creates devotion, and union with the beloved leads to a higher realisation, but the anxiety of being separated after being united fosters the highest devotion. It is the same passionate longing for the presence, not just the vision of, a sensual Krishna, that defines the metaphysics of Krishna *bhakti* of the *Bhagavata Purana* and from which was to arise *madhurya bhakti* or loving devotion to Krishna and which took the form of *bhakti shringara* of Chaitanya in Orissa and Bengal and *bhakti shangar* of Vallabhacharya in Gujarat and Rajasthan. While *viraha* is the basis of *bhakti*, what separates the *bhakti* of the *Bhagavata* from that of the *bhakti yoga* of the Gita is not only the passion in the longing of the devotee but equally the sensuality of the beloved who is longed for. If the lover is amorous the beloved is equally passionate, if the devotee is given to ecstatic longing the deity who is longed for is no less sensual. The *gopis* long for Krishna and Krishna in turn longs for the *gopis*. Krishna is the paragon of sensuality and a repository of joy, and to love him is to indulge in him with all one's senses and partake of his joy. Romantic love in the

Bhagavata rests on the foundation of the beauty and primacy of sensuality and the richness and grandeur of emotional gratification of the lover and the beloved. To love Krishna is to energise all one's senses. The *Bhagavata's* concept of *navadha bhakti* arises from the homology of *bhakti* and *shringara* in the persona of Krishna. To be devoted to Krishna is to love him as a romantic lover would love her beloved. The Tamil convention of the *bhakti* poet assuming a female persona is given a doctrinal basis in the *Bhagavata* when it says that the joy of worshipping Krishna through love becomes established perfectly in women, for women alone can taste this joy and only then can a man taste it in women.

While the *Bhagavata Purana* is a compendium of Krishna's *lilas* and a source of romantic delight it is in the *gopi geet*, the songs of the *gopis*, that we find the essence of *shringara bhakti*. In their songs, at the end of the *raas lila* when their separation from Krishna is unbearable, the *gopis* address Krishna thus:

> *your love sports and captivating smile was a source of delight*
> *and even the contemplation of that is so auspicious*
> *for it so touched our hearts that remembering those moments*
> *disturbs our minds.*
> *we were drawn to you and away from our families*
> *by the sound of your flute and captivating songs,*
> *is it not treachery on your part*
> *to leave us all alone in the night?*
> *those moments spent with you in solitude*
> *under the tree where even Lakshmi resides*
> *touched our lives and made them blossom*
> *our minds are drawn towards you.*

The innocent and total surrender of the *gopis* in the *Bhagavata* becomes the hallmark of *bhakti shringara*. From these simple beginnings it was to evolve both aesthetically and theologically, resound in courts and temples, inspire poets and painters alike, and wherever Krishna was celebrated with love and devotion the songs of the *gopis* were never forgotten.

The *Bhagavata Purana* remains a corpus of seminal importance in the romantic tradition and especially in the establishment of *shringar bhakti,* or ecstatic devotion through the idioms and metaphors of romantic love. However, in the *Bhagavata*, even in the 10th chapter, Radha makes only a tentative appearance and attention is focused entirely on Krishna, while in the post-*Bhagavata* period of Indian literature Radha comes to occupy centre-stage. For about a thousand years after the *Bhagavata* the Indian artistic mind explored and indulged in the many nuances of Radha both as a romantic heroine and as a goddess. There developed both a theology as well as an aesthetic doctrine around the persona of Radha. It was a period when the Indian mind perceived both beauty and divinity in Radha—she was both

kamini and *devi*—it was a period in our history when socio-historic conditions could sustain and promote the sensuality and sacredness of Radha's amorous dalliance with Krishna. As we shall note later, in the 19th century the primacy of woman as *nayika* was to be replaced by the concept of woman as *nari* and the overt sensuality of Radha was to be questioned. A pertinent observation that can be made at this point is that conditions in the second millennium of the Indian civilisation were conducive to the artistic celebration of romantic love through the persona of Radha, conditions that were to change as the millennium started drawing to a close. These conditions were economic prosperity and stability, a certain political malaise and indifference towards political conquests and the growing presence of Islam in the country, each of which was to contribute to an ambience where the love of Radha and Krishna could be celebrated in its manifold artistic expressions. However, it must be said that while social conditions may facilitate and promote a certain ethos and foster a certain artistic mood, the ultimate epistemological commitment must come from the sensual mind in accepting, understanding and internalising a specific aesthetic sensibility. The sensuous and delicate love of Radha for Krishna was not just a cultural refuge or sensual titillation but, more importantly, a recognition of the primacy of emotion and especially that of romantic love, as a supreme state of the human condition.

It is important to stress that the romantic relationship between Krishna and the *gopis* established in the *Bhagavata Purana* which has produced the finest romantic poetry and idyllic paintings should not be considered a mere love story or a romantic drama, neither is it just a product of poetic fantasy or creative imagination. Krishna's dalliance is not just a romantic adventure but the expression and enactment of the most sublime and sensitive state of the human persona. Krishna's love is a *lila*, a divine sport, which gives primacy and transcendency to the emotion of romantic love. To love and be loved, the poignancy of longing and the pleasure of fulfillment, the anticipation and the excitement and the many other facets of romantic love in the *Bhagavata* are nothing short of theophany.

Reminding us that the romantic emotion could not be contained in any particular genre, and that it was neither the preserve of the gods nor of kings, is the refreshingly sensual and secular 11th century work *Chaurapanchashika*. Attributed to the Kashmiri poet Bilhana, the work attained wide popularity especially in northern and western India, was translated into regional languages and was illustrated as well. The *Chaura* is a collection of 50 verses held together by the haunting refrain *adyapi*, even now, which resonates from one verse to another holding them together, and creates an ambience of passionate love. The intensive particle *api*, best translated as 'even' frees Bilhana's pulsating love from the constraints of time, makes his nostalgic ruminations come alive and the beloved almost palpable. The recurring *adyapi* ensures that the poet is not describing romantic love of a distant past but a love that is felt even now, not only for Bilhana but equally for us, as we celebrate his poetry and are captivated by his amorous remembrance. Using *bahuvrihi* compounds Bilhana packs the romantic and remembered moments spent with his beloved into a charged verse full of sensuously descriptive and sonorous words. Bilhana uses images of sounds and odours, tastes and textures, and brings to life the movements of her limbs and flickering of her eyes. The opening verse of *Chaura* prepares us for the flood of sensual images that are to follow:

> *Even now*
> *I regret her*
> *gleaming in garlands of gold champak flowers*
> *her lotus face blossoming*
> *the line of down delicate at her waist*
> *her body trembling and eager for love*
> *when she wakes from sleep*
> *magic I lost somehow in recklessness.*

Bilhana's lyrics exude the fragrances of musk and sandalwood oil, body rubbed with saffron paste, mouth savouring of camphor and betel nut, flower-heavy plaited hair, the nectar of night-blossoming jasmine and love's sanctum fragrant with lotus pollen. If these fragrances are richly evocative, Bilhana presents the touch and the texture of romantic moments with equal sensuality, for these moments include soft arms clinging like vines on the neck, a lotus bed of passion, her beloved locked tight in his limbs, wine-smeared lips, lush breasts, heavy hips and bodies burning with fires of parted love. Bilhana's passionate moments have every colour of love, hot red blood from tooth marks on lips, languid body rising to a golden glow, face gleaming white like a clear autumn moon, *kohl*-blackened eyes, black bees wild in their desire, streaks of light from jeweled lamps, arms bound by golden bracelets, vermilion lips, hands painted red like young leaves of *ashoka* and body rubbed golden.

Detail, **Ragini Gauri**
see page 188

With sensually charged images such as these Bilhana's beloved comes alive and is almost palpable, as we share his richly nostalgic moments, *adyapi*, even now.

The next important development after the *Bhagavata* was the *Gita Govinda* a short song that was to have a mammoth and indelible impact both in the fields of *shringara rasa* and *bhakti shringara*.[2] The *Gita Govinda* has rightly been called the supreme example of romantic poetry in the Indian tradition and the culmination of the Sanskrit poetic tradition. Written in perfect classical and lyrical Sanskrit by Jayadeva in the 12th century, the *Gita Govinda* is a romantic work of unsurpassed beauty and unmatched elegance that is

---

2. I am grateful to Dr. Kapila Vatsyayan for initiating me into the layers of meanings of the *Gita Govinda*.

Detail, **In Anticipation of the Nayak**
see page 151

chanted, sung, painted, commented upon and performed even today eight centuries after it was composed. Legends abound about Jayadeva and his romantic relationship with his wife Padmavati, and such was the impact of his creation, that even within his lifetime he was regarded as a saint by the Vaishnavas and soon afterwards the *Gita Govinda* was to acquire doctrinal status for the Bengal Vaishnaivites. Treatises have been written about this work and there have been innumerable exegeses but our interest is mainly in its impact primarily on *shringara rasa* and secondarily on *bhakti shringara*. Among the many cardinal features of the *Gita Govinda* the three of utmost importance in the dynamics of *shringara rasa* are the humanisation of Krishna, the emergence and dominance of Radha as a *nayika* and the role played by the *sakhi* or the love messenger.

No longer masquerading as a generic *gopi*, Radha in the hands of Jayadeva is the cynosure of our attention as she humanises Krishna from a *devata* to a *nayaka* and in so doing makes the romantic emotion in the *Gita Govinda* at once sensual and spiritual. The amorous dalliance of Krishna by the time of Jayadeva was not only given a *Puranic* status but was also the subject of folk songs and ballads, songs of wandering pilgrims and the *yatras,* particularly in Bengal and Orissa of the 12th century, and there is no doubt that Jayadeva was privy to both the classical and folk sources of Krishna lore. The sensuality and the earthiness of Krishna both in the *Bhagavata Purana*, and even more so in the *Gita Govinda*, was probably a contribution of the folk ethos reminiscent of the Prakrit tradition. In fact the post-*Gita Govinda* romantic literature, as we shall see, championed the folk rather than the classical idiom. Some have even suggested that Jayadeva's lyrics are translations in Sanskrit of songs from *bhashas*. Whether or not this is true, we must in the spirit of the folk tradition, joyously celebrate the *Gita Govinda* as a magnificent romantic poem of the beautiful love of Radha and Krishna and accept human love as a reality in itself, rather than look for metaphorical or allegorical meanings in this love.

Jayadeva champions the robust and earthy love of Radha and Krishna through words which richly resound with music and evoke beautiful images. The Krishna of the *Puranas* arises from a primeval agricultural psyche and even though Krishna dallies with the *gopis* in Vrindavan his plurality as seen in the *raas lila* leaves no doubt that he is none other than the godhead. Krishna of the *Bhagavata* is the coming together of the form and the formless, the one and the many, clearly establishing himself as a symbol of divinity and not a mere human being. But Jayadeva's Krishna is none of this. He is first and last a human who grows line by line, verse by verse, *prabandha* by *prabandha* throughout the twenty-four cantos. Nowhere is the human passion of Krishna seen better than in the 12th canto when he tells Radha:

Leave lotus footprints on my bed of tender shoots, loving Radha
Let my place be ravaged by your tender feet
Love me Radhika. (12.2)
Consent to my love; let elixir pour from your face. (12.4)
Offer your lips' nectar to revive a dying slave, Radha. (12.6)
Radha, make your jeweled girdle cords echo the tone of your voice. (12.7)
Soothe the long torture my ears have suffered from cuckoo's shill cries. (12.7)
Glance at me and end my passion's despair. (12.8)

We realise that even the mighty Krishna is given to *rati khedam*, the despair of love, for he is a mere mortal passionately in love with Radha, unable to accept, *vyathayati vrtha maunam* (10.12), Radha's silence, and to seek his love's fulfillment is his *vidheyi vidheyatam* (10.10), destined rite.

Kapila Vatsyayan aptly describes Radha's unique status in the *Gita Govinda* when she says:

> Radha is not the special [*gopi*] with whom Krishna runs away
> in the *Bhagavata*. Nor do all the references to her ranging from
> the *Atharvaveda* to Hala's *Gathasaptasati* provide a prototype for
> the character which Jayadeva creates in the *Gita Govinda*.
> Nowhere is she drawn like any of her prototypes. She stands in
> a one to one relationship with Krishna whether jealous or
> impetuous, forbidding or captivating, she is the woman in love,
> separation and union. None of the nascent sketches of (her)
> character in earlier literature provides us with a predecessor.
> Jayadeva fills every limb of the character (of Radha) with sap
> rich and sensuous but human and endearing.
> (*Chhavi* 2, 1981: p. 257)

If Radha is the epitome of a *nayika*, graceful in love's fulfillment and dignified in love's separation, richly sensual in her romantic expressions and yet serenely spiritual in the realisation of that love, the *sakhi* or the love messenger in the *Gita Govinda* on the other hand plays a unique and important part as an intermediary in the dynamics of love in Jayadeva's creation. The *sakhi's* only concern is to see Radha and Krishna united and joyous in love and to this end she not only carries messages but comforts and even admonishes them. While Bharata in the *Natyashastra* and Vatsyayan in the *Kama Sutra* describe the requirements and functions of the *sakhi*, Kalidasa creates the cloud messenger in his *Meghadutam* and the *Bhagavata Purana* is replete with the accounts of the *gopis*, it was left to Jayadeva to create the artful, selfless and compassionate *sakhi*. When Radha cries out poignantly *sakhi he keshi mathanam udaram, ramaya maya saha madana manoratha bhavitaya savikaram* (2.11), O Sakhi make Krishna make love to me, I am engrossed with the desire for love, her call does not fall on deaf ears. The *sakhi* carries her message to Krishna in the fourth *sarga* of the *Gita Govinda* with the words *madhava... sa virahe tava dina*, she is distressed in your absence. Such is her state, the *sakhi* tells Krishna, that she slanders sandal, considers the Malayan wind to be poison, draws a likeness of you with musk, evokes you in deep meditation, laments, laughs, collapses, cries and trembles. Radha and Krishna function in their own aesthetic spaces but it is the *sakhi* who links the two. The *sakhi's* message is not just for Krishna but equally for us, for Jayadeva points out in no uncertain terms that *shrijayadeva bhanitam idam...sakhi vacanam pathaniyam* (4.9), if your heart hopes to dance to the haunting song of Jayadeva study what

Detail, **Krishna appeases an offended Radha**

see page 116

the *sakhi* said about Radha's suffering, leaving us in no doubt that the *sakhi* is not just a literary device but an indispensable persona in the dynamics of love and in our celebration of that love. We are not to be mere voyeurs in the beautiful romantic relationship of Radha and Krishna, but in identifying with the *sakhi* we raise, for ourselves, the celebration and realisation of *shringara rasa* to lofty aesthetic heights. The unique status of Jayadeva's *sakhi* paved the way for the doctrine of Bengal Vaishnavism and Jayadeva's aesthetics were transformed into Vaishnava theology. This short love lyric suddenly changed from *kavya* to *shastra*, a transformation unique and unmatched in the Indian tradition, leaving no doubt about the exalted status of the *Gita Govinda*. The *Gita Govinda* was created as a love poem with aesthetic foundations and little could Jayadeva have known that it would become a doctrine of *bhakti shringara*. The evocation of *bhakti shringara* in the *Gita Govinda* is a multi-step process. The romantic emotion arises in the *pratibha* of Jayadeva and it is from this creative imagination that the romantic text is created. The second is the evocation of that romantic emotion in the reader from a celebration of the text through dance and music. And in the third and final step, the reader who is chastened by that romantic emotion then transfers that same emotion in an ecstatic and romantic adoration of Krishna. However, we must stress its aesthetic strengths and leave its religious implications for another journey.

The aesthetic strengths of the *Gita Govinda* are numerous; its mellifluous language, sonorous rhythms, rich images and the delicacy of the emotions portrayed place it at the pinnacle of classical Sanskrit poetry. The images of Jayadeva are not only richly nuanced but interlinked. In Jayadeva's hands the love of Radha and Krishna is not merely the throbbing emotions of the lover and beloved but equally the sap that flows through lotus flowers and mango blossoms; the song of Govinda resonates not only in fragrant bowers but equally in the cry of the cuckoo; the whisper of their joyous dalliance is shared by the bees that swarm the *bakula* trees; when the lovers are overcome by passion they are not alone for the *tamala* tree garlanded with fresh leaves is equally overcome by the passion of musk, and the intoxication of spring through the fragrance of the *madhavika* flowers is not only for Radha and Krishna but produces infatuation even in the minds of sages. It is an enchanted world that Jayadeva creates, for these richly evocative images pulsate in a symphony of colours. From the dark blue of the night when the drama begins we move to the yellow and ochres of the midday sun and we arrive at night again, the dark night of the soul where white garlands on dark skins are the white cranes in cloud-covered skies. The dawn follows with its hues and we return to the golden glow of the morning meeting. Colours in the *Gita Govinda* are not mere poetic hues but evoke states of the mind. The love of Radha and Krishna in the *Gita Govinda* does not remain confined to the passionate emotions of two individuals in love but becomes a sustaining principle of the universe, the domain of their love expands from confined romantic arenas to cosmic spaces, the drama of love unfolds not in profane but in sacred time and thus on purely aesthetic grounds the *Gita Govinda* rises from mere sensuality to an exalted spirituality.

Jayadeva had brought romantic poetry in classical Sanskrit to a climax and none was to rival him in this genre of poetry. However, in the ethos that Jayadeva had created romantic Sanskrit poetry flourished and one poet of the 15th century who made a significant contribution was Bhanudatta. Bhanudatta, who wrote the *Rasamanjari*, continued the tradition of romantic Sanskrit poetry and built on the traditional *nayikabheda* or classification of romantic heroines. He went on to provide an elaborate taxonomy, not only of romantic heros and heroines, but of the many and varied romantic situations. *Rasamanjari* far from being an arid and prosaic document shows a deep poetic awareness and sensitivity of the many moods and seasons, the changing colours and resonances of the mind of the *nayika* and the *nayaka* which bring into play *sarojasundarachatmakara* (74), the wondrous arts of love. The poetry of the *Rasamanjari* leaves no doubt that romantic activity was no idle pastime or trivial sport but a sincere commitment and a lifelong dedication of the romantic personae, who totally believed in their love and defined their lives in its pursuit and fulfillment. To such a person the celebration of romantic love was the raison d'etre for life and living. This is the central message one derives from the *Rasamanjari*.

Bhanudatta recognises that romantic exchanges rarely need words but are even more beautifully conveyed by suggestive signs and gestures. The hero desirous of having a romantic rendezvous is asked by the beloved to meet her at sunset:

When the lover holds in his hand the golden lime fruit
the moon faced nayika puts a dot on the sun that is painted on the wall. (112)

And when Bhanudatta wishes to caution the *nayika* of the possibility of scandalmongers at a tryst he says:

My friend you may gladly proceed to the bower to see Krishna
but be careful of the humming bees hovering there during the day
and the chakoras roaming at night with their garrulous beaks

Bhanudatta uses the facility of Sanskrit in conveying two meanings with one word. For instance in using the word *sneha*, meaning both oil and love:

God created the moon faced Radha like a flame of light for this earth
As ill luck would have it this flame is dying
O Krishna! Refresh this flame with your oil/love
So that the three worlds are not immersed in darkness. (99)

Bhanudatta while providing an elaborate taxonomy intersperses his *nayikabheda* with descriptions of beautiful romantic moments, like:

The modest *nayika* is in a dilemma. To fall asleep is to lose sight of the adored one, to remain awake is to risk physical possession (9). The *nayika*, lest the morning should bring the love play to a close hastily covers the lotuses in her ears with the hem of her garment so that their opening may not announce the dawn of day (10). O traveller the sun being piercingly hot today it is proper for you to rest on the bank of the river adorned with rows of jasmine creepers entwining *tamala* trees (23). The sweet eyed *nayika* turned pale like the leaves of a palmyra tree when she learnt that the clove creepers which grew at her trysting place had shed their leaves with the advent of the month of *chaitra* (27). The deer eyed *nayika* adorned herself with flowers and ornaments, scented her curly hair and put betel leaves beside her bed. Her fair body bedecked with gold and *ketaki* flowers lighted up the chamber (66). By sweet trickery she puts her mother-in-law to sleep, covers the flame of the lamp and by producing sounds like the cooing of pet doves makes a sign to her lover to come (68).

The concluding chapter of *Rasamanjari* is called *Darshana* in which Bhanudatta describes the various ways in which the beloved is visualised, in a dream, through a picture or in an actual meeting, but for the avid *rasika* the *Rasamanjari*, in providing a vision of the variegated moods and colours of the mind of one who is in love, and the various arts and rituals it inspires, is indeed a *karna bhushanam*, an ornament for his ears.

In the centuries after Jayadeva there were two major movements in the country: the *bhakti* cult which swept across most of north India and produced its own genre of poetry in the hands of singer saints such as Tulsidas and Mira and in the field of romantic poetry, *ritikavya*. The Radha Krishna model of romantic love which was rooted in the *Bhagavata Purana* and which was brought to a climax by Jayadeva in classical Sanskrit now moved on to the *bhashas* and was expressed especially in Hindi and its dialects. The aesthetic space of romantic love was already created and *ritikavya* celebrates that love as it moves fluidly between religious devotion and urbane romanticism. The *ritikala* poets embraced the romantic love of Radha and Krishna and north

India resonated with their beautiful compositions as the love of Radha and Krishna took on yet another dimension. It is important to recognise two different strands in Radha Krishna poetry of this period. While *ritikavya* celebrated the romantic love of Radha and Krishna in sensuous and worldly terms *bhaktikavya* was entirely devotional in character. While recognising this difference one hastens to point out that *ritikavya* transcends sensuality by tending towards spirituality and *bhaktikavya* in being religious does not negate the earthly and the romantic, and therefore, in a sense, these two distinct poetic expressions must be considered two fibres of the same fabric of Radha Krishna lore or two streams in the river of romantic love. However, it would be fair to say that the audiences for each genre of poetry and of the paintings that they inspired would be different.

Radha in the hands of *ritikala* poets was the perfect *nayika* or romantic heroine of courtly love, she was both *kamini* and *ramani,* a desirable woman, and she was projected in all her amorous manifestations and romantic moods. Schomer is right in saying that "by being so many different women, Radha (in *ritikavya*) becomes depersonalised and universalised, a symbol rather than an individual. She is no woman in particular but stands for every woman in love"[3]. *Ritikavya* not only expressed the sensuality of romance but also provided a taxonomy of prescribed models of romantic love. *Ritikavya* is built on the well-worn idioms and rhetoric of Sanskrit romantic poetry that preceded it but it went on to create a distinct and striking style of poetry and hence the term *riti*, style or mannered. In enunciating a strongly secular tone and in staying clear of overt devotion, *ritikavya* occupies a unique place in romantic poetry in the Indian tradition. *Ritikavya* was court poetry and flourished under the patronage and in the courtly ambience of the many kingdoms of north India. Its words were sonorous, its lyrics mellifluous, and in the courtly ambience *ritikavya* was not just literature but a performance and in turn provided inspiration to other performing and visual arts such as dance and painting. The romance it portrayed, whether it was of longing or togetherness, was courtly not pedestrian, the ethos it created was one of graceful dignity and refined finesse within the ambience of a court or a *haveli* and not the idyllic environs of Vrindavana, the mood it painted was singularly devoid of banality, the romantic personae it brought to life were idealised and not stereotyped, and love in their depictions was not just sensual but equally spiritual. The *ritikal* poets presented a variety of beautiful romantic moments that defined courtly love; they did not set out to write a love story. The changing social conditions of *ritikal* are evident through the depiction of the love messenger in the poetry of this period. The *sakhis* in *ritikavya* were not *gopis*, playmates of Radha, as they were in earlier poetry, but women of the town, of a lower social order, who were able to move freely from *nayaka* to *nayika* as they fulfilled their role as ideal functionaries of the elite. In many

---

3. *The Divine Consort*, John Hawley & Donna Wulff (editors). Beacon Press, Boston, 1982:93.

Detail, **Krishna plays Holi**
see page 121

situations they become the point of entry for the audience in both poetry and painting. The change in the social structure of the *sakhi* however did not rule out the possibility that she would also become the object of a male gaze during the transactions of romance, but at all times she remains the poet's voice making accessible to us the world of courtly love. She makes sure that we are not mere voyeurs but participants in the beautiful romantic moments that unfold before us. At one level the romance is secret and clandestine but at another it is the *sakhi* who makes it public for us. This is particularly true in *ritikavya*. So great was the appeal of *ritikal* poetry that it did not remain confined to courts and *havelis* but eventually reached the common people of the Hindi heartland and entered the songs and conversations of the peasant and the potter, the mother and the bride at fairs and festivals. In this sense they even surpassed the appeal of Jayadeva. The lore of Radha and Krishna and their beautiful romantic love through *ritikavya* became the heart-throb of north India and it was as if the poets had recreated the celestial Vrindavana in the *braj* country. Of the many poets in this genre the names that stand out are those of Vidyapati (1352–1448), Keshavdas (1555–1617), Bihari, (16th century) and Ghanananda (1673–1760).

Vidyapati (1352–1448), who was called the second Jayadeva even in his lifetime, continues the romantic ethos of poetry perfected by Jayadeva, but makes significant innovations. Although Vidyapati was a court poet of Siva Simha of Mithila, he departed from the norm of writing in Sanskrit and chose to write in Maithili instead. This was an important departure for, in getting away from courtly Sanskrit, Vidyapati not only made poetry accessible to the ladies of the court but took poetry to the streets and people of Mithila. Vidyapati's Maithili had a certain sweetness and earthiness that endeared it to the common people of Mithila and spoke to them with a disarming directness. What is more important is that Vidyapati, more than Jayadeva, showed in his poetry a rare, tender and sensitive understanding of the heroine's psyche. While Jayadeva was a Krishna *bhakta* Vidyapati upheld Radha as a perfect *nayika* and through her reached out to every woman of Mithila. Whether he is describing the *nayika's* slowly awakening youth, her sensuous beauty, her coy charm or her naive innocence, her surrender to love and her anguish when neglected, Vidyapati presents it from a woman's point of view. Vidyapati truly had a woman's heart and the beauty of his *nayika* is not only sensual but spiritual, not just physical but also emotional, and while his poetry did not inspire painters it entered the hearts and songs of the people of Mithila. Vidyapati's romantic lyrics are earthy not courtly; in his world birds and *sakhis* intermingle with the loves and laments of the lovers. Notice how the parrot is part of the lover's world:

Awake Radha awake
Calls the parrot and its love
For how long must you sleep
Clasped to the heart of your dark stone?
Listen the dawn has come
And the red shafts of the sun
Are making us shudder.

Vidyapati sings of a fragrant world shared by bees where love is carried not just by words but by the dust of pollen:

Here is love
And there is fragrance
There the mangoes are in bloom
Here kokilas
Are singing in the pancham
The season is ripe.
Bees float in the air
Inhaling pollen
Sucking honey.
The god of love
Is secretly setting
Flower arrows to his bow.

Vidyapati describes spring nights of longing that are made up of flowers in groves, humming bees, trumpeting elephants, moonlight, sandal paste and a bed of *kunda* flowers. For him Radha has the fragrance and delicay of the *malati* flower as is very clear when he says that the forest has burst open with white *kunda* blooms but the bee is enraptured by *malati* and her honey. Vidyapati captures the excitement of spring for Radha with these lines:

Blue lotuses
Flower everywhere
And black kokilas sing
King of the seasons
Spring has come
And wild with longing
The bee goes to his love.
Birds fight in the air
And cowherd girls
Smile face to face
Krishna has entered
The great forest.

Whether in longing or rejoicing Vidyapati captures the beauty of the romantic moment for Radha:

The moon spits fire
Lotuses droop
And loaded with fragrance
Mingle in sad love
Kokila bird of spring
Why do you torture?
Why do you sing
Your love provoking song?
My lover is not here
And yet the god of love
Schemes on and on.

For Vidyapati there is correspondence between the mind of the *nayika* and the landscape of Mithila for one evokes the other, one is a reflection of the other. Thus it is that when the winds blow through the trees of Mithila even today they seem to whisper one of Vidyapati's heart throbbing songs.

In the genre of romantic poetry the *Vasanta Vilasa* occupies an important place for several reasons. Written in old Gujarati in the 15th century and illuminated by paintings the *Vasanta Vilasa* forms a part of the *phagu* literature and celebrates the longing and joys of a *nayika* in the season of spring. It reflects the romantic and secular ethos of Gujarat of that period. The *Vasanta Vilasa* is also one of the earliest works to be written and illustrated on paper rather than on palm leaves. While it draws upon motifs and metaphors of the tradition it maintains a measure of independence from classical Sanskrit poetry. Without the sophistication and finesse of court poetry the *Vasanta Vilasa* has a certain disarming joy and spontaneity. The poem revolves around the anguish of a *nayika* whose beloved is on a distant journey and opens with one of the finest evocations of spring and its effects on a yearning *nayika*. Spring in the *Vasanta Vilasa* is when:

bees have been set humming by the honey in flowers,
the mango trees resound with the cuckoo's call,
the fragrance of the lotus is wafted abroad and southern breezes play about,
plantain bowers have been erected,
thresholds adorned with coloured rice and powder,
homes have festoons of leaves,
coloured water sprinkled,
swings with golden chairs have been fastened to champaka trees,
the water is delightful from streams of musk and currents of camphor,
women fill bowls with sandal paste to adorn themselves and
Kama rules as vasanta presides
bees tinged with saffron circle above the bakula buds
the buds of the champaka trees have blossomed with golden colour
like a stream of flame to light Kama's way.

The splendour of spring is unbearable to a lovelorn *nayika* for whom:
the necklace is a burden, the ornaments are hot coals,
sandal does not remove her care and the moon gives her no pleasure,
clothes do not please her, food is only leavings, water does not taste sweet,
Kama agitates her heart day and night,
the night does not pass at all.

The importance of the *Vasanta Vilasa* lies in its being a mediaeval document of an earthy romantic emotion in a *bhasha*, demonstrating that this genre of poetry while borrowing from classical sources stayed self-assuredly on its own, and played an important part in the lives of the non-Sanskrit speaking people of India, and leaves no doubt that the celebration of the romantic emotion was without any boundaries.

While it was none other than Bharata who in his *Natyashastra* had touched upon the subject of *nayikabheda* and provided a typology of the different types of romantic heroines it was left to *ritikal* poets to give substance to it and enlarge it to a delightful taxonomy. Such a taxonomy was not merely an arid compendium of people and places, or an album of romantic events, it was like a bouquet of flowers from the garden of love. It helped in not only underscoring the many sides of romantic love and highlighting the delicate and tender facets of the mind of the heroine but it also led to a beautiful and deep understanding of the various shades and nuances of the romantic emotion itself. A defining feature of the romantic emotion is that it is uncertain, fleeting and transient, the beauty is in the present moment as there is no promise of the future. It is this uncertainty, as much as the various types of heroes and heroines, that creates the endless situations and moods of romantic love and leads to elaborate taxonomies. The romantic emotion was the living *rasa* of the heroine that animated her like the sap of the tree, and just as a tree responded to the whisper of the winds and the rhythms of the earth, the changing of the seasons and the loving care of the gardener who tended it, the *nayika's* persona was equally alive and sensitive to the smallest change in the ambience, circumstance and moods of love. For, many indeed are the colours of romance, variegated its hues, various its responses, and numerous its manifestations. The poetry of *nayikabheda* takes us inside the mind of the *nayika* and forms an important part of the treasure of *shringara rasa kavya*.

Keshavdas (1555–1617) is the prototypical *riti* poet. He was the court poet of an Orchha prince Indrajit and it was there that he produced his monumental work *Rasikapriya*. *Rasikapriya* is an encyclopedic compendium and taxonomy of *nayakas* and *nayikas*, their moods, meetings and messengers and is considered a *lakshan grantha*, foundational work, in *riti kavya*. While rooted in Sanskrit rhetoric Keshavdas makes a significant contribution to romantic literature in choosing to express himself though *brajbhasha*, a language which is ideally suited to conveying the earthiness and sweetness of romance. Using variable metres and appropriate metaphors, through

Detail, **Nayikas Shangar**
see page 152

enunciation of romantic theory and demonstration of how it can be put into practice, Keshavdas makes every nuance of romantic love come alive through melody and meaning in his verse. Keshavdas clearly enters the mind of the *nayaka* and the *nayika* for he expresses the hidden as well as the manifest features of every nuance of love. His is an enchanted world of the joys of dalliance and the pangs of pathos, the muted voices of messengers and the whispers of lovers, the arrogant heroine and the truant hero, of clandestine meetings in groves or in the comfort of a *haveli*, of words on *champa* leaves and the sanctity of *tulsi* groves. In describing the *ashtanayikas*, the eight types of romantic heroines, Keshavdas uses the inflections of *brajbhasha* to great advantage. While painting the variegated and tender emotions of the *ashtanayikas* Keshavdas not only shows an understanding of feminine sensitivity, but beautifully connects that pulsating love of the heroine to the world around the *nayika*, for the love that pulsates in his lovers is no different from the sap that enlivens the world around them. Romantic love for Keshavdas is not a trivial or titillating emotion, not just a psychological state but the animating principle of life itself. He offers this taxonomy of the *ashtanayikas*:

> *The svadhinapatika, who is greatly loved by her beloved gets her soles scrubbed by pumice stone and painted red by her beloved and who is kept in the mirror of his heart as betel leaves in a basket.*
>
> *The ukta, who is troubled because her lover is absent, worries about his health or the rain in the middle of the night which has kept him from coming.*
>
> *The vasakasajja who adorns herself and waits expectantly around sandalwood trees entwined by clove creepers and yearns for her beloved with every sound of the breeze and leaves and looks like rati in a tulsi grove.*
>
> *The abhisandhita, the heroine who is arrogant when approached, does not glance at him even when he falls at her feet but thereafter is sorrowful without him, and finds that even sandalwood, lotus and moon burn her body.*
>
> *The khandita who reproves her beloved when he misses his rendezvous and arrives only in the morning, and whose eyes reddened by the henna of another raises suspicions of unfaithfulness.*
>
> *The prositapatika, whose beloved is away on business but who will return, but whose heart is hard like a log of wood which does not burn even with the fire of separation.*

The vipralabdha, whose beloved does not come in spite of a tryst arranged
by her sakhi, finds her sixteen adornments are like embers and flowers have
turned to darts and gardens to fearful forests
And inscribes some words on a champa leaf.
The abhisarika, who sets out to meet her beloved. When driven by love
she is premabhisarika, by pride garvabhisarika and by passion
kamabhisarika. Adorning herself with sandal paste and a garland of
flowers she makes the chakors forget the pain of parting, ignoring snakes
entangled around her feet and the thunder of clouds, she is driven to him.

Keshavdas' poetry is never far from *puranic* myth, indicating that for our romantic poets the sacred and the secular were one continuum. Mortals share the same love that move our gods and goddesses. In a speech by a lover who dreams of his beloved he says that his *nayika* is as gentle in her speech as Sarasvati, as loving as Rati and as dedicated as Parvati and more beautiful than Menaka and Urvashi.

The strength of *Rasikapriya* lies in its encyclopedic presentation of lovers, a treasury of their emotional states, a taxonomy of their meetings and messengers, an atlas of their joyous togetherness and their painful separation and a veritable anthology of variegated amorous situations and states. Thus it was that it became so popular with kings and nobility and provided an inspiration for miniature painters who found in it endless themes and countless motifs to depict the many facets of romantic love.

Following in the footsteps of Keshavdas was another notable *ritikal* poet, Matiram who lived in the mid-17th century, was a court poet of Rao Bhav Singh of Bundi and among his works are *Rasaraj, Lalit Lalam* and *Alankar Panchashika.* Matiram continues the style and tenor of his predecessor and outlines in a taxonomic fashion the various *nayakas* and *nayikas.* In a beautiful passage he describes the beauty of Radha's face thus:

it was none other than Brahma who has created the face of Radha
a face so beautiful that it caused the moon to feel jealous
one night the moon spread its rays to steal Radha's beauty
but having been caught committing this theft
was arraigned in Brahma's court
and was punished with black spots on its face.

Another significant *ritikal* poet whose gem-like verses shine in the repertoire of *riti kavya* was Bihari. Born towards the end of the 16th century in Orcha and having spent his creative life at Agra and Amber, Bihari's couplets it is said may appear insignificant but inflict a deep wound like the arrow of a hunter. For Bihari love was not mere sensual gratification but a spiritual outpouring for as he says: "The spoken words are of no account for they are false. That is why Brahma has made eyes for expressing what lies in the heart". In another *doha* Bihari says:

I never saw such eyes with glances more piercing
than Kama's arrows;
O Krishna their loveliness indeed surpasses
the eyes of a gazelle.

And then again:
Though without collyrium the coquettish eyes of that girl
adept in the art of love making
have put to shame those of the khanjana bird
even the lotus pales before their loveliness.

Facing page:
Detail, **Reflections of Love**
see page 163

Colours were important to Bihari for they conveyed more than words could
speak:
Her pink cheek is so tender and fragrant
that the rose petal that got stuck to it
could not be distinguished.

Also:
How perfectly the yellow champa garland blends with your hue dear girl
It can be seen only when its flowers fade.

And in this invocatory verse Bihari brilliantly uses the language of colours to
pay homage to Radha:
Radha take away the pain of existence, the cycle of the world, from me
you whose golden reflection turns Krishna's blue complexion into a glowing green

In other *dohas* Bihari uses words as a painter would use colours and
says that the radiance of her limbs makes the white *malati* flowers turn
golden, the crimson-streaked eyes are like twilight, the river turns a saffron
yellow whenever she plunges into it, her limbs glisten like yellow jasmine,
her feet are redder than lac dye, her ruby red feet shed dust as a *dhupariya*
flower has blossomed at each step and her ravishing eyes are as dark as black
bees.

Bihari follows all the usual conventions of *riti kavya* to describe the
beauty of a *nayika* but for Bihari sensuality was never far from spirituality as
the human body was only a reflection of the world around it:
Her dazzling splendour shining through her flimsy dress
is breathtaking as a kalpa tree
reflected leaf and branch in the waters of the placid ocean.

Bihari wrote in *brajbhasha* and he colours his words, ornaments his
phrases and imparts a certain fragrance to his verses, and his *dohas*, brief but
elegant, are sheer music to our ears as they weave through every situation and
mood of romantic love. His *Sat Sai* was a landmark in romantic poetry for not

only was it copied, translated and commented upon, it also inspired miniature artists to render it into paintings, and it can be said that if Keshavdas' *Rasikapriya* gave painters endless romantic situations Bihari's *Sat Sai* provided inspiration for lyrical representations of romantic love.

Ghanananda, a later *ritikal* poet, broke away from the rigid conventions of *ritikavya* and brought a certain earthy freshness and bubbling spontaneity to romantic poetry. It is said that he was in love with a courtesan by the name of Sujan and that his poetry was not mere poetic composition but a record of his personal heart-throbbing romantic experiences and in turn he wrote for that specially endowed *rasika*:

who is forever drenched
in the sweet essence of love
whom meeting vexes
as much as parting
who can master language
yet not be enslaved by convention
such a man alone
can enjoy
Ghanananda's verse.

Ghanananda's disarming lyrics bring the passion and the power of the romantic gaze:

My lover's face is like a lotus flower
round which my eyes like black bees
roam longingly
and my eyes gazing on it
are as a lovelorn chakor
gazes on the moon.
Even before we met
my eyes bartered me to my lover
our love is no longer secret
I am defamed everywhere.
Ever since my eyes have seen my lover
though open
they see nothing but him.
He wounds me with his glances
and shows no pity
he remains indifferent
whether I laugh or weep.
Lover when you were with me
my eyes drank your beauty and lived
but now when you are gone
those very eyes burn with anxiety.

Although romantic moments are fleeting, the lover's dedication and commitment to his beloved in Ghanananda's words are steadfast:

The playful chatak
loves only the svati rain
compared to it
nectar seems like poison to him
so constant is he
to his vow.
The lily clusters bloom when the sun rises
and in its absence
even the light of the moon
seems like darkness to the lilies.

Many are the hues of Ghanananda's *nayika* and his words are washed by her colours:

Your lips are ever red
your laughter's brilliance has the splendour of camphor
millions of sweetly scented things
mingle in your perfumed breath
from the loveliness of each of your limbs
Holi's coloured water ever rains.

Ghanananda's well-sculpted words full of the colours and sounds of romance, the gaze and the touch of love, the longing and loving of throbbing hearts makes those beautiful romantic moments come alive.

A genre of romantic poetry that is unique in its concept and expression alike is the *barahamasa* or seasonal poetry of the twelve months. It is not insignificant that Vedic word *rta* and the Sanskrit *ritu* come from the same etymologic root which denotes cosmic order through movement or growth. If the Indian mind perceives a certain order in the movements of the universe it also feels an attachment with the environment and a living link with the changing seasons. Poets like Kalisada and Harshavardhana have celebrated the seasons in their compositions. The *Ritusamhara* is at once a poem of seasons, as of love, while the *Meghadutam*, is a prime example of *dutakavya*, where there is a beautiful depiction of the cloud acting as a love messenger. The seasons for us have a living presence embodying the mysterious essence of growth and decay and regrowth, tied to the movements of the cosmos and the rhythms of the earth, touching the deepest longings and aspirations, moods and feelings of humans, providing a scenario upon which we celebrate and understand life and love. Of all human emotions, that of romantic love is closely tied to the changing seasons, each month bringing a special message to the beloved, every season a special reminder of the joys of love and longing, the changing seasons reflecting the varying moods of romantic love and the songs of the seasons echoing a melody that resonates through the heart of the lover and the beloved. *Shadrituvarnan* or the description of the six seasons, *vasanta, grishma, varsha, hemanta, shravan* and *shisira* is an important part of the *kavya* literature in Sanskrit. However, Sanskrit literature did not have *barahmasa* poetry. It was *apabhramsha* literature, precursor of Hindi, that developed a rich description of the seasons and tied it to romantic love. In this genre there is *chaumasa*, poetry which had either four or six seasons or *barahmasa* which was a description of the seasons of the twelve months. The oral *barahmasa* of the *bhashas* later becomes an important part of the literary poetic tradition, both secular as well as Hindu, Jain and Sufi religious poetry. While religious *barahmasa* remains didactic in nature and was used to impart religious instruction, the village *chaumasa* and *barahmasa* were romantic and were village women's rain songs, especially in North India from Gujarat to Bengal, where they sang of their isolation from their husbands either in the rainy four months from *ashadha* to *ashvin* or through the twelve months. These rain songs are based on the absent husband who is away from home either on business or duty, and the wife either longs for his return in the rainy season or urges him not to leave at all. Seasonal poetry of this genre also was a feature of folk theatre. There was some variation not only in the number of seasons but in their chronology as well, and one of the poetic conventions was that while Sanskrit *shadritu* poetry described the erotic joys of the lover and the beloved when they are together, the *chaumasa* and *barahmasa* dealt with the *premika's* longing and fear of separation from her beloved. *Viraha barahmasa* or the seasonal poetry of longing remains the most evocative in this genre of romantic poetry and in this group the *barahmasa* compositions of Keshavdas who wrote the *Rasikapriya* stand out among others. *Barahmasa* poetry is not only poignant love poetry on the one hand but shows the close resonance between the psyche of the heroine and the mood of the seasons, each season not only possessing a different colour but a distinct message for those in love. In expressing her lament and relating it to the colours and moods of the seasons the heroine equates the throbbing of her heart with the pulsating sap of the trees, the trembling longing within her to the movement of the clouds and the agony of her forlorn state to the pain of lonely birds. Thus she is not alone in her anguish, her piquant cry is heard by the birds and the blossoms that surround her and who understand and share her pain perhaps more than her beloved. In *barahmasa* poetry we see the strong and sympathetic resonance between the romantic mind of the *nayika* and the natural world around her,

Detail, **Abhisarika Nayika**
see page 173

Romantic Moments in Poetry

it is a world that shares her romantic urges and longings, and she defines her love with the same life and energy that animates the trees and the birds and who stand in mute testimony to her love.

Keshavdas in his *barahmasa* converts the lunar calendar into romantic poetry that vividly celebrates the months as it evokes the pain of the *nayika* at the impending separation from her beloved. Starting with the month of *chaitra* he portrays the heroine urging her beloved not to leave her in that month as every month has something special which would make separation painful and unbearable and as the poet goes through the twelve months the heart-throb of the *nayika* pulsates with the sap and songs of the world around her.

Chaitra: *charming creepers and young trees have blossomed and parrots, sarikas and nightingales make sweet sounds.*

Baisakha: *the earth and the atmosphere are filled with fragrance and all around there is fragrant beauty, but this fragrance is blinding for the bee and painful for the lover who is away from home.*

Jyestha: *the sun is scorching and the rivers have run dry and mighty animals like the elephant and the lion do not stir out.*

Ashadha: *strong winds are blowing, birds do not leave their nest and even the sadhus make only one round.*

Shravana: *rivers run to the sea, creepers have clung to trees, lightning meets the clouds, peacocks make happy sounds announcing the meeting of the earth and the sky.*

Bhadrapad: *dark clouds have gathered, strong winds blow fiercely, there is thunder as rain pours in torrents, tigers and lions roar and elephants break trees.*

Ashvin: *the sky is clear and lotuses are in bloom, nights are brightly illuminated by the moon, people worship Durga and it is time for ancestral worship.*

Kartika: *woods and gardens, the earth and the sky are clear and bright lights illuminate homes, courtyards are full of colourful paintings, and the universe seems to be pervaded by a celestial light.*

Margashirsha: *rivers and ponds are full of flowers and joyous notes of hamsas fill the air, this is the month of happiness and salvation of the soul.*

Pausha: *the earth and the sky are cold. It is the season when people prefer oil, cotton, betel, fire and sun shine.*

Magha: *forests and gardens echo with the sweet notes of peacocks, pigeons and koel and bees hum as if they have lost their way, all ten directions are scented with musk, camphor and sandal, sounds of mridanga are heard through the night.*

Phalguna: *the fragrance of scented powders fills the air and young women and men in every home play holi with great abandon.*

The 16th century was important in the history of romantic poetry for it was then that Vallabhacharya founded the *pushtimarga* sect of Vaishnavism and both *shangar* and *shringara*, adornment and romantic love, were legitimised and given pride of place in Krishna *bhakti*. Krishna as Shrinathji was adored and venerated not only through ritual but celebrated through the arts, especially music and painting. The *haveli* at Nathdwara was Krishna's temple and it resounded with songs of his *lila* and was radiant with picturesque *pichwais* and miniature paintings of his many deeds. The *pushtimarga* tradition was to play an important part in the religious and cultural life of western India, but our concern at this stage is with romantic poetry and we come face to face with a poet who was also considered a saint, whose poetry combines the aroma of sensuality with the fragrance of *bhakti*, who re-created the *Bhagavata Purana* through music and verse and whose contribution to the rich treasure of romantic literature is unique. That poet was Surdas. If the *Bhagavata* established Krishna as the prototypical romantic hero Surdas' *Sursagar* ensured that Krishna *bhakti* would not be devoid of the beauty of *shangar* and the pulsating warmth of *shringara* and would thereby have a certain *madhurya* or sweetness. Surdas' dates are uncertain, 1478–1563 being one suggested life span. However, what is certain is that Surdas through his poetic creations changed the tenor of the *Bhagavata Purana* from that of a sacred text into romantic poetry and in so doing not only enhanced the beauty of romantic poetry but gave *bhakti* a new, more intimate dimension. Surdas while remaining a Krishna devotee did not lose sight of the romantic and human aspects of Krishna's persona. It was none other than Vallabhacharya who recognised his talent and initiated him into the *pushtimarga* tradition and he become one of the first to join the hallowed group of the *ashtachap kavis* of Shrinathji. In weaving *shringara* and *bhakti* together in his lyrical songs Surdas paved the way for the rich and beautiful evolution of the *pushtimarga* tradition. It is only Surdas who can bring out the subtle nuances of philosophy and romance, in the togetherness and separation of the *gopis*, who are at once lovers and devotees at the same time, as is seen in the following lines:

> *Gopis: we, whose minds you have stolen*
> *have not kept any distance from you*
> *who are the knower of the Vedas and the Upanishadas.*
>
> *Krishna: I am never away from you*
> *for you have drowned me in your love*
> *I left heaven and took birth*
> *in Braj for your sake*
> *you see difference when there is none*
> *between us; you and I are one*
> *two bodies but one spirit*
> *living in Braj how could I forget*
> *Radha's ancient love for me?*
> *Your minds are my abode*
> *It is you who have imprisoned me there.*
>
> *Surdas,* (73.1613–17)

Surdas is able to bring out the subtle nuances of the Vaishnava philosophy of *bheda-abheda*, different-and-yet-not-different, of transcendence and immanence, through his well chosen words using the paradigm of romantic love. If the *gopis* are drawn by the flute of Krishna, Krishna in turn is equally attracted by the songs of the *gopis*:

> *I reside in the hearts of those*
> *who have abandoned pride and sing my praise*
> *in a voice that is choked with emotion*
> *drowned in love for me.*
> Surdas (74.1618)

The poetic world for Surdas is the Vrindavana or the enchanted forest of the *Bhagavata Purana*, which is a microcosm of the heavenly and eternal Vrindavana, one is not a reflection of the other, for both are real and Surdas being equally a *rasika* and *bhakta* participates in both these worlds. Surdas continues the trend started by Jayadeva that the poet is not only a *rasika* but also a *bhakta* at the same time, the difference being that while Jayadeva was not a part of any established *sampradaya*, Surdas on the other hand was writing from within *pushtimarga* Vaishnavism and therefore sets up a trend that others of the *sampradaya* follow. Surdas, therefore, is able to bring both aesthetic and religious truths together in his compositions. The message in Surdas' songs is not different from the structure and sensuousness of his words. Krishna is both lover and godhead for Surdas and thus it is that he, and the *asthachap kavis* that followed him, were able to weave *shringara* and *bhakti rasa* together in their minds and their songs. There are subtle theological differences between the *pushtimarga* Vaishnavism and Chaitanya's Bengal Vaishnavism, but they need not detain us here. Suffice it to note that both work on a foundation of *shringara rasa*, and turn away from *shanta rasa* in their celebration of Krishna. The convention of *bhanita* or the signature line in Surdas' songs leaves no doubt that he is actively participating in the dramatic action of the poem, as in:

> *Sura says that you are the all knower as the Vedas and Upanishadas declare*
> *Sura says that while smiling, Krishna said words he never meant*
> *Sura says return our minds to us so that we can go home with willing steps*
> *Sura says that a home without you is like a dry well in a forest.*
> Surdas (73.1613–17)

While Surdas was the brightest star in the poetry of the *ashtachapkavis*, that poetry continued to be evocative and romantic as we note in this composition by Chaturbhujdas:

> *The son of Nanda plays his flute on*
> *the banks of the Yamuna*
> *And the touch of lips brings forth*
> *melodious notes.*
> *The maidens of Vraja are drawn forward by*

its magic, heedless of their appearance.
In their haste, their necklaces of pearls
snap and swing loose on their necks as they run.
Waters ceased to flow, the winds held still
in the groves of Vrindavana
That which was still moved, while
the moving stands still.
Trees bring forth fruits and flowers bloom
Barren trees grew green, love like a
spring ripples down Giriraj.

This poetry, like many others in its genre, shows how romantic love for the *pushtimargis* was not merely an emotion that was shared by two individuals but was the very animating principle of life itself. For the flute of Krishna which touches the hearts of the *gopis* also quickens the plants and the trees of Vrindavana and caresses the waters of the Yamuna.

Perhaps a contemporary of Surdas, but one who walked in the hallowed dust of Bengal and not Braj, was Chandidas, a poet who sang with moving intensity of the love of Radha and Krishna, whose passionate compositions inspired Chaitanya, and whose songs are sung in *kirtans* even today. Chandidas was a village priest connected romantically to Rami, a washerwoman, and in the spirit of the Sahajiya Vaishnavas of Bengal he raised her to a mother goddess. Chandidas combines sensuality with a special sensitivity as he weaves passion in his poetry:

I never touch a black flower
In my diffidence.
Sadness grows.
I hear everywhere
Whispers about my dark love.
I never look at a sombre cloud
Fearing Krishna.
I do not wear kajal.
I screen my eyes
while going to the stream.
As I pass by the kadamba shade
I seal my ears
Hearing the flute.

Chandidas displays a certain fondness and poignancy about the *kadamba* tree for that is the haunt of Krishna and even the whisper of winds through its leaves excites Radha:

Darkness and clouds
Shroud the frightening night
Alone, I suffer

Under the kadamba tree.
I scan distances in vain,
Krishna is nowhere.
Split the earth open
And I will conceal myself.
My youth runs away,
Yet still my heart suffocates
Waiting for Krishna.

While romantic poetry in the *bhashas* was resonating in north India there was an equally significant romantic movement that was making its presence felt in the same region and that was Sufi romantic poetry.[4] The first poets of these romances, the Chisti Sufis, were important figures in the cultural and religious life of the Delhi Sultanate in the 13th and 14th centuries. Borrowing both from the Persian *masnavis* and the Sanskrit *rasakavyas* the Sufi romantic poets created a new genre in the *bhashas* with its own unique epistemology, poetics and conventions. They wrote in Hindavi and composed in the *chaupai-doha* style borrowing topoi, conventions and aesthetic theories from both Persian and Sanskrit but remaining uniquely distinct. Sufi romantic poetry was essentially court poetry and was to be understood and celebrated in the unique Sufi concept of music and mysticism, where the invisible divinity is to be realised through sensual experiences. In this genre of poetry are Maulana Daud's *Chandayan* (1379) Qutban's *Mrigavati* (1504) and *Raj Kunwar* (1503) Malik Muhammad Jayasi's *Padmavat* (1540) and Manjhan's *Madhumalati* (1545). Hindavi Sufi poetry, grounded as it was in the metaphysics of an Islamic godhead and the political ambience of kingship, created a new romantic narrative structure. This poetry, unlike the Sanskrit and *bhasha rasakavyas*, was created entirely for the noble and the aristocratic literary culture of the Delhi Sultanate and the *shringara rasa* that they celebrated was called *raja rasa* or the *rasa* of kings and for kings. Poetry and *sama* or music were only for the royalty of a sensitive *tabiyat* or temperament and musical gatherings for Sufi poetry was a common practice in the cultivated life of the Delhi Sultanate both in courts and hospices. The performance of Sufi poetry was part of the grand occasions of courtly life and it is fair to assume that this poetry did not reach the common person of the time. The setting for such a performance is described thus:

Detail, **The Bewitching Gaze**

see page 176

---

4. I am indebted to Prof. Aditya Behl for leading me through the epistemology of Sufi romantic poetry and letting me quote from his forthcoming book.

There should be a large and open roofed space with trees all around it, perfumed with musk, ambergris, camphor and rose. The audience should all sit facing the head of the assembly according to their social rank. The connoisseurs who understand and appreciate music and dance should sit on the left and the performers must be in front of them. The sponsor should be generous, noble, knowledgeable and dress better than everyone else.

It is within this elite and discriminating literary culture that we must begin to seek our theory of reading for Sufi romantic poetry. Sufi romantic poetry, more than poetry in Sanskrit or the *bhashas*, had a nuanced texture and *dhvani* or layers of meanings, available only to the sensitive aesthete. Among the Sufis such a view has Quranic sanction. As Jayasi says, the bee comes from the forest to smell the fragrance of the lotus, but the frogs that live next to the flower will never get it. Sufi poets extol romantic love, but even more, the pain of separation that comes with love. Manjhan puts it eloquently when he writes:

> *From love all creation sprang*
> *love filled each created form*
> *Only he enjoys life's reward on earth*
> *in whose heart is born love's anguish*
> *Do not think separation is pain,*
> *from it joy comes into the world*
> *Blessed is the man whose sorrow is the sorrow of separation.*

Sufi romantic poetry while celebrating earthly love always has the scent of the invisible world beyond. An important difference between the romantic emotion of Sanskrit and the *bhashas* on the one hand and that of the Sufis on the other is that the Sufi romantic emotion, called *prema rasa*, has an admixture of both romantic emotions and ascetic practices. Further, the Sufi poets stress that it is only the experience of *viraha* or longing that drives the seeker onwards along the Sufi path. The beauty and the strength of romantic literature for them is to realise the epistemic value of longing and it is around this fundamental concept of longing that their romantic narrative is structured. Language, and especially that of romance, becomes the ground for understanding and representing the revelation of divinity to humans through the proper understanding of romantic love. In the hands of the Sufi poets the romantic emotion experienced through literature is merely instrumental in the training of the self towards God. The basic ideology of Sufi romantic love is that each object of desire is loved for the sake of one higher than itself, and through this process of unrequited love, the individual annihilates himself and this leads him all the way up to Allah. This concept of annihilation is brought out in these lines of Jayasi when he describes the *joahar* of Padmavati:

Detail, **The Bewitching Gaze**
see page 176

They prepared the funeral pyre
and gave generously in alms and charity
seven times they circled the pyre
in life, beloved, you embraced us
we will not leave your embrace in death
we and you, lord, will be together in both worlds
they left this world steeped in their love
and heaven glowed ruby red.

Thus the typical Sufi hero loves two women, one lower and worldly, and the second higher and other worldly, one plain and the other divinely beautiful, and in ascending in his love from one to the other, he has a religious experience of the ultimate. The differences between *prema rasa* of the Sufis and *shringara rasa* of Sanskrit and the *bhashas* are obvious. *Shringara rasa* while elevating *viraha* or longing does not advocate annihilating the self but instead celebrating and ennobling the self.

Poetry and music have a special relationship in the Indian tradition as all poetry is meant to be performed through music, mime, gesture and dance and never inwardly read. Poetry therefore, has always been a performing art. However, it is in the classical musical form of *khayal* that poetry, and romantic poetry in particular, finds an important place. Called *bandish, cheez, asthayi* or *rachana* the origin of poetry as a part of classical music is traced to the 13th century Sufi saint Baba Farid. In the Sufi tradition, music and poetry are an indispensable part of their mysticism. Through the centuries *khayal bandish* evolved in the hands of Muslim and Hindu musicians and it was in the 17th century court of Mohamed Shah Rangila that musicians Adarang and Sadarang perfected the present form of *dhrupad* and *khayal bandish*. Created under intense musical states of contemplation by music masters and preserved in their *gharana* by their students, *khayal bandish* has a tough grammar and is composed mostly of vowels with very few consonants. Using Persian, Hindi or Urdu, *khayal bandishes* remain rooted in the people's sensibility. Through brief but well chosen words enshrined in the appropriate *raga*, they convey beautifully both the joy of union and the pathos of longing, and give a new dimension to romantic poetry. It is left to the musician to make the *bandish* come alive through the human voice.

If the minimalist lyrics of a *khayal bandish* convey the romantic emotion through a combination of poetry and music, and the texture and timbre of the human voice, a *thumri bandish* brings a romantic situation alive through the *abhinaya* and movements of a *kathak* dance. Composed generally in the *bhashas* and particularly in *brajbhasha* and *avadhi* in Benaras and Avadh, a *thumri bandish* evokes the many nuances of the romantic moods of a *nayika* and suggests the locale where the romantic activity is taking place. A variety of etymologies for the word *thumri* have been offered. One such poetic etymology suggests its evolution from '*thum*' or Radha's rhythmic and

musical gait and '*ri*' or whispered conversations between her and her *sakhis*. The abundant *nayikabheda* literature provided a rich source for musicians and the *ashtanayikas* come vibrantly alive in *thumri bandishes* set in *ragas* such as *Khamaj, Pilu, Sohani,* and *Bhairavi.* It is left to the musician and the dancer to convey the heart-throb of the romantic heroine through the musical but minimal lyrics of a *thumri.* For instance, a *proshitapatika nayika* sings in *raga Pahadi:*

Detail, **Bhadrapad**
see page 184

> *my beloved has gone abroad*
> *and has not returned even after promising that he would*
> *and my home seems like that of an ascetic.*

A *svadhinapatika nayika* sings in *raga Purvi:*

> *My sweetheart colour my sari red*
> *Colour it the same shade as your turban*
> *I want to be colourful and smart*
> *Get me more saris and colour them red.*

A survey of romantic moments cannot be complete without looking briefly at romantic letters. Even though they may not be in verse they are none the less very beautiful. *Patracarca* or epistolary art has an ancient history that can be traced back to the enigmatic hieroglyphics of the Indus Valley seals. One encounters a variety of letters in Sanskrit and Prakrit, and this includes letters such as *vijnanapatras* or letters by Jain devotees on certain auspicious occasions, *rajapatras* or epistles by kings, *dutakavyas* or an entire poem like Kalidasa's *Meghadutam* in the form of a message, *patrakavyas* or long letters in verse like the *Suhrilekha* written by Nagarjuna to king Udayana extolling the

virtues of Buddhism, but our interest here is only in romantic letters. Such romantic letters are associated with Kama and therefore are called *anangalekha, madanalekha* or *manmathalekha*. They were written on leaves such as those of the lotus and *tamala*, petals of flowers or *bhurja* bark.

Both Bharata in the *Natyashastra* and Vatsyayana in the Kamasutra refer to *patrahariduti* or love messengers and in Sanskrit and Prakrit literature messengers can be friends, servants, traders, birds and even clouds. As early as the *Bhagavata Purana* we encounter the long and moving love letter written by Rukmini to Krishna, asking him to come and rescue her before she is married off to Shisupala. In his *Lalitamadhava* Rupa Gosvamin, the 16th century Bengal Vaishnavite recreates this episode and Rukmini writes a letter that is taken to Krishna by a brahmin:

> *O cloud of dark colour, let your sonorous sound deceive the opponent*
> *and deceive the peahen with a downpour of nectar. I am your*
> *expectant, do quench my thirst.*

In the *Padmapurana* we come across this love letter written by Madhava on *mala* flowers to Sulochana whom he wished to marry:

> *O damsel I have crossed the sea on my horse... please accept me as*
> *your life partner... no other person other than me can fathom your*
> *excellence, as the beauty of a lotus is only appreciated by a bee but not*
> *by frogs. The planet Gemini and the cloud appear in the sky but the*
> *lily admires only the moon.*

Kalidasa celebrates love letters in his own unique way, when he writes in *Kumarasambhavam* that Vidyadhara maidens are seen to have incised the throbbing of their heart on the bark of *bhurja* trees. In another Kalidasa play Priyamvada asks Shakuntala to engrave a message with her nails on a lotus leaf, charming as a parrot's breast, which she will then carry concealed under flowers to Dushyanta. Not only do nails serve as a stylus but are a suggestion of Shakuntala's longing for her much cherished embrace by her beloved. In that letter she wrote:

> *O ruthless one, I know not your heart, but day and night Kama*
> *exceedingly heats my limbs with my yearning for you.*

In Banabhatta's *Kadambari* is found this delightful description of how a love letter is written. Pundarika plucks twigs from a *tamala* tree and pounds these leaves on a stone to extract their juice. He then writes with this juice on his *angavastra* and deputes Taralika to take it to his beloved Mahashveta. In the genre of epistolary creations romantic letters occupy a special place and as Rabindranath once said, "Letters like tiny jasmine flowers appear to be very small in shape but the environment wherein they flourish is as expansive as the creeper of jasmine." For this environment is not only the preparation of the materials on which the letter will be written and the tenderness with which it is inscribed, but equally its imaginative delivery and the thrill of its recipient. Within the few words of that romantic letter is hidden a whole gamut of emotions, an entire universe of excitement and anticipation, a complete alphabet of romance. More than poetry and not in as many words, and even more than what words and gestures can convey, a romantic letter is able to convey a certain urgency and immediacy, sincerity and intimacy of love, and therefore forms an important part of the corpus of romantic literature.

And finally in the genre of romantic poetry we cannot overlook a genre of beautiful poetry that carries the theme of *nayikabheda* and Radha Krishna lore to new dimensions, poetry that bridges literature and painting and enters the sonorous world of music, that evokes not only visual images but leads to soundscapes—*ragamala* poetry. The precursors of *ragamala* poetry were *dhyana mantras*, seed formulae that gave a verbal form to abstract musical concepts and provided poets, and later painters, with poetic images of *ragas*, thereby giving music both a poetic and pictorial dimension. *Ragamala dhyana mantras* gave an anthropomorphic life to *ragas* and through their romantic suggestion and nuance, music was given both an oral and a visual form. The entire tradition of *ragamala* poetry and painting is an affirmation that the various arts in India are inter-related and that richly sensuous romantic poetry can breathe life into music and that music in turn is tied to poetry, and both to painting. Ranade[5] is right in stating that the *ragamala* tradition is part of a larger Indian ethos of combining music, painting, drama and literature, other examples of which are the *chitrakathis* of Maharashtra, *pabuji-ka-phad* from Rajasthan and the *jadupatuas* of Bengal. A *raga* in the hands of *ragamala* poets and painters is no longer an abstract concept but a person—man, woman or child—who resonates with every shade of the romantic emotion. Even as early as Bharata's *Natyashastra* emotion, colour and a presiding deity were linked. The *Naradiya Shiksha* moves a step forward and equates *swara*, musical note with *varna*, colour. It was the legendary Hanuman, who lived probably in the 7th century, who devised a system of six male *ragas* with five consorts or *raginis* each. Later, sons and daughters, or *ragaputras* and *ragaputris*, were added to the family. Narada's *Raga Sagara* probably of the 8th century is perhaps the earliest document of the *dhyana mantras* where a *raga* is given a deified form and addressed through these prayer formulae. *Dhyana mantras* invoked the mood and the ambience of the *raga* in words rather than through musical notes. Some others feel that the 14th century work *Sangitopanishadsar* of Sudhakar, a Jain musicologist, is the

Detail, **A Fond Welcome**
see page 166

---

5. I have profited from the many discussions I have had with Dr. Ashok da Ranade

earliest work to have *dhyana mantras*. Among other texts which were sources of *ragamala* poetry were *Ragamala* of Kshemakarna (1570) and *Sangitadarpana* by Damodara Misra (1625). Thus it was very early in the tradition that music was given a form of a *mantra*, even as a *mantra* already had a musical dimension, attesting to the fact that performance and literature are flowers of the same tree of creativity, or limbs of a larger body of the arts. It was from these *dhyana mantras* that *ragamala* poetry in Sanskrit and later in the *bhashas* arose, and then from this poetry was to come a number of *ragamala* paintings. *Ragamala* poetry not only adds to the rich storehouse of romantic literature but is further evidence of the genius of the Indian mind in giving a *nirvikalpa* concept like music a *savikalpa* form. In the 16th, 17th and 18th centuries a number of *ragamala* texts were developed, mostly in Rajasthan, but also in Malwa and the Deccan, and came to be known generally by the name of the city such as Jaipur, Amber, Sirohi, Chawand and so on, and these were later to provide the basis for *ragamala* paintings. A few examples of *ragamala* poetry should suffice to illustrate its generally formulaic style and its pithy but sensuous visualisation:

Kakhuba Ragini
Tortured by separation, wearing a yellow garment
gone to the forest carrying flowers
and reciting his beauty
she returns not
her fair body excites everybody's mind.

Dhanasri Ragini
Taking a lovely drawing board
she draws his picture in many forms
the great beauty
wth the loveliness of the blue lotus.

Vasanta Raga
With crest on head and lute in hand
Madana is resplendent
and as he dances enthrals our minds
Mango tendrils flower on all sides
the cuckoo calls, the peacock cries
a girl beats the mridanga and describes his fair body.

Gauri Ragini
Sprays of the heavenly wishing tree in hand
adorned with a girdle of sweet toned bells
and beauty enhanced by a splendid robe
she, who ever pleasure gives
is declared to be Gauri.

Thus, romantic poetry in the Indian tradition is a rich storehouse of the heart-throb of the *nayikas* and the *nayakas* and a chronicle of their beautiful moments, be they of longing or living, of ecstasy or anguish. It is a charmed world of the sighs of the lovelorn heroine and the cries of the *chakravaka* bird as it seeks its mate, of the footfalls of the *sakhi* as she carries love messages and the song of the peacock as it heralds the advent of the rain, of the perfume of sandalwood paste and the music of the bangles of the *nayika* as she awaits her beloved. It is poetry that is richly sensuous and equally spiritual, and takes us not only into the charmed spaces of a *haveli* but to the hushed ambience of Vrindavana where Krishna and the *gopis* dally. In its lyrics we see the colours and the seasons of heartfelt emotions, we participate in the games and *lilas* of love, through its words we hear the music of Krishna's flute and the footsteps of romantic dalliance. Romantic poetry leads us into Vaishnava theology and Sufi mysticism, through it we learn of *shringara* and *prema*, and read poetic creations not only in ancient Prakrit and classical Sanskrit but also in the *bhashas*. A survey of romantic poetry is a journey into the minds of our poets from Amaru of the 4th century to Jayadeva of the 13th century and beyond, into the courts of Hala and Bharatrhari, into the kingdoms of Rajasthan and the foothills of the Himalayas. And as the music of romantic poetry resonates we are lifted from the everyday mundane world to the realm of *ananda*, where love is not just passion or superficial excitement but an exalted state of living and being, celebrated for its own sake, we are soaked in its aesthetic creations and we cannot but exclaim *raso vai sah hyevayam labdhva anandi bhavati*, he is *rasa* having obtained which one attains bliss.

Romantic Moments in Painting

Detail, **Raas Lila**
see page 113

history of romantic paintings in the Indian tradition is a journey into a celebration of love by painters and patrons, *rajas* and *rasikas*; it is an odyssey where *nayakas* and *nayikas*, the parrot and the peacock alike enliven inanimate spaces and transform them into a living drama of romantic love; it is a voyage into the artistic creations of a people for whom romantic love was an exalted state of living and being, of a civilisation where to exult in the passions and the pathos of love was a cherished experience; it is a document of the story of the grand themes of Vaishnava love and equally of the mystic truths of Sufi romances; it is recognition of the love stories of potters and peasants as much as those of the royalty and the nobility; it is a vivid and vibrant visualisation of the taxonomies of love enunciated by our poets, of feasting our eyes on the adornments of love for in the impulse to adorn is the very breath of love, of every mood and situation of lovers and of the colours and seasons, *ragas* and *raginis* of love; it is the artistic depiction of every nuance and meaning of what it is to love and be loved. And yet, a journey such as this is more than just a historical chronicle, for these paintings speak of the deepest longings and ecstatic devotion of its people, for whom to love was to worship, and for whom no worship could be devoid of love, and moreover for whom to indulge in and experience romantic love was ultimately to know oneself.

The chronology of romantic painting in the Indian tradition follows a different path from the history of love poetry, just as the written word in the tradition evolved differently from the spoken word. The chronology of painting for us is not just one of style or format, although that is important in the understanding of the evolution of romantic painting, but it is equally also the saga of the two *brahmans*, the *nirguna* and the *saguna*, for the aesthetic experience from these romantic paintings is our ultimate concern and not a superficial, hedonistic titillation through art. And as one ponders over these two resplendent *brahmans* of painting one enters the majestic edifice of Indian philosophy itself. Romantic painting is essentially visual poetry, and although the two evolve differently, they remain intimately tied, one cannot exist without the other, and furthermore, one needs poetry to understand painting. To a philosopher of the arts the transformation of the initial abstract *dhyana* of the poet into *sabda*, still within the mind of the poet, and from that unspoken *sabda* to a spoken *sabda* or *kavya*, and then from that spoken *sabda* or *kavya* to a visible and palpable *rupa* such as *chitra* or painting, is the story of the mystery and the beauty of artistic creation, a phenomenon that cannot be totally probed or intellectually analysed. The *dhyana* and the unspoken *sabda* grow within the mind of the poet and are shaped by forces within that creative mind, forces that not only include psychological stimuli but even more importantly *samskaras* or latent psychic impressions from a previous birth. These are included under the poetic concept of *pratibha* or the creative genius of the poet. Once a *sabda* is spoken and leaves the poet's mind and becomes *kavya*, and from *kavya* assumes a visible and palpable form such as painting, it becomes part of the public domain, and is therefore influenced by a variety of forces which include socio-economic factors, political ambience, cultural trends and even religious beliefs of the society in which that painting is produced. This explains to a great extent why painting evolves differently from poetry. The story of romantic painting is therefore, also the story of the people and the patrons, the *raja* and the *praja*, of kings and nobility, of political intrigue and religious affiliations, but above all it must not be forgotten that romantic painting, like poetry, remains a testament to love and an object of beauty. Our primary interest is in understanding how romantic painting, as an object of beauty, grew and evolved in the Indian tradition and also how, and to whom, it provided aesthetic pleasure.

It is usual to divide the history of painting in India into classical or mural painting and post-classical or miniature painting and this approach has some merits at least didactically. Recent archaeological work has uncovered pre-historic rock painting in Bhimbetka near Bhopal, while the murals in

Ajanta, Lepakshi and Badami of the early centuries of the last millennium have been known for a long time. Some consider these murals as the roots of Indian painting. It was, however, the Buddhists and the Jains who stressed the importance of the written over the spoken word and started creating manuscripts of their canonical traditions. These manuscripts were illustrated and these painted palm and *bhurja patra* Buddhist manuscripts and their *patlis* or wooden covers should really be considered the precursors of miniature painting in the Indian tradition. It has been suggested that this tradition started even before the Christian era but since there are no surviving manuscripts from this period it is difficult to be certain. However, we know for certain that the methodical transcription of Jain texts started as early as the 6th century AD after the conclave of monks held at Vallabhi in Gujarat, also there is historical evidence of a 11th century Jain manuscript made in Jaisalmer. From the available material it is known that a manuscript that was commonly illustrated with miniature paintings, in the 11th and 12th centuries in the Buddhist areas of eastern India, of the Pala dynasty and in Nepal, was the *Prajnaparamita*, a canonical text that did not lend itself easily to illustration. Painters illustrated this manuscript with many deities of the Buddhist pantheon and this was meant to help in the meditative practices of the monks and lay devotees. These illustrations were iconic in representation and were two-dimensional reproductions of the then contemporary Buddhist sculptures. Eventually Buddhist monasteries, where these manuscripts were produced, were destroyed or fell into disuse by the 14th century, and with it the making of these manuscripts came to an end.

At this time the thrust of manuscript illustration shifted to western India where Jain manuscripts on palm leaves were already being produced. Illustrations in these manuscripts were similar to those in Buddhist documents, bearing no relationship to the text and serving as magical, protective or auspicious charms, and thus playing an esoteric rather than an aesthetic role. Paper was first introduced in India in the 12th century but it was only in the 14th century that it was adopted enthusiastically by Jain scribes for creating Jain manuscripts in western India. The geographical entity called western India comprising Gujarat, Malwa and Rajasthan of the 14th and 15th centuries was a prosperous and peaceful region, well connected by trade routes to the north and the east of the sub-continent, and by sea routes to Egypt and shores beyond, and given to the preservation and celebration of its religion and culture. Jain merchants and bankers were munificent patrons of their temples and religious *bhandaras* or libraries and since at this time the Muslim influence was beginning to be felt, Jain piety was turning to the making of small objects and manuscripts which could be secretly preserved in the Jain *bhandaras* and away from Muslim eyes. While Hindus preferred to give donations to brahmins and keep their manuscripts in their *pustak khanas*, Jains on the other hand endowed their temples and libraries, and with their love of the written word the donation of manuscripts as *shashtradan* was the most common gift. Western India was teeming with artists and scribes who under Jain patronage produced many illustrated canonical manuscripts which featured miniature illustrations. The two most commonly produced Jain manuscripts were the *Kalpasutra* and the non-canonical *Kalakacharya Katha*. The latter text features a story of the abduction of Kalaka's sister by the evil Persian Sahi king Gardabhilla, but the abortive romance in this story is subordinated to the virtues of the Jain *dharma*. Working on paper but in the palm leaf format, perhaps drawing some inspiration from the mural tradition, these artists were totally indigenous in their ideas and methods, and must be considered the *adishilpis* of miniature paintings, for even in the cramped space of a few square inches of the manuscript they were able to produce, through line and colour, the typical lissom Gujarat female figure with full-breasted body in three-quarter profile, with the head with its projecting farther eye while the sharp nose remains in true profile. The three-quarter profile and the projecting eye is sometimes referred to as *dedh chashme ka chehera*, the face with one-and-a-half spectacles. These artists were drawing their inspiration from sculpture where the norm was the full frontal face and the human image had essentially an iconic purpose and in using the three-quarter profile the early artists were fulfilling the need for iconic figures in illustrated religious manuscripts. The human figures though depicted in angular and wiry outlines had a certain linear energy. Even within the small space of a few inches the artist imparted a certain life and vitality to these figures, with controlled and polychromatic colouring within the taut and wiry line, while not neglecting adornments through jewellery and garments. This type of figure, conservative but yet expressive, was to remain the model for western Indian artists for about 200 years. It is here within the restricted palette of Jain manuscripts, where the text dominates the page and the scribe clearly has the upper hand, that the genius of the Indian artist in creating a beautiful space is seen. It is a space that is shared both by gods and humans, animated by birds and creepers, set against a background of solid colour. Even within that small space the manuscript illustrators were able to establish an entire landscape with turretted pavilions and ornate woodwork reflecting the prevailing styles of architecture in Gujarat, textile canopies and furnishings, all of which express a certain Indian sophistication. In the hands of the western Indian artists one sees a paradigm shift in the Indian artistic tradition, from the iconic murals of ancient India to the charmed space of miniature painting. The refined sensibility that these spaces show reflects not only the skill of the artist but such refinement as could only have come from the cultured lifestyle of the patrons. It is here that one must seek the beginnings of the rich world of miniature painting which was to evolve over the next five hundred years and which was to give expression to the romantic ethos of India, where the artist and the patron interacted in the creation of the art, and where not only the subject matter but also the artistic tastes of the patron played a part, and where these creations of romantic love were appreciated in cultured and cultivated audiences.

Facing page:
Detail, **Ragini Gunakali**
see page 190

The question of the Persian influence in these Jain miniatures must be addressed at this point not merely for chauvinistic reasons but for aesthetic considerations as well. It is known that in the 15th century the Muslim court of Malwa had contact with Persia. Persian artists came to Malwa and brought with them their manuscripts. The miniatures in the Jain manuscripts of this period however were a product entirely of the Indian mind and did not admit too many outside influences. The only Persian feature in these manuscripts is possibly in the borders, where the Indian artist may have been influenced by Persian tiles in the mosques of western India. The *Kalpasutra* of the Devasanopada *bhandar* and now dispersed is the most noted example of this type of painting where horsemen derived from Turkoman paintings in Persia are seen in great abundance in the borders. The Jain style that developed in western India remained robust and indigenous till about the middle of the 16th century, and then relaxed after coming under the influence of a new Hindu style. The point that needs to be stressed at this early stage in our journey of miniature paintings is that the concept and the techniques of miniature painting sprang from purely Indian roots and ethos and retained their Indianness for several hundred years before being touched by outside influences. This is even more true of the romantic tradition where the patron, the artist and the connoisseur alike shared a common Indian ambience and sensibility in the celebration of *shringara rasa*, the romantic emotion. Indian artists borrowed from Persian artistic idioms only those that suited the Indian ethos and rejected others such as the high horizon. It is worth stressing that one must look nowhere other than the soil of India to find the roots of *shringara rasa* in both poetry and painting. Equally, in no other civilisation has *shringara rasa* in poetry and painting been raised to such great aesthetic and religious heights as we have done in India.

While Vaishnavism, and in particular the celebration of Krishna's romantic persona as set out in the 10th chapter of the *Bhagavata Purana*, was a subject very dear to the western Indian painters, they were to take on secular love themes as well such as the *Vasanta Vilasa phagu* and the *Chaurapanchashika*. The *Vasanta Vilasa phagu* in particular was a direct outgrowth of the western Indian style of painting and is an assertion not only of the robustness of that style but equally of the desire to visually celebrate *shringara rasa*, making that scroll the first known expression in miniature painting of the joys of spring and of romantic love. The Freer Gallery scroll of the *Vasanta Vilasa* is dated 1451 and thus becomes one of the earliest expressions of the romantic ethos in the miniature genre, and the colophon of the scroll goes on to say that it was executed in Ahmedabad in the reign of Qutub-ud-Din, the son of Ahmad Shah, the founder of Ahmedabad. Using the well-established idioms of the western Indian style but not being bound by them, the artist of the *Vasanta Vilasa* created charmed miniature spaces that resound with romantic moments and bring the spring landscape to life. The artist of these paintings showed that he could translate the poetry of the *phagu* into visual terms, the poetic images

Detail, **Vasant Vilasa**
see page 132

of spring and love were given a new visual idiom. This was an important landmark in the history of miniature painting as from now on there would always be a synergy between the world of nature and that of humans, one reflecting the other, one resonating with the other, and even more, one depending on the other. The poetry and the paintings of *Vasanta Vilasa* are a testament that the sap of love that flowed in the hero and the heroine was no different from that of the trees and the blossoms, and the birds and the bees that surrounded them. In one painting, as a young couple are enraptured in their youthful delights, the painter depicts a parrot on the cornice of the pavilion, a black bee behind the man and a peacock dancing nearby. When Kama the god of love sounds his war conch the artist shows bees circling above the *bakula* buds or over the jasmine blossoms, a parrot pecking at a fruit and a *kokila* perched on a tree. When the poet writes that the *champaka* buds have burst into blossom lighting the path of Kama the painter is equal to the task and shows colourful trees. The empty bed, the heroine in conversation with her *sakhi* or talking to a bird, a parrot in a cage, a crow bringing news to the expectant heroine, standard artistic idioms of the languishing heroine in later paintings, make their first appearance in the *Vasanta Vilasa*. And so too the passionate embrace of a couple, their animated conversation, garlands, love potions, betel leaves and the other paraphernalia of love find a place in the paintings of the *Vasanta Vilasa*. It is difficult to imagine that the wiry and hieratic figures of the Jain manuscripts, although in two dimensions only, could be transformed by the artist of the *Vasanta Vilasa* into characters that pulsate and throb with romantic love. That is a tribute not only to the genius of the western Indian artist and the sensibility of the patron but also to the ethos of romantic love that was innately Indian. In the *Vasanta Vilasa* we see the first flowering of the romantic idiom of the tradition of miniature painting, the first star of what was to become over the next five hundred years a dazzling cosmos of painted visions of romantic love.

Detail, **Chaurapanchashika**
see page 134

Now that by the middle of the 15th century, the idioms of romantic love in miniature painting were well-established, the tradition was to evolve one step further, and that step was the style of painting that has come to be called the *Chaurapanchashika* style. It has been said, and quite rightly so, that paintings of the *Chaurapanchashika* were a turning point in the evolution of miniature painting in India. The 14th century saw the emergence and the establishment of the western Indian style of painting. Staying faithful to the basic artistic idioms that they had developed and which had stood them in good stead when it came to illustrating Jain manuscripts and the *Vasanta Vilasa*, these western Indian painters made two important artistic changes that were to take miniature paintings on a very different course and leave an imprint on the tradition of miniature painting that was to follow over the next five centuries. First, they broke out of the *pothi* or palm leaf format and created a squarish rather than a horizontal space, a move which not only gave them more space but significantly greater freedom to indulge and celebrate both the human form and its adornments and the landscape in which it was set. Secondly, while continuing to produce canonical manuscripts they introduced the concept of *chitravali* or picture books, where a series of folios from a manuscript would be illustrated with the text reduced to only a line or two of inscription at the top of the painting. With these changes the Indian miniature artist came into his own and the scribe was now in a secondary position. Miniature painting now triumphantly embarked on a course from which it was not to look back. The style of the Jain manuscript illustrations and the *Vasanta Vilasa* was resilient enough to permit evolution to the next stage of miniature painting which was the *Chaurapanchashika*, but yet leave its unforgettable stamp.

The paintings of the *Chaurapanchashika,* which were found near Pratapgadh in north India, were probably executed between 1540–1580, (although some date them a hundred years earlier) and were painted in western India, probably in the heyday of the Mewar kingdom. Some art historians assert that the *Chaurapanchashika* style of painting was a pan-north-Indian style and not restricted just to western India. They are sometimes also referred to as the *kulahdar* group of paintings, from *kulah* or a small conical cap that the men are shown wearing, and are a direct outgrowth of the western Indian style of manuscript illustration. Drawing its inspiration from the 12th century love poem by the same name, the paintings of *Chaurapanchashika* retain a remarkably native and earthy Indian romantic ethos and are undoubtedly a product of a Hindu court and culture, both in style and content, while incorporating some pre-Akbari Muslim artistic styles, and can be considered the first truly Indian art of post-classical northern India. Champavati, the heroine in the painting, seems self-assured and poised with an undercurrent of passion and in her, in the words of Barrett and Gray, the "Indian artist invented perhaps his most enchanting symbol of feminine coquetry, demure and studied, at the same time advancing and in retreat."[1] There is in these paintings a declaration of frank sensuality and moments of uninhibited romance that seem to resonate Bilhana's hauntingly nostalgic refrain *adyapi*, even now. The two central figures in the composition have hand gestures reminiscent of dance drama and although the static figures are set in a two-dimensional space there is about them a sense of movement and counter-movement. The assured line depicting a square face, a large backward sweeping eye, a large triangular nose, a sharp protruding chin which curves softly down into the neck, well-endowed breasts that intersect, cut-away *choli*, the triangular lower projection of the *patka*, the diaphanous *odhni* that balloons over the head, the *chakdar jama*, colourful Gujarat textiles, a vivid palette with the intense red and green background, have all come to be recognised as the signature of the *Chaurapanchashika* style. The most important innovation however of the *Chaurapanchashika* artists was the turning of the head in full profile and dropping of the farther projecting eye, one artistic idiom that was to give more freedom to the artist, not only to narrate a story, but even more importantly to convey the moods of the *nayaka* and the *nayika*. From the *dedh chashme ka chehera* the face was now *ek chashme ka chehera*, the face with one spectacle, a face that could do justice to the many colours of love and romance, and the miniature artist could give full play to the eye, especially of the romantic heroine, and was thus able to match the romantic poet in depicting the language of the eyes.

The *Chaurapanchashika* style of painting continued for a couple of hundred years and was versatile enough that it was used not only in western India but also centres such as Gwalior and Jaunpur and was capable of expressing hieratic and secular themes alike. The Hindu tradition of painted manuscripts in the 15th century was clearly lagging behind. The Hindu penchant for orality, preference for donations to *brahmins* rather than to temples and for keeping their manuscripts in their personal possession meant that few Hindu manuscripts of antiquity have survived in India. Even after paper was available Hindus preferred palm leaves for their religious books and this tradition was particularly strong in Orissa. However, the prolific production of Jain illustrated manuscripts and the ethos of the written and illustrated manuscripts in western India was to rub off on the Hindus. The

---

1. Barrett and Gray, 1978: p. 68

Bhagavata Purana was compiled around the 9th century and by the 12th century Jayadeva's *Gita Govinda* was already resonating on the east coast and the magic of *shringara bhakti* had cast its spell in Orissa and Bengal. This was the precursor of the Chaitanya movement. Dwarka in Gujarat was already a centre of ritual Krishna worship and it did not take long for both the *Bhagavata Purana* and the *Gita Govinda* to travel from the east to the west coast, through trade and caravan routes, carried by monks and traders, and introduce Hindus in western India to the joys and charm of ecstatic Krishna *bhakti* as espoused in the *Bhagavata* and *Gita Govinda*. The Jain manuscript illustrators had given the Hindus the artistic idioms and tools to celebrate Krishna's romantic dalliance, not only through song and dance as it was being done on the east coast in Bengal and Orissa, but equally through the medium of miniature painting; Hindu artists and patrons were quick to respond and learn these new skills. What is equally important is that the people of western India were ready to embark on a new artistic and spiritual journey. Sociologists of the arts point to the growing Muslim presence in this region and the influence it was having on the Hindu psyche. Under this Muslim influence temple building had ceased, ostentatious expressions of *bhakti* had to be curtailed and the times demanded a more private and even secret celebration of Krishna. The Krishna of painting, rather than of sculpture, was a new icon for the Hindus and opened a whole new aesthetic universe. However, even above and beyond sociological forces that ushered in Hindu miniature painting in western India, the advent of Krishna in painting inaugurated a new aesthetic which was to beautifully complement the Krishna of poetry and song. Painting as an aesthetic medium could achieve what sculpture could not, that is, express with great sensitivity the many shades and nuances of the romantic emotion. Sculpture in Khajuraho and Konarak, to name just two examples, reached a high water mark in sensuality and eroticism, and the sensuous females in the sculptures of the Rani ki Vav in Gujarat and that in Belur and Halebid to name two southern examples reached iconic perfection. Yet, such and other images fell short of being able to depict the depth, the beauty, and the many nuances of the romantic emotion. While sculpture could be imbued with a certain sensuality and religious life, either in a temple or in a home shrine, only painting could bring the delicate romantic emotions to life, and the Hindu artists and aesthetes of western India must be credited with creating a new genre of painting which changed not only the aesthetics but, even more importantly, the epistemology of both Vaishnavism and romantic art. The artists of the western Indian school of painting who produced the erudite Jain manuscripts, the beautiful *Vasanta Vilasa* and the romantic

Detail, **The Adoration of Krishna**
see page 111

Chaurapanchashika were laying the foundation not only of the beautiful tradition of romantic painting that was to follow but also of *pushtimarga* Vaishnavism. Their artistic idioms were meant not just to display the iconic and the narrative but to portray nuances of emotion and were to survive for several centuries. From within the western Indian style emerged important changes, changes that were to define the entire tradition of painting and romantic painting in particular.

Once *Vasanta Vilasa* and *Chaurapanchashika* were produced and the artistic idioms proved resilient enough to portray the romantic emotion in painting, the doors were open for western Indian artists to produce *chitravalis* of the *Balagopalastuti, Bhagavata Purana* and the *Gita Govinda,* for the ultimate expression of romance was to be found in these texts. The romantic hero in these texts was none other than Krishna and a celebration of his romantic dalliance in Vrindavana was to become a supremely delightful aesthetic experience both for the artist, the patron and the aesthete. Once Krishna was portrayed in paintings as the divine lover, that beautiful and divine love was affirmed and realised not only through song and dance but now equally through painting. The painted Krishna could now be held in one's hand, the many and varied romantic moments could now be shared visually in intimate audiences, one could return again and again to enjoy the many colours and splendours of the enchanted Vrindavana and if this visual experience was accompanied by the songs of Krishna one could then become immersed in a total aesthetic experience of Krishna. Through the aesthetic medium of paintings Krishna had acquired a new dimension and the romantic emotion a new meaning. Unlike the Jains, Hindu piety did not extend to endowing illustrated manuscripts to temples, although the possibility that Hindu patrons commissioned manuscripts and kept them in their private possession cannot be ruled out. However, the reading of the *Bhagavata* was a popular religious activity, then and even now, and one is therefore led to believe that the illustrated *Bhagavata Purana* was produced more for its aesthetic delectation rather than for its religious merit, and by extension one can credit the aesthetic sensibility of its patrons even more.

While the earliest Muslim settlement in the subcontinent goes back to the 8th century, it was not until the 13th century that a definite Muslim presence was felt as different Muslim sultans ruled over different parts of India including Gujarat, Bengal, Delhi, Malwa, Mandu and the Deccan. The Sultanate period with its establishments at Delhi, Jaunpur and Mandu was the next phase in the evolution of painting. The Sultans were benevolent dictators and patrons of the arts and promoted artists to create paintings from both the Hindu and Muslim traditions. They were bibliophiles and a calligrapher of the Koran occupied an exalted place in Muslim courts. The Sultans and later Muslims were equally fond of secular books as well. They were responsible in part for the creation of the *Vasanta Vilasa* and the *Chaurapanchashika* and these works are sometimes considered a part of the Sultanate legacy. However, a special contribution of the Sultanate period, of interest to us as we trace the romantic emotion, was the illustration of the Sufi romances, where we see a syncretic coming together of Indian and Persian styles along with Hindu and Sufi artistic sensibilities. A popular Sufi romance that was illustrated was *Laur Chanda* written by Mulla Daud late in the 14th century in Avadhi and illustrated within a century, early in the 16th century, probably at Jaunpur in north India. The inspiration for *Laur Chanda* was a Hindu ballad but in the hands of Mulla Daud it became a popular Avadhi love story. While Persian elements can be seen in its cloud patterns, exquisite arabesque and tile like ornamentation on textiles and objects, *Laur Chanda* remains essentially Indian and borrows from the western Indian style of painting with its two-

dimensional representation, intense colouring, fondness for exuberant adornment, decorative architectural designs and vibrant textile patterns. The human figures are derived from the western Indian style with the men wearing the *kulahdar* turban and *chakdar jama* and women with the typical transparent *odhni* and the triangular downward pointing *patka*. *Laur Chanda* remains a major contribution of the pre-Mughal Sultanate period painting. Another Avadhi romance that was popular with the artists of eastern Uttar Pradesh was *Mrigavati*, written by Qutban in 1504 and illustrated soon thereafter. The style of the *Mrigavati* although derived from the western Indian school is distinctly folkish. While it may lack the refinement of *Laur Chanda* it makes up for this lack in its earthiness and vitality and it seems therefore, that while *Laur Chanda* was produced for a courtly audience, the *Mrigavati* may have been done for a more bourgeois clientele. This, therefore, establishes the fact that patronage for book illustrations of romantic literature of the 16th century came not only from the royalty and the nobility of the Sultanates but equally from the bourgeoisie who were able to see and enjoy the aesthetic merits of this type of artistic activity. The audience for these illustrated Sufi romances was the whole spectrum of the population from the pious Sufi masters to the enlightened kings and the nobility of courts down to the plebeian, unenlightened pleasure-seeker. It is therefore correct to state that the celebration of romantic stories, whether recited as poetry, sung as a ballad, performed as a dance drama or painted as a *chitravali*, was an essential ingredient of Indian aesthetic sensibility and culture and reached all levels of Indian society.

Detail, **Padmavati**
see page 130

When Babur entered India in April 1526 he inaugurated a dynasty that was to have far-reaching effects on the history of the subcontinent as well as on the history of Indian painting making it one of the glorious epochs of India. When his son Humayun returned from Persia he brought back with him one of the finest Persian painters, Mir-Sayyid Ali of Tabriz and this was a turning point in the history of Mughal painting. However, the most pivotal event was the birth of Akbar in 1542 for he went on to become not only one of the greatest emperors of India but one of the most enlightened and munificent patrons of painting. Akbar learned painting when he was in Kabul and when he ascended the throne he set up one of the finest ateliers where he personally supervised the productions of paintings. Akbar's ateliers not only had artists but calligraphers, illuminators, gilders, margin-makers and bookbinders and it mainly produced books and illustrated manuscripts. One of the first works created in Akbar's ateliers was the monumental *Hamza Nama* and this set the style for all Mughal paintings that were to follow. Akbar's atelier was visited not only by Persian painters but also by European emissaries. They brought with them European prints and paintings and it was through this that Mughal artists mastered the technique of portraiture, both linear and aerial perspective and chiaroscuro in Mughal painting. Akbar's atelier produced some of the most dramatic and vivid paintings of histories and heroic tales, of heroes and harems, of battles and sieges, and reflects Akbar's sense of history, his pride in his ancestry and his sense of mission as India's emperor. Abu'l Fazl writing about Akbar's portraits from his atelier quoted Akbar who said that "those who have passed away received new life and those who are still alive have acquired immortality." Abu'l Fazl also said that for Akbar there was none better than an artist in knowing God, for each time he draws a living being he must draw each and every limb of it, but seeing that he cannot bring it to life must perforce give thought to the miracle wrought by the Creator and thus obtain a knowledge of him. With the kind of reverence that Akbar had for artists, miniature painting had found its greatest patron and painting had gained a certain spirituality. By 1580 the fully-formed Akbari style of painting had emerged, combining Indian, Persian and European aesthetic strands. Jehangir, though self-indulgent and sensuous, was an avid lover of nature and introduced a refined and elegant naturalism in Mughal paintings that was not to be surpassed. He preferred paintings rather than books and individuality rather than group work among his artists and this led to many different styles of painting. "Observed realism, physical accuracy and psychological insight were extremely important to Jehangir."[2] His son Shah Jahan, the builder of the Taj Mahal, inspired sumptuous and magnificent portraits and under his patronage portrait painting attained a high water mark. "Style rather than substance, outward appearance rather than inner character, decorative exuberance rather than restraint, technical virtuosity rather than spontaneous expressiveness are some of the salient features of Shah Jahani paintings",[3] a good example of which is the *Padshanama*. Aurangzeb's austere and conservative attitude was responsible for the decline in painting during his reign but it indirectly helped painting at the Rajput courts as artists left the

2. Pal, 1993: 181
3. ibid, 185

Detail, **The Embrace of Love**

see page 167

Mughal atelier and sought patronage under the art-loving Rajputs. The Mughal school drew upon the resources of regional centres of painting especially in the north and in turn influenced them to create not only a provincial Mughal style patronised by the nobility, but a bazaar or popular Mughal style which was to incorporate many Hindu themes and thus pave the way for the Rajput paintings of the 17th century. Thus, under the grand Mughals painting reached a high degree of sophistication and technical perfection. Their finesse and style was magnificent and although they painted poets, musicians and even some romantic manuscripts like *Raj Kunwar*, they will be remembered more for their brilliant portraiture rather than for their contributions to the ethos of *shringara rasa*. The Mughal artist worked in a tightly-run court ethos where the king as patron of the arts was the ultimate authority with only minor inputs from the women and the lesser nobility and royalty. The Mughal artist could draw pretty faces but did not understand the many nuances and moods of the beautiful emotion of love; this was left to the later Hindu-inspired paintings of the Rajput courts. However, the legacy of the Mughal ateliers was to ensure that miniature painting was high art and it became, after the end of the grand age of Indian sculpture, the chief artistic idiom of the visual arts in later medieval India.

Mughal patronage of painting largely came to an end when Delhi was sacked by Nader Shah of Persia in 1739. As the Mughal empire was disbanding and the ateliers were losing their hold on the artists, provincial centres still remained active. One such centre where the Mughal artistic style continued was Avadh. Under Shuja-ud-daula (1753–1775) Avadh in eastern India became a powerful state virtually independent of Delhi and in its atelier a nostalgic though perhaps a decadent style of Mughal painting still continued. The prosaic composure of the Mughal line blended with local trends and manners and an added emphasis on the architecture of that period to produce some fine court scenes. A similar provincial Mughal atelier also flourished in Murshidabad in Bengal where brusque and prosaic formulae were similarly used.

Before we move on to the Rajput paintings, which was to see the efflorescence of the tradition of miniature painting, we must visit briefly the Deccan schools of the 16th century of Ahmednagar, Bijapur and Golconda. The patronage of the Asaf Shahi kings of Golconda was particularly important in stimulating painting in that state, while that of Ibrahim Adil Shah II was instrumental in promoting it in Bijapur. The Deccani or the southern style was influenced by a number of factors—the Mughal from the north, the Vijaynagar murals from the south and Turkish and Persian from the west—but in its art and culture the Deccan exhibited a certain innate independence. The Deccani artists were known for their brilliant and intense colouring, lavish costuming, lush vegetation, compartmentalised gardens, ornate borders and the vigour of their compositions. Like the Mughals, they produced a number of opulent court scenes and portraits but they also produced some beautiful *Ragamala* paintings, all of which shows that there was a certain self-assured pride and confidence in their unique culture, refined taste, baroque-like ambience and a cultured sensibility. By the end of the 16th century Golconda had become the richest province and the opulent jewelry on the dancers and courtesans is one indication of its wealth. By the middle of the 17th century as their political fortunes dwindled and artists left for northern patrons, the Deccani ateliers were impoverished and, although Hyderabad under the Nizams was buzzing with artistic activity in the 18th century, the Deccani ateliers became a pale shadow of their earlier glory.

This brief survey of the Mughal and Deccan schools raises an important question when it comes to the aesthetics of romance, as to why despite a well-honed technique, munificently-endowed ateliers, opulent courts and a refined sensibility, the expression of the many and beautiful nuances of romantic moments was not important to these artists? Suggestions of romantic liaisons in harem scenes and in *Ragamala* paintings in the hands of these Mughal and Deccani artists are more lustful than romantic, pretty rather than beautiful, and lack the refined and delicate depiction of romantic love that is seen in the Rajput painting that was to follow. The only exception perhaps was the illustration of *Laila Majnu* by Mughal artists. The answer probably lies in the Islamic attitude towards love, an attitude that did not elevate romantic love to a higher state of living and being. Vaishnavism on the other hand exalted the love of Radha and Krishna and their many romantic dalliances. It has been said in the *Vedas* that *rupam rupam pratirupam babhuva*, every form is a replica of the primal form, in the same way every *nayaka* and *nayika* who engaged in romantic activity were considered to be following in the footsteps of the divine couple. Romantic love in the hands of Vaishnavas had not only divine sanction but royal patronage and societal acceptance as well and no aesthetics of romance, whether it was poetry or painting, would be complete without celebrating the love of Radha and Krishna. Painting in the hands of the Rajput ateliers was visual poetry and arose from a deep-seated poetic sensibility and therefore there could be no Hindu atelier where the mellifluous flute of Krishna was not heard, no Hindu court where the sweet whisper of Radha was not present and no Hindu poet who would not identify with the heart-throb of the *sakhi* and celebrate ecstatically the romantic moments of Radha and Krishna.

In their account of the development of Rajput paintings art historians write about issues of patronage after the decline of the Mughal ateliers and the pervasive influence of the Mughal style in Rajput paintings. However, what is not stressed is that Rajput painting, whether in Rajasthan or the hill states of Punjab, saw the resurgence of the Krishna of love, a Krishna that was already celebrated by poets in eastern India in the *Bhagavata* and the *Gita Govinda* and by painters of the western Indian school in the 14th century. Rajput patrons assured the centrality of Krishna in the celebration of *shringara rasa*. To the Indian psyche amorous feelings could not be separated from the flute of Krishna; the sensuousness of romance was tied intimately to the sights and sounds, the aroma and the ambience of the enchanted forest where Radha and Krishna dallied; the joy of belonging and the pathos of longing could only be understood through the various moods of Radha, and one could only experience the depth of *shringara rasa* by recreating Vrindavana within one's heart. If *shringara* for us has *madhurya* it is only through Krishna, if *viraha* is *adhyatmika* it can only be through Radha. Radha and Krishna are particular and universal, human and divine, sacred and secular at the same time. This is the reason why the love of Radha and Krishna is so central, so meaningful. In partaking of their love we bring something of their sweetness into our own lives, in remembering Vrindavana we bring some of its enchantment into our own minds, in enjoying the various *lilas* of Krishna there is a reminder, that within the Krishna of love is also a child given to pranks, and in letting their abundant love touch us we are bringing boundless joy into our own little lives. The Rajput courts gave a new dimension to this very rich and magnificent love. The songs and the stories, the poetry and the *puranas* took on a visual and palpable form in Rajput courts and *havelis*. One could hold and feel the paintings and enjoy them in elite company, recount the deeds of Radha and Krishna and exult in their many dalliances. If Jayadeva had created an enchanted Vrindavana, the Rajput artists painted magnificent courts and *havelis*, if Jayadeva wrote evocative poetry, the Rajput artists created visual poetry, if Jayadeva's words were music to the ears, the Rajput creations were a visual feast. The Rajput courts continued the ancient Indian tradition of tying visual art to textual sources and creating art that was not only sensually rich but spiritually evocative, but they broke new ground and inaugurated a new era in Hindu art when they chose to represent visually the many nuances and shades of romantic love, especially that of Radha and Krishna. In the Rajput courts a new chapter in the aesthetics of Vaishnavism was written. Besides creating paintings of the *Bhagavata Purana* and the *Gita Govinda* Rajput artists produced refined and visually charming paintings from the *Rasikapriya*, *Rasamanjari* and *Sat Sai*. *Ragamala* and *Barahmasa* were other favourite texts of the Rajput ateliers. In placing romantic love within the myriad taxonomies offered by the *riti kal* poets, Rajput artists moved romantic love from the idyllic Vrindavana to the *havelis* and courts. It has been said that in satisfying the spiritual and aesthetic needs of their Hindu patrons and placing Radha and Krishna in a courtly ambience, the artists who created these Rajput paintings, whether they were Hindus or Muslims, were working within a conceptual and emotional framework that was well-established centuries before their time.[4] It is worth noting that although there were sharp doctrinal and religious differences between the Hindus and the Muslims, when it came to painting, Hindu and Muslim artists worked together harmoniously in many ateliers. Some of the finest paintings with Hindu themes have been painted by Muslim artists. This was due, in great measure, to the culture of tolerance that prevailed in many Mughal and Rajput courts. In the exuberant Vaishnava ethos religious differences were put aside. What mattered most was to capture the spirit of romantic excitement and ecstasy. Ancient texts such as the *Kama Sutra* stipulate that the cultured elite should be well versed in the art of painting. While agreeing in principle with this statement we would like to emphasise that while the artistic idiom of ancient India in the visual arts was sculpture, and that while this was able to depict feminine eroticism and fertility with finesse, the sensitive and elegant visual depiction of *shringara rasa*, the romantic sentiment reached a high water mark only in the paintings of the Rajput courts. Another aesthetic feature for which the Rajput ateliers must be given credit is the boldness and sensitivity with which they used colours. Pal is right in saying that "the most compelling aspect of Rajput painting is the primacy given to colours, chosen more for their intrinsic qualities and emotional values than for their fidelity to nature."[5] The Rajput artists created a female form that was emotionally evocative, sensually rich and aesthetically pleasing. One important development in the creation of this form was the tortuous or the twisted figure of the nayika. Anand Krishna[6] traces this to the depictions of beautiful women in early Sanskrit literature. He cites this passage from Kalidasa's *Kumarasambhavam* where the poet is referring to Parvati:

her entire body displayed amour as if like a newly sprouted kadamba blossom,
as she stood before Shiva, having large eyes,
she looked prettier as she stood with her face turned in the sachi-krita attitude.

In *Vikramorvasiyam* King Pururava recalling an amorous posture of Urvasi addresses a wild creeper:

O! lata you have done a great favour to me
as you came in her way and that the large eyed one
turned her face back in the paravritta ardhamukha posture
and that way I had a chance of catching a glimpse of her.

Anand Krishna feels that the *paravritta ardhamukha* depiction of the *nayika* which brought out her sensuality and helped in igniting romantic feelings in the *nayaka*. If Indian sculpture depicts mythic figures in their iconic

---

4. Pal, 1978: 10
5. ibid, 28
6. Personal communication

splendour using the full frontal view, Indian painting converts the profile into a perfect vehicle of romantic lyricism. While the icon stands on a lotus pedestal expressing its majesty and divinity, the lissom *nayika* assumes the form of a winding, swaying lotus plant when she twists and turns as she expresses her tender, wistful feelings of love. A woman's sensuality is tied to the sap of the trees and creepers. While the *salabhanjika* in sculpture offers her fecundity to the *ashoka* tree the *nayika* in paintings identifies herself with the lotus plant as she responds to the touch of her beloved or wilts when she finds his absence unbearable. The romantically sensitive and sensually aroused heroine in the hands of the Rajput painter is like the lotus plant when she expresses and experiences her sensuality; the life that animates her is no different from the sap that informs the plant and thus, the *nayika* and the plant are trans-substantiated.

It has been said by some that while the female form in Indian painting receives a lot of attention from art historians and connoisseurs alike, the artistic strength of the male form is relegated to the background. Romantic poetry is full of the sensual qualities of Krishna. However, in romantic painting this charge may largely be true and needs to be defended by philosophers of the arts. The centrality and primacy of the male gaze in romantic paintings is obvious. The reasons for this are cultural, sociological and psychological. Male chauvinism in Rajput courts cannot be denied. But there are philosophical—both metaphysical and epistemological—grounds why we in the Indian romantic tradition attribute sensuous beauty mainly to the female. A woman is the metaphor of *prakriti*, objectivity and materiality, while a man is the symbol of *purusha* or pure subjectivity and self-awareness. When it comes to *shringara rasa* that *purusha* is none other than Krishna, or *raseshvara*, the embodiment of the romantic emotion. In Indian thought the radiant and resplendent *purusha* stands serenely and magnificently alone and represents the self-assured, self-realised conciousness. Therefore, while the woman in love, whether it is Radha or the *gopis*, is the paragon of perfect beauty and it is her sensuality that is celebrated in painting, Krishna as the *purusha* and the prototypical romantic hero is not only the tranquil and serene self but equally the personification of the emotion of romantic love, and it is his acts of love that are depicted, his valour and strength that are venerated and his *lilas* that are admired. Krishna in his romantic attributes retains his mystical *bheda abheda*, different yet not different persona, and it is this that is the source of his beauty.

It is important to understand the Rajput psyche to really appreciate Rajput paintings. Present-day Rajasthan which was the original homeland of the Rajputs not only had a harsh terrain and climate but was surrounded by Muslims and this was, in no small measure, responsible for the Rajput character of a true *kshatriya*, a warrior with fierce loyalties to his clan and pride in his Hindu origins. Another feature of the Rajputs was that many aspects of their culture were sustained by popular as well as courtly patronage and this was responsible for the prevalence of many folk stories and songs, such as that of Dhola Maru and this was to have an influence in their paintings as well. Despite this the Mughals were able to subdue the Rajputs and one Rajput kingdom after another was annexed by the power and political intrigue of the Mughals. The first to surrender was Amber as early as 1562, and one of the last was Jodhpur in 1581. Although the Rajputs conformed to Mughal courtly standards and were influenced by Mughal artistic styles and idioms, they maintained their unique Hindu ethos, and this is especially seen in their celebration of *shringara rasa*, the romantic emotion, in painting. And the life-breath of *shringara rasa* for the Rajputs, as it is for all Hindus, is the love of Radha and Krishna and in turn it is this beautiful love that not only defines Rajput romantic painting but lifts it out of the ordinary and makes it sublime. B. N. Goswamy, in distinguishing Mughal from Rajput art, sums it up succinctly when he says:

> [The distinction between Mughal and Rajput painting] is of temper and style rather than of theme and subject matter... The emphasis on the poetic and lyrical aspects apart, [Rajput art] is permeated with what could be loosely termed Hindu modes of thought. [The Rajput's] approach is bardic while the Mughal's method is that of a chronicler... It is not only what is brought in that is significant but also what is left out...in Rajput work the Hindu way of seeing asserts itself...events do not necessarily move in a linear fashion...one senses that in rendering a moment the painter is not losing sight of the moments that have gone by and those that are yet to come...when he turned his hand to the subject, it seems that he dipped into his mind to recall the received notions of the very purpose of drawing a portrait, which was to capture an inner reality, the essence of the person rather than the accident of appearance.[7]

Before we examine the all-important legacy of Rajput paintings it is important to briefly visit *ragamala* paintings for they incorporated the romantic emotion in a very special way. To understand, capture and comprehend the divine qualities of music, its practitioners believed that each melody had not only a *nadamaya* or a sound form but also *devamaya* or a deified form and thus it was that a link between a *raga* and a deity was created. As *ragas* proliferated various taxonomies were developed to group these ragas and one of them was to regard music as a family with masculine *ragas*, feminine *raginis* and their children as *ragaputras*. There were six main *ragas*, namely, Bhairav, Kaushik, Hindol, Dipak, Shri and Megh. In masculine *ragas* the notes have an ascending tendency with cadential notes resting on the stronger pulses while in feminine *raginis* the phrases tend downwards with the cadential notes resting on the weaker pulses. *Ragas* are pentatonic while *raginis*

---

7. In Desai, 1985: xxi

are heptatonic. It is these visual forms of music that are sought to be portrayed in *ragamala* paintings. The *ragamala* painters sought inspiration from the Krishna lore, the poetry of *barahmasa* and the many themes of *nayika bheda*. While the principal figures are the *nayaka* and the *nayika*, of equal importance are the objects which enhance the mood and symbolise various aspects of romance. Two earthen-ware jars hold cool water and represent the sensuous beauty of a female. Buzzing bees represent the passion of lovers and lotus blossoms are an epitome of love. Rain is the season when the Rajput warrior as well as the merchant return home and it is therefore the season of love. With rain comes lightning which becomes the expression of passion. The peacock with his display of colours evokes the mating dance of the male. The bedchamber with its empty bed and bolsters further suggests the joy of love-making. A platter of betel and other condiments, garlands and sandalwood paste are useful accessories in a romantic rendezvous. Apart from these generic elements of *shringara rasa* specific *ragas* and *raginis* of the romantic mood call for definite visual manifestations. A swing with attendants and musicians suggests raga Hindol while a lady at her toilet adorning herself with jewellery is a sign of anticipation and is *raga* Bilaval, a *nayika* feeding a deer is a lovesick woman singing a lonely tune and is reminiscent of *raga* Todi, a thunderstorm with the cry of peacocks and birds gathering for shelter in trees evokes the fear and longing of a *nayika* as she finds comfort in feeding a peacock as in *raga* Madhumadhavi, when a coy *nayika* extinguishes a lamp in preparation for amorous pleasures it is *raga* Dipak, while to lessen the pangs of separation a *nayika* plays on the *vina* and composes a song evokes Gurjari *ragini*, when she makes a bed of flowers for her beloved it creates the mood of *ragini* Gormalar, a woman startled by the cry of a cuckoo and deriving comfort from the company of peacocks is *ragini* Kakubha. And when the hero discharges a flower arrow at the rooster who announces daybreak it is the mood of *ragini* Vibhasa. *Raga* Bhairava is supposed to have emanated from the throat of Shiva and is portrayed by the *bhairava rupa* of Shiva. *Raga* Shri named after Laxmi was originally related to the bounty of harvest but later came to symbolise fortune and is represented by a court scene in which amid royal splendour the king and queen listen to music, *ragini* Maru was considered to have emanated from the sounds of the swords of warriors and is depicted by

Detail, **Ragini Madhu Madhavi**
see page 196

the love story of Dhola Maru. While *ragamala* paintings may not be the most perfect visualisation of music they did create a beautiful, warm and lyrical visual form and in incorporating both the Radha Krishna theme and equally that of *nayika bheda* they are a unique idiom of Indian romantic painting.

It was in Mewar in the 17th century that Rajput art was to blossom. Mewar was blessed not only with a beautiful landscape and romantic architecture but equally with distinguished rulers who were not only valiant warriors but munificent patrons of the arts. The kings of Mewar belonged to the Sisodia clan of Rajputs and included such glorious names as Rana Kumbha, Rana Pratap who moved his capital to Chavand, Amar Singh, Jagat Singh, Raj Singh and Ari Singh. The Mewar kings refused to submit to the power and hegemony of the early Mughals or the religious bigotry of Aurangzeb and maintained a distinctly Hindu ambience in their courts. A popular adage of the Mewar courts was *sat bara, nau toohara*: seven days and nine festivals, for the observance and celebration of festivals was very important to them. Not only did this take their minds off the political and social realities of the state but it provided artists images to capture these celebrations in paintings. One of the earliest extant Mewari paintings is the *Chavand Ragamala* executed by Nisardi in 1605 and is a synthesis of Mughal, western Indian and local artistic idioms. *Rasikapriya* was the most commonly illustrated romantic text in Mewar. The Mewar artist paid scant attention to linear perspective but very often employed a bird's eye perspective. The strength of the Mewar artist was bold colouring and stylised rendering of trees and blossoms. The somewhat archaic and earthy Mewari style of painting was given a boost by another noted artist of this school, Sahibdin, and later Manohar, and it was they who gave a distinctive style to the Mewari school, a style that persisted almost into the 19th century. It was a style characterised by a tensely rhythmical line, a flamboyant use of strong emphatic colours, vigorous simplifications of *havelis* and bold and primitive idioms for plants and trees.

East of Udaipur, the new capital of Mewar, were the twin states of Kotah and Bundi (formerly known as Haraoti) which became important sites of Rajput painting. The earliest painting from this state is a *Chunar Ragamala* of 1591 but Mewar came into its own in the 17th and 18th centuries. Rao Chattar Sal (1631–1659) of Bundi was a patron of the arts and the Bundi artistic idiom was characterised by reddish-brown flesh tints and an architectural complex featuring open verandahs, domed pavilions, manicured gardens, lush plantain trees, water pools, tumultuous skies and male figures wearing long *jamas*, narrow *patkas*, *churidar pyjamas* and turbans with broad sashes and female figures with narrow waists, almond eyes and wearing a *gaghra* or *pishwaj*, high *choli* and *odhni* and ornamented by pearls. The Bundi *kalam* was noted for sumptuous luxuriance, a predilection for greens and oranges in juxtaposition, a delight in natural profusion and the use of recessions, shading and round volumes. The Bundi style was lyrical and had refinement, its figures showed grace and there was a certain subdued elegance about its compositions. Bundi had close contacts with the Deccan and Bhao Singh (1658–1681) of Bundi was the governor of Aurangabad under the last Mughal, Bahadur Shah. This contact resulted in a number of Deccani artistic influences in Bundi painting such as patterned floorings, pillared balconies, domed edifices and marked Mughal mannerisms. In the 18th century the bright and bold colouring of the Bundi artists was to give way to paler shades and this period is sometimes referred to as the white period of Bundi painting. It was in 1624 that Kotah broke off from Bundi to form an independent state and the beginnings of the Kotah *kalam* belong to the reign of Rao Jagat Singh (1657–1684). Kotah artists excelled in portraying hunting scenes and between 1720 and 1870 this was their main artistic output. The Kotah atelier also produced fine romantic paintings. The conservative and somewhat archaic style of Rajput painting of the 17th century found its way into Malwa in central India, part of present-day Madhya Pradesh, where under the rubric of the Rajput *kalam* yet another distinctive school of painting emerged. Although Sultanate manuscripts were executed in Mandu, capital of Malwa, and even though the Mandu court was overthrown early in Akbar's reign, its remoteness protected it from Mughal influences. The Malwa *Rasikapriya* of 1634 with bold monochrome backgrounds and simple architecture is a good example of the Malwa style and was able to bring to life the foundational text by Keshavdas. Therefore, it remains an important school in the development of the romantic idiom. The 17th century Malwa style is rightly considered to be a pure, classic statement of Indian shapes and sensibilities with painted domes and bright hues.

The tradition of romantic painting both in Rajasthan and in the Punjab hills did not feature portraits or studies of personalities but in the ateliers of Kishangarh this rule was broken for a romantic personality who epitomised not only exquisite beauty and unmatched grace but even more the passion of romantic love. That person was Bani Thani and the artist who immortalised her was Nihal Chand. The other notable artist at the Kishangarh atelier was Bhawani Das. Nihal Chand was a Muslim who emigrated from Delhi sometime between 1719 and 1726. Kishangarh which lies between Amber and Ajmer was founded by Kishan Singh in 1609. The state prospered during the 17th century but it was under the reign of Savant Singh that the atelier of Kishangarh came into its own. Savant Singh was born in 1699 and as a youth he was a gallant Rajput and even found favour at the Mughal court of Farrukhsiyar. It was there that he noticed the elegance of courtly attire and copied many of its features for himself. At the age of 20 he started to write devotional Krishna poetry under the pen name Nagari Das. Among his poetic words are *Rasik Ratnavali, Bihar Chandrika* and *Nikunj Vilas*. When he was 35 an event took place that was to change his life. His stepmother was impressed by a young dancer with a sweet voice and brought her to Kishangarh. Not only did she possess unsurpassed beauty but she also adorned herself tastefully and this earned her the name Bani Thani. Bani Thani was also a poetess who wrote under the name Rasikbehari, and it is not surprising that Savant Singh fell in love with her. Savant Singh acceded to the throne in 1748 but his heart was not in matters of the state. In one of his poems he wrote: what is the use of carrying worldly burdens lest it turn my mind away from Vrindavana? Savant Singh abdicated his throne in 1757 to spend the rest of his years in Vrindavana in the company of Bani Thani. He died in 1794 followed by Bani Thani a year later. For Savant Singh, Bani Thani was the embodiment of Radha and if he was able to capture her beauty in poetry, his artist Nihal Chand was to transform that beauty into a portrait that immortalised not only her beauty but her love. Nihal Chand's style was eminently fitted to express the mood of sensitive and romantic adoration. Nihal Chand also created many other paintings in which Bani Thani and Savant Singh were transformed into Radha and Krishna. It would not be wrong to say that Bani Thani was the one of the few historical persons who became idealised in painting as a romantic *nayika*. Nihal Chand also incorporated many of the sylvan and idyllic features of Roopnagar into his paintings, and his style and his depiction of Bani Thani endured for centuries.

Detail, **Bani Thani**
see page 161

Marwar or the present-day Jodhpur was founded by Rao Jodha (1444–1488) of the Rathor clan in the 13th century and in 1564 was annexed by Akbar. The earliest dated output from the Marwar atelier are *ragamala* paintings, although the illustrations of folk stories such as Dhola Maru and religious subjects such as the *Bhagavata Purana* may have started much earlier. The earliest *ragamala* set from Marwar is the Pali *ragamala* dated 1623, and which derives much from the Jain and the early Rajput traditions, is considered by some to be the prototype of Marwar paintings. Jaswant Singh, Ajit Singh and Bijai Singh were the early patrons of Marwar art and the late Jodhpur style reached its climax under the reign of Man Singh. Jodhpur artists were particularly fond of illlustrating the Dhola Maru story. It was in 1586 that Rai Singh of Bikaner gave his daughter in marriage to the son of Akbar, the heir-apparent Salim. This alliance placed the Bikaner court in close association with the cultural life of the Mughals but was not until the 17th century that it also developed an important school of painting. Under the patronage of Raja Anup Singh (1669–1698) Bikaneri painting reached its height. Its artists were swayed more by Mughal influences and there is an overall softness about the Bikaneri *kalam* with its demure female figures. An important group of artists at the court of Bikaner were what are called the Umrani Ustas, among whom was the noted Ruknuddin. They were mainly responsible for developing the characteristic style of the

17th century Bikaneri painting. Bikaner also had close contacts with the Deccan and this was also to have an influence on its compositions. The state of Amber assumed considerable political importance after Akbar married the princess of Amber in 1563 but Amber was not noted for its artistic creations until Raja Sawai Jai Singh II, who ruled from 1699 to 1743, and who moved his capital to the planned city of Jaipur in 1727, encouraged painting in his kingdom. Jaipur painting tends to be flat against the backdrop of the Amber fort and it produced a number of *ragamala* sets with broad red borders but of all the Rajasthani schools it failed to develop a style of its own and relied more on the decorative rather the poetic.

While different states of Rajasthan had individual artistic styles and idioms, which in turn stemmed from variations of taste and traditions, as historians are quick to point out, there is a certain thread of continuity from one state to another particularly when it comes to the celebration of the romantic emotion. The Rajput royalty and nobility of Rajasthan were sensitive patrons and recreating the various nuances of romance was important to them. Like the Mughals they had a need for portraits and court scenes as well but it was more important for them to keep the romantic ethos alive in their lives. They may have subjugated their political identity to the hegemonic Mughals but when it came to their private sensibilities they cherished their Hindu traditions and ensured that the Vaishnavite Krishna of love had a living presence in their courts and kingdoms. The love of Radha and Krishna for them was not just a beautiful love story but a foundational principle for life and living just as the various romantic texts were not just literature that was to be appreciated but almost a theology that gave purpose and meaning to their lives. They saw the changing seasons through the depiction of the *barahmasa* paintings and celebrated music through the *ragamala* paintings. The Krishna of love resonated in their minds, *shringara rasa* animated their artistic sensibilities and the beauty and nobility of romantic love in their courts became a refuge in the otherwise arid lives of Rajput men and women. Miniature painting was the chief artistic idiom of the Rajput courts and has left behind a rich and unique legacy of art in the Indian tradition.

The viewing of these miniature paintings was an activity of importance in the Rajput courts. While some kings who were so inclined would see the painting even as it was progressing and make important artistic suggestions, most were shown the finished creation. The king would reward the artist with money, a splendid robe, a sumptuous dagger, an elephant or sometimes even a village. The paintings were then wrapped in silk and stored in vaults. On festive occasions or in *mehfils* or gathering of poets the paintings would be brought out, passed from one person to the other and enjoyed in elite company, in the presence of poets and musicians who would recite and sing appropriate poetry. It was on such occasions that many romantic episodes were recreated, the true colour of romance was brought out and the paintings really came alive. If romantic dalliance needed privacy, the celebration of romantic art was best carried out in elite, cultivated and sensitive company. While soirees would include both men and women of the court, the women in their *zenana* would also entertain artists and enjoy romantic paintings.

While the 17th and 18th centuries saw the emergence of miniature painting in the Rajput courts of Rajasthan and a golden chapter in Indian art was written, the Rajput ethos travelled to the Himalayan hill states through trade routes and, because of the collapse of the Mughal empire, led to the production of beautiful miniature paintings, generally referred to as Pahadi paintings in the 18th and 19th centuries. Although an early Rajput style manuscript of the *Devi Mahatmya* of 1552 has been found from this hill region it is difficult to be sure about how much contact there was between the plains of Rajasthan and the hill kingdoms of the Himalayas as these states were sheltered from the conquests and invasions that the rest of the country suffered. Equally, while the Mughals held control over these hill states, Mughal interference in this area was very limited. And then again while Rajput painting in Rajasthan saw the complete evolution from early manuscript illustration to the fully evolved and refined miniature painting, it appears that Pahadi painting did not go through this transformation. Another feature of the Pahadi *kalam* was that there was greater homogeneity between the output of different kingdoms, as artists from one kingdom frequently travelled to another. The Pahadi kingdoms showed a greater predilection for worship of the goddess and had a well-developed tradition of making bronze images; this was also to have an effect on miniature artists. Broadly speaking, three phases in the development of miniature painting in the Pahadi *kalam* can be recognised, the early beginnings in the kingdom of Basohli, the middle phase in Guler and the late phase in Kangra.

Detail, **Madanika Darpana**
see page 154

Basohli was an ancient state and its present capital was founded in 1630 near the right bank of the river Ravi. Raja Kirpal Pal was born in 1650 and ruled from 1678 to 1695. He inaugurated the first atelier of Pahadi painting in his state of Basohli and commissioned a manuscript of the *Rasamanjari,* and is considered the father of the Pahadi *kalam.* Art historians while recognising that paintings of the *tantric devi* series may have been produced much earlier in the *pahadi* region, have debated why, in spite of temple building and folk painting in the hill states, miniature painting as an art form did not develop. Patronage, religious affiliations and outside influences must surely have played a part. The Basohli atelier had artists from Kashmir and possibly even from Nepal as well as *tarkhans* or carpenters who were proficient in architectural drawings and wood sculpture. This explains the unique style that developed in the atelier of Basohli which incorporated all these influences. Besides the robust, ethnic and primitive figures that are a signature of the Basohli *kalam* the use of shiny green beetle wing particles on jewellery was a feature of the Basohli *kalam* not seen anywhere else. Raja Kirpal Pal was a learned ruler and like Akbar he developed a fondness for possessing illustrated manuscripts on a variety of subjects. Raja Kirpal Pal was aware not only of Mughal styles and sensibilities of the Aurangzeb period but equally of Rajasthani tastes and particularly that of Mewar. Besides the *Rasamanjari* which was the favourite text of Kirpal Pal, the *Bhagavata Purana* and *Gita Govinda* were also illustrated at Basohli. Throughout the 18th century Basohli rulers showed a special fondness for the *Rasamanjari* and this kingdom was to produce some of the finest illustrations of this romantic text by Bhanudatta. Even though it is entirely possible that artists from neighbouring states may have played a role in the development of the so-called Basohli style, the style remains unique and is one of the finest artistic expressions in miniature painting of the 18th century, with its characteristic ethnic types, bold colour schemes, wooden architectural motifs and frank and robust figures. Kirpal Pal's son Dhiraj Pal continued his father's tradition and the Basohli *kalam* flourished under him as well. Artists from Basohli migrated to other states, to Nurpur in particular, and also to Mankot, Bilaspur, Kulu and Chamba, where they continued the Basohli *kalam*.

The second phase of the development of the Pahadi *kalam* was to take place in the kingdom of Guler. Geography as much as patronage was responsible for the development of the Guler *kalam*. Founded by Hari Chand in 1405, Guler is located south of Kangra by the river Beas and since it was easily accessible from the plains it was subject to outside influence. It was Govardhan Chand (1743–1773) who founded and patronised the atelier at Guler. However, the Guler style was mainly shaped by Pandit Seu and his illustrious sons, the older Manaku and the younger Nainsukh. Information gleaned from *bahis* at pilgrimage centres suggests that Pandit Seu and his family came originally from Kashmir and were Raina *brahmins* and his initial training was in a Mughal atelier of Muhammed Shah. Pandit Seu brought these skills to the Guler court of Raja Dalip Singh and it was thus that a new Guler *kalam* was inaugurated. Nainsukh was born in 1710 and had prodigious skills and after working initially with his father moved to Jasrota in 1740 where he attached himself to Balwant Singh, a young prince who belonged to a breakaway branch of the ruling family. There is some debate whether Balwant Singh belonged to Jammu or Jasrota. Nainsukh stayed with his patron Balwant until the latter's death in 1763. This was to be a very fruitful partnership and a number of beautiful portraits arose from this association. After the passing away of Balwant Singh Nainsukh moved to Basohli where he worked for Amrit Pal and painted a delightful *Gita Govinda*. Nainsukh brought a certain delicacy, refinement and lyricism to Pahadi painting, which is in sharp contrast to the earlier Basohli style, but his mastery lay, in Goswamy's words, "in being able to seize a detail and exalt it." The Alakananda river which flows through Guler had a special fascination for the Guler artists. Nainsukh and his brother Manaku left an indelible stamp on Pahadi painting and it would be no exaggeration to say that their creations rank among the highest achievements of Indian art in the 18th century. In 1780 the fully evolved Guler *kalam* was taken to Kangra and in that state under the patronage of Raja Sansar Chand (1175–1823) miniature painting reached perfection in the early decades of the 19th century. In 1805 when the Gurkhas of Nepal besieged Kangra, Sansar Chand had to take the aid of Ranjit Singh, and although the Gurkhas were defeated Kangra was annexed by Ranjit Singh. Later Kangra painting therefore began to show Sikh influences. Sansar Chand, now a defeated person, led a retired life. Along with his daily routine of prayers he spent his time listening to music and examining paintings. He spent his last days in the company of a dancing girl by the name of Jamalo in his palace at Nadaun overlooking the Beas. While the Kangra *kalam* exudes a refined sensuousness and lyrical grace, drawing its inspiration not only from its idyllic landscape but equally from the living presence of the Krishna of love, it is in the depiction of the graceful and elegantly sensuous female that it reaches its greatest heights. The Modi *Bhagavata* ranks as the highest watermark of the magnificent Kangra *kalam*. The Kangra *nayika* not only had an elegant and sensuous charm and unsurpassed beauty but a refined romantic sensibility, whether she was experiencing the pain of pathos or the pleasures of love, and in the genre of romantic figures that Indian artists have produced she represents the most beautiful and the most exalted. By the middle of the 19th century the Pahadi *kalam* had lost much of its finesse and vitality and the glorious era of miniature painting was coming to an end. It is important to visit briefly Garhwal where the atelier was founded by two brothers Sham Das and Hari Das who came in 1658 to the court of Raja Prithipat Shah in the company of the fleeing Prince Suleman Shikoh, son of Aurangzeb's brother Dara. The Garhwal atelier, however, was dominated by Mola Ram (1743–1833) who in his long life produced some scintillating paintings imbued with life and colour and resonant of Krishna.

An important school of painting that is intimately tied to Krishna and must not be missed in our survey of romantic painting is the Nathadwara school. At Nathadwara we see the rare coming together of *shringara rasa* and *shringara bhakti* where Krishna is venerated in his divine form as well as celebrated in his human form. Nathadwara celebrates Krishna as Shrinathji and is the home of *pushtimarga* Vaishnavism founded by the 15th century saint Vallabhacharya. The essence of *pushtimarga* is in Vallabha's own words, "He dwells not in wood, in clay or in stone; in *bhava* He dwells, which holds the first place of all" emphasising the emotionally ecstatic and richly adorned, rather than the contemplative worship of Krishna. Whether in the image of Shrinathji or the various rituals that are performed, the place of Radha's love is never forgotten. The mirror held in front of Shrinathji as he dresses for the *shringara darshan* is compared to Radha in whose heart Shrinathji is ever present. The metal box on a stand contains twelve folded *bidas* of *pan* which represent *dvadasha nikunja lila,* the twelve bowers where Krishna and the *gopis* held their *lilas,* the lotus garland around his neck is Radha herself, the U-shaped *tilak* mark on his forehead is supposed to be the impression of Radha's foot left there when Krishna bowed to her, the tiny pitcher wrapped in a red cloth is Radha's *madhurya bhava.* Painting as a regular activity seems to have started in *pushtimarga* from the time of Gopinathji, Vallabha's elder son who propagated *chitraseva,* the worship of painted icons. However, the Nathadwara school of painting came into being later during the latter half of the 18th century. The Nathadwara *kalam* is known for two main types of paintings, *pichwai* and miniature paintings. While *pichwai* or the painted fabric always features the iconic Shrinathji, miniature painting shows Krishna both as the iconic Shrinathji along with devotees and the *tilkayats* of the temple as well as Krishna the cowherd and his various *lilas* with the *gopis.* Deriving inspiration from the Rajasthani schools such as Mewar and Kotah the artists of the Nathadwara school of the 19th and early 20th centuries were also influenced by European paintings. It is not uncommon to see Radha and Krishna in Nathadwara paintings set in a European landscape.[8]

It has rightly been said that Hindu patrons had very low expectations of their scribes[9] and the text that was inscribed either on the front or the back of the painting was often carelessly done. It was in Kashmir that standards were first established in this field. Very little is known about early painting in Kashmir. There is a strong possibility that a Sultanate style of painting existed in the Kashmir valley in the 15th century. Rajauri was an important centre in Kashmir and this was on the Mughal route from Punjab to Kashmir. In the 18th and 19th centuries a number of illuminated manuscripts were made in Kashmir where a synthesis of Hindu and Muslim styles could be seen. These manuscripts were small and the calligraphy was well done. Some Kashmiri artists revived the ancient practice of writing in gold and silver ink on blue or black paper.

The odyssey of romantic painting that we have undertaken will not be complete unless we visit two other centres of art where the romantic ethos was alive even as the era of miniature painting was coming to an end— where the love of Radha and Krishna is written in the very earth and Krishna lore is in the wind, where no formal ateliers existed and painting was an activity of the common person, where simple motifs expressed grand truths and paintings adorned not the precincts of courts but the walls of homes—Madhuban and Kalighat. Madhuban is a district in the Mithila region of northern Bihar where *Brahmin* and *Kayastha* women have

---

8. I am grateful to Amit Ambalal for leading me through the nuances of Nathadwara painting.
9. Losty, 1982: 119

continued a tradition of wall and floor painting and have recently successfully transformed their techniques of painting onto paper. While floor paintings are done in every home in Mithila, the painting of murals is a speciality of the women of Mithila and these murals are created in corridors of homes and around home shrines, but one mural in particular very special to the Madhubani artists is the mural on the *kobhar ghar*, a chamber in the bride's village where the newly married couple spend the first few days. These murals are executed on surfaces freshly covered with a mixture of cow dung and mud. Traditionally the colours were derived from plants, flowers and vegetables and brushes were made from rags tied to twigs whil a bamboo sliver was used for fine line work. The *kobhar ghar* featured not only Radha and Krishna along with other mythological images and images of *samskaras* or ritual events of initiation, but in particular it was full of fertility symbols like the fish, bamboo, lotus, parrots and blossoms. Through these symbols and within geometrical patterns the Madhubani artist created images that are aesthetically pleasing and magico-religiously potent, which more than make up in their earthy robustness, what they may lack in artistic refinement. These images, which were not intended for courtly connoisseurship, had a living presence in the lives of the villagers. Madhubani painting is an important visual document of the love of Radha and Krishna, emerging from the minds and hands of rural women, women who are unsophisticated at one level but beautifully sensitive at another. In Madhubani art each leaf or blossom, every parrot and fish has its own space even if it means sacrificing perspective; in abstracting rather than stylising, the Madhubani artist breathes life into plants and animals which are so much a part of her environment. In eliminating the sky and the earth, time and space, Madhubani art acquires a mythic character even though it remains rustic, although considered folk art by some standards it has a modern and primitive ethos at the same time. Madhubani artists are short on words, nor do they lay claim to any literature, but they have a rich treasure of an oral tradition, of stories and songs, passed on from mother to daughter; they also have hidden springs of racial memories, and it is from this that their images arise. The folk style of Madhubani art while departing from the stylisation and refinement of Rajput miniatures and also from the sculpturesque forms of ancient murals exudes an earthy warmth, simple sweetness and a loving intimacy. Madhubani creations do not have the stately mansions and regal courts of Rajput and Mughal painting but instead feature the loving relationship between mankind and nature. To the Madhubani artist the *rasa* that animates Radha and Krishna is the same sap that resonates in trees and blossoms, fish and parrots and in us humans. The strengths of Madhubani are its earthy, robust figures in warm colours and this especially comes alive in the *kobhar ghar*. What is interesting to note is that the *kobhar ghar* not only features gods and goddesses and fertility symbols, both of which are necessary for a successful marriage but equally the tender loving figures of Radha and Krishna indicating that marriage according to the people of

Madhuban was not only a sacrament to be celebrated but a romance to be cherished.

If Madhubani art has carved a place for itself in the annals of Indian romantic painting Kalighat art has a special place particularly as it stands at the threshold of the traditional and the modern in Indian romantic painting, and even more so as it was the doorway to modern Indian painting inspiring artists such as Jamini Roy. As the ateliers at Mughal and Rajput courts were losing their patronage, artists started looking for newer pastures. Kolkata, which in 1773 had become the capital of British India, was attracting a number of artists. The building of the Kali temple in the early 19th century and the requirements of the pilgrims, the Battala press which produced woodcuts, the advent of photography, the presence of British patrons and the rise of the Bengali middle class in the 19th century provided the inspiration for traditional scroll painters or *patuas* to settle around the Kali temple and create images on paper and in clay, not only for pilgrims but for their eclectic patrons as well. These Kalighat artists belonged to a hybrid Hindu and Muslim caste, taking inspiration not only from their own stock of images but also other artistic traditions, both Indian and European and successfully transforming their style of scroll painting to produce distinctive mythological and secular images. Even though they favoured Kali and other goddesses Kalighat artists were not untouched by the love of Radha and Krishna. Kalighat paintings are generally in vertical format made on newsprint paper and their figures have strong lines, solid colours, an informal and bold iconography and minimum background landscapes so that the figures stand out as if telling a story, narrating a moment, true to their origins from *patas* or scrolls. By the end of the 19th and early 20th century with the advent of lithographs and modern Indian paintings, Kalighat art came to an end.

Thus in this brief history of romantic painting, we have undertaken a journey where we met art loving patrons, visited ateliers where romantic themes came to life, encountered family rivalries, political intrigues and military conquests that played a part in the artistic and cultural life of the courts, walked on trade and caravan routes with artists as they moved from one court to another seeking patronage, wondered about the differences in the Rajput and the Mughal ethos of painting, touched the rich treasure of romantic poetry from which these paintings have arisen and which transformed these paintings into visual poetry and realised that the only door to the intimate worlds of these paintings is through that richly evocative poetry, enjoyed the line and colour, the symbols and motifs that the artist used in sensitively portraying romantic love, took in the landscape in which romantic love unfolds and saw that human love not only resonated with the blossoms and the birds but equally in courts and *havelis*, dipped into the milieu in which the artists functioned and inquired about the paper, the paint and the tools with which they must have worked, considered their relationships with their patrons, were dismayed to find that ravages of climate had destroyed some of their finest creations, came face to face with the most exalted of human emotions, that of romantic love between a man and a woman, a love that is richly sensual and yet serenely spiritual, a love that is celebrated both in the pleasures of belonging and the pathos of longing, realised that there were a thousand nuances and a hundred hues of romance, explored the poetically elegant and richly sensuous female form, imagined the courtly atmosphere of the cultured elite where these paintings were enjoyed, became aware that there were many ways in which romantic love was expressed and experienced, a love that was sparked with the first sight of the beloved but which was locked in a timeless gaze, but above all reaffirmed the Vaishnava spirit of *shringara bhakti*, and along with *sakhis* exulted in the love of Radha and Krishna and recreated the enchanted Vrindavana in our hearts and minds where their love causes the trees to bloom and the birds to sing, saw Radha and Krishna as the lover and the beloved but were wonderstruck at their biune unity, and sang along with Radha

Facing page:
Detail, **Nayika Watching Pigeons**
see page 165

> *the god of love has woven in a garland your heart and mine,*
> *given us two bodies but one atman*
> *for you are me and I am you*
> *two so that we may enjoy our love*
> *but really one*
> *for in the enjoyment of love we may be two*
> *but in the perfection of love*
> *there can be no duality*
> *only the advaita of love.*

These beautiful paintings, whether in a museum or a book like this, are obviously removed and fragmented from their context and stand in mute testimony to the ethos and ambience in which they were celebrated, but bereft of the meaning and dignity that they possessed in their original environment. To merely appreciate its artistic attributes and read the formal features of the painting would be to embark on a journey that was never intended. The modern but sensitive reader should ideally attempt to become a *sahradaya*, a connoisseur whose heart vibrates in resonance with that of the artist and the patron in whose atelier these paintings were produced, and try and restore as much of the context as possible, so that these paintings regain some of their lost glory. The cultivated aesthete must try and understand the piety and poetry from which these paintings have arisen, shun voyeuristic tendencies and instead share the tender feelings that are being expressed through line and colour and enter the intimate worlds of *nayakas* and *nayikas* that these paintings depict. Only then will these paintings come alive and speak of the heart-throbbing, soul-stirring romantic moments that they so charmingly depict.

Romantic Moments in Painting

Virag
The Changing Colours
of Love

We have surveyed romantic love through poetry and painting and enjoyed its ethos and its expressions, even as we have celebrated the *shringara rasa* that it evoked. It is not difficult to see that as the tradition evolves, while the fabric of *shringara rasa* remains basically the same its texture varies, while the melody of love remains the same its lyrics change, while the palette remains constant the colours of the *rasa* change. It is that change that we shall explore in this concluding section. It has been a beautiful journey that we have undertaken, a journey of romantic moments in poetry and painting, a voyage that has taken us through the many hues of the romantic emotion, its variegated nuances, its changing ethos, its many songs and delightful stories, the different heroes and heroines, its chequered milieu, now sacred and now secular, but always arising from that primal need to love and be loved, and have found in that pulsating, throbbing love the meaning and expression of life itself. We have given the romantic emotion the pride of place in our arts and have called *shringara rasa* the *raja rasa*, the king of *rasas*, the supreme emotion and have been bold enough to weave in a single tapestry both romantic and devotional love with the same thread, we have worshipped god and loved our beloved with the same notes of our love song and have used the same blue colour of the clouds of *ashadha* to paint Krishna the godhead and Krishna the romantic hero.

The *dashama skanda* of the *Bhagavata Purana* brought to a peak the conventions and the style of *aham* Tamil poetry and not only established the primacy of *shringara rasa* but wove into it *bhakti rasa* creating the unique motifs and metaphors of *bhakti shringara* or ecstatic devotion through the aegis of romantic love and not the arid contemplative devotion of *bhakti*. In *bhakti shringara* Krishna is both the lord and the beloved and the *gopis* love him just as a *nayika* loves the *nayaka*.

There are two features of *shringara rasa* that are special to the *Bhagavata Purana*. First the locale of love is the sylvan Vrindavana and the beautiful love of Krishna and the *gopis* takes place amidst verdant groves and the meandering

माल स्य त त ो नि वृ तु ह र े : ॥२४२॥ न म न स्का ल त दा ला प ल ब्धि वे ष्ट त द ा लि का: ॥ त रु णा व ग ा यं त्यो ना त्मा ग ा र णि स स्म रु: ॥४३॥ पुन: पुलि न म ा वि श्र य का लिं द्या: कु स म भा व ना: ॥ स म ता ज गु: कु स ंत दा ग म न का शि ता : ॥ ॥ इ ति श्री भा ० ह ० कृ ष्णा न्वे ष ण ना म त्रिं श ो ध्या य: ॥ ॥

Yamuna river, their amorous whispers are shared by singing birds and blossoming trees. A second feature of the love in the *Bhagavata* is that it is the gopis who collectively love Krishna and Radha as the supreme *nayika* makes only a tentative appearance. The *raas lila* is the highest experience of that love of the *gopis* and as the *raas* ends the *gopis* continue to love and worship Krishna, although now instead of the pleasure of belonging they suffer the pangs of longing and the excitement of *samyoga* turns into the poignantly beautiful *viyoga*.

Bhagavat Purana
Sirohi, 19th century
Collection: Author

After the *Bhagavata* the ethos of *bhakti shringara* was firmly established and spread throughout the land. About five centuries later Jayadeva added another important milestone in the evolution of *bhakti shringara*. In a short poem of unsurpassed beauty Jayadeva added two new features to the dynamics of *bhakti shringara*. Jayadeva gave primacy to Radha and established her as the supreme *nayika* and secondly he located *bhakti* equally in the poet and the *gopis*, making Jayadeva not only a poet but the consummate *sakhi* in his loving devotion and adoration of Krishna. In doing this Jayadeva was continuing the tradition started by the *aham* poets who, in their love for Krishna, assumed the persona of a woman. The *Gita Govinda* continued the idyllic and sylvan ambience of the *Bhagavata* emphasising that the love of Radha and Krishna is no different from the sap that animates the blossoms and the birds in the enchanted Vrindavana. The human mind and heart resonate in the *Bhagavata* and the *Gita Govinda* with the world around and a loving association is established between the two where the vibrating and pulsating sensuality is never divorced from deep-seated spirituality.

Jayadeva in the first canto of the *Gita Govinda* clearly establishes the primacy of Krishna in *shringara rasa* when he says *srijayadeva bhanitam idam adbhuta kesava keli rahasyam* (1.45) the song of Jayadeva is about the secrets of Krishna's wondrous love and further *shreni shyamala komalair upanayann angair anangotsvam* (1.46) it is he who initiates the festival of love with his limbs which are dark and tender. It is the sound of Krishna's flute that is not only a love call but a call to eternity. For the flute of Krishna unlike the *vina* of Sarasvati, expresses a melody and words, it is *nirvikalpa* rather than *savivikalpa*, it invites rather than instructs, it beckons rather than insists. For if love is a festival it needs an initiation, no different from the *diksha* that a religious teacher gives and the *siksha* that one obtains from a guru. Jayadeva further asserts that to recount the many deeds of Krishna he chooses *madhurkomalakantapadavali* a string of sweet, delicate and loving words. Keshavdas in his invocation to the *Rasikapriya* states all *rasikas* should forever serve Krishna for none other than Krishna contains the nine emotions, once again emphasising that it is he who is the embodiment of all emotions and true emotional fulfilment can come only from celebrating him. It therefore follows that the elaborate taxonomy of love that Keshavdas offers is really a chronicle of the many moods and meetings of Radha and Krishna. When Surdas writes *surdas bali bali jori para nandakunvara brhabhanu kumvariya*, Surdas is delighted even at the thought of the love of Radha and Krishna, he enunciates the credo of the *ashtachap kavis* of the Nathadwara tradition. Vidyapati who loved and admired Radha, whether it was her naive innocence, her need for love, her surrender to rapture, her anguish when wronged, upholds the romantic persona of Radha through his passionate love songs and says sweet as honey is the talk of a girl in love. There is no doubt that if Vidyapati's words are sweet it is because Radha is the paragon of sweetness herself.

Detail, **Krishna appeases an offended Radha**
Gita Govinda, Mewar, AD 1714
Collection: Author

Clearly implied in the word *upanayann* of Jayadeva when it is applied to romantic love, deriving its etymology from having one's eyes opened, is the concept of understanding, insight or wisdom, for without this one is likely to lose one's path and go astray in the many paths of love, without the vision of love that Krishna inspires one is likely to be led into blind alleys in the forest of hedonistic desire rather than rejoicing in the Vrindavana of romance, and without Krishna's gentle touch it would be easy to mistake sensuality for sexuality in romantic love. It is only Krishna who can ensure that romantic love is sensuous and spiritual, it is only Madhukara who can make love sweet and profound, it is only Ghanashyama who can ensure that love is vast and universal as the dark blue cloud of *ashadha*, it is only Venugopala who can make that love as mellifluous as the sound of his flute, it is only Giridhara who can lift human love to the realms of the divine, none other than Yogeshvara who is equipoised in *samyoga* and *viyoga* of love, who other than Keshimathanam can destroy lust and purify it to amorous desire, only Upendra who can wield the thunderbolt of love and make it as soft as the lotus, who other than Govinda can tend romantic thoughts as gentle as the cows and only a Janardana who can make the torment of love into the pleasure of the soul.

From now on Krishna and Radha become the prototypical heroine and hero of all romantic themes. The *nayikas* and the *nayakas* that appeared in the rich literature of the *bhashas* that followed and especially in *riti kavya*, were fashioned in the likeness of Radha and Krishna, and had a certain softness in their demeanour, a sweetness in their gestures, a delicacy in the portrayal of their emotions, a cultured sensitivity in their actions and activities, a lyrical charm in their interactions, a measured grace in their movements, and above all a noble restraint in their passions. The *nayika* in the many and varied manifestations of her emotions was always demure, though sensuous she was never flirtatious, frankly passionate in her love but never erotic, ecstatic but never lustful, intensely sensual but yet serenely spiritual. The *nayaka* on the other hand is equally graceful, mischievous but never malicious, truant at times but always committed, given to the many innocent games of love but never devious, demanding yet never aggressive. Whether it is the pathos of longing or the pleasure of belonging, the joys of togetherness or the pain of separation, the thrill of the sensuous touch or the burning desire for a caress, there is in the persona of the loving couple a decided grace and sensitivity, never a hint of crassness, at no time even a tinge of lewdness. Romantic love for them was more a giving of themselves rather than receiving, it is a treasured offering, a joyous sharing, a *yajna* where no sacrifice was too great, no pain unbearable, where in the pleasures of love they maintain a loving duality but in the perfection of love they melt into one. And while this love surges in their breasts it also resonates in the world of blossoms and birds around them. In sitting under a tree or holding its branch they are emphasising that the *shringara rasa* that flows within them is the same loving sap that animates the trees. When the lament of the deserted heroine is compared to the poignant call of the *chakravaka* it suggests that there is a bond between them, when the peacock dances under gathering rain clouds and the *nayika* longs for the return of her beloved she knows that

Bundi
18th century
Collection: Author

she is not alone in her feeling. When tender creepers wind around tall trees they are only imitating the passionate embrace of the lovers, and when intoxicated bees hum around lotus pollen they are singing a paean of love.

If Krishna as *nayaka* initiates us into the many nuances of romantic love Radha equally is a mirror of the beautiful mind and body of the *nayika*, sensuous in her *samyoga* but serene in her *viyoga*, regal in her manner and yet coy in her demeanour, changing with the seasons yet steadfast as *dhruva*, the pole star, offended when wronged but easily forgiving, courageous when she braves the storm and sets out as an *abhisarika* and giving of her *shangar* when she adorns herself as a *vasakasajja*, looking every bit a *yakshi* when she holds the branch of the *kadamba* tree as she waits for Krishna.

Detail, **Rasika Priya**
Mewar, 1730–1740
Collection: Author

Following Jayadeva's *Gita Govinda* there were two important theistic developments in the realm of *bhakti shringara*, developments that not only changed the theology of Krishna worship but equally its aesthetics, and these were the evolution of the *pushtimarga* of Vallabhacharya in western India and *Gaudiya* Vaishnavism of Chaitanya in eastern India. The nucleus of the *pushtimargis* was Nathadwara and the celebration of Krishna and his many *lilas* mainly through painting, but also through music, was their main activity. It is significant that many *pichwais* and paintings of the Nathadwara school celebrate the iconic Krishna as lord and the romantic Krishna at the same time emphasising in yet another way that ultimately Krishna, whether sensual or spiritual, was one. The ethos of the poets and painters of Nathadwara spread into neighbouring Rajasthan and became the driving force of its many ateliers but with one difference. The love of Radha and Krishna moved from the earthy and pastoral environs of Vrindavana to the courtly and more formal norms of the *havelis*. Instead of the blossoms and the birds *shringara rasa* evolved within canopied *havelis*, the unsophisticated gopis of Vrindavana were replaced by the elegant attendants and courtiers, and the simple love games of Radha and Krishna evolved into a love that was marked as much by intrigue as romance. *Sakhis* that held branches of trees now held fly whisks, blossoms of the forest were replaced by furnishings of the court, the birds and the trees were exchanged

Shri Nathji
Nathwada, early 19th century
Collection: Author

for trappings of courtly elegance, the sound of birds gave way to court music and instead of the dance of the peacock, court dances. *Rasikapriya* and *Rasamanjari* and other poetic works in this genre provided the artists with endless situations and taxonomies within which to place and celebrate courtly love. The nobility and the royalty of Rajasthan were committed to the pursuit of *bhakti shringara* but more as patrons rather than true aesthetes. However, were it not for their patronage, the rich treasure of magnificent courtly paintings of Radha and Krishna would not have been created.

In eastern India the theology and aesthetics of *bhakti shringara* took on a slightly different colour. Chaitanya took on the persona of a *gopi* and even dressed as one; the supreme pleasure for a *gopi* was to delight in the amorous

coming together of Radha and Krishna. For Chaitanya, Radha and Krishna were meant to be together, never separate, one amorously tied to the other, never parted. The world for the Bengal Vaishnavas was only complete when they danced or sang in ecstasy at their amorous togetherness. The many manifestations of *viyoga* or love in separation that inspired the court painters of Rajasthan could not be a part of Chaitanya's ecstasy. They expressed themselves more through song and dance and while upholding the amorous relationship of Radha and Krishna raised Radha and Krishna on a pedestal. Radha became a consort and was no longer a lovelorn *gopi*. If *madhurya* captures the essence of the romantic love of Radha and Krishna, the *Gaudiya* Vaishnavite concept of *achintya bheda abedha*, the mysterious relationship where they are different and yet not different, defines the role of Krishna in that love and in the dynamics of *bhakti shringara*. Krishna is human and divine, sensual and spiritual, one with his devotees and not of them, immanent and transcendent, worldly in his *lila* and otherworldly in his *maya*. It is this dual persona of Krishna, that moves between *lila* and *maya*, that is imponderable, an enigma, a riddle, a mystery that the Gaudiyas celebrate.

Radha Krishna
Jaipur, late 18th century
Collection: Art of the Past,
New York

Gaudiyas emphasise that it is the rational mind that seeks comfort in secure and sunlit spaces and shuns borders and shadows, for rationality thrives in asserting and maintaining dualities rather than transforming those very dualities into a rich and majestic non-duality. To understand Krishna and his love the Gaudiyas insist that one must be prepared to transform that rational mind into the Vaishnava mind that celebrates the romantic coming together of Radha and Krishna and brings that love into their daily lives.

With the advent of modernity,[1] while the theology and the religious adoration of the sacred Radha remained intact, her aesthetic celebration did

1. I have benefitted from Karine Schomer's Where Have All The Radhas Gone? in *The Divine Consort*, Hawley and Wulff (eds.) Beacon Press, Boston, 1982

undergo a significant change. A number of factors were to contribute to this change in Radha's romantic aesthetic sensibility. With the dawn of modernity in India there was a greater social and national awareness and the attention of poets shifted from the romantic *nayika* to the socially repressed *nari*; from the *kamini,* the idealised and desirable woman in love, to the *abala* or the woman who was wronged and subject to social injustice and emotional deprivation. In that sort of climate there could be no celebration or patronage of the coy and romantic *nayika* of traditional love poetry and painting. Poets of the *chayavad* group while celebrating love preferred a more universal woman rather than the Radha of *riti kavya*. Mahadevi Verma as an example of the *chayavad* genre even converts the poignant *viraha* of love into a more universal pain of women. Art was driven more by social realism rather than idealised romance, where poets made an obvious choice of breaking away from tradition and looking to the world around them, where the love of *riti kavya* became irrelevant and where romantic love was only a small part of the complex whole of the human condition. Modernity also brought in a change of patronage from the elite, cultivated and liberal nobility to the puritanical, boorish middle class and in this ambience the lovelorn *nayika*, pining for her beloved and exulting in his company, had no place. And then there was the revivalism, where poets and scholars revisited the ancient epics and *riti kavya* lost much of its sparkle. And finally the 19th and 20th centuries saw the emergence of the nationalist movement where patriotism rather than romanticism was the order of the day. And, as the millennium ended, feminism in all its hues was already well-established and the Indian woman was a free and liberated person affirming her identity, moving closer to Durga or even Kali in her persona rather than to Radha or Parvati, subverting romance to sexuality, tender love to seduction and medieval suppression to modern assertion. Even if modern poets and patrons consign the tender lovelorn Radha to the dusty, musty corridors of our past, her heart-throbbing, soul-stirring romantic love for Krishna can never be totally irrelevant, her selfless celebration of love for its own sake can never be without meaning and the romantic moments that she shared with Krishna have a certain timeless beauty and will forever remain part of our aesthetic treasure.

Chitramanjari:
A Bouquet of Paintings

राम हलस्रवेण वजारिडिछि गोपारमिछि

Fluting in Vrindavana

Gita Govinda, Gujarat, late 16th century
Collection: Author

In one of the earlier representations of the *Gita Govinda*, the Gujarat artist though working with paper, prefers to use the *pothi* format to present the full moon night in Vrindavana. It is the moment before the *raas lila* as Krishna plays his flute and *gopis* have gathered in the moonlight. Although they occupy spaces within the trees they are in consonance with the verdant world around and the love that flows within them is not different from the sap that animates the trees. And as love resonates within their heart their bodies move in joyous rhythms as the celebrated *raas* is about to start while the two *gopis* closest to Krishna are spellbound by the sights and sounds of the enchanted forest. This early image from the *Gita Govinda* may lack the artistic finesse of later creations but it possesses an earthy vitality and charm, and a robust colouration that characterises the western Indian artistic idiom. The faces are in full profile and the farther eye is missing indicating a later provenance but the folio is a good example of the ethos of early Gujarat miniature painting.

His infatuating flute resounded with honied tones like the nectar from his quivering lip, his hair was surrounded with a ring of peacock tail feathers, his lovely robe was like a dark cloud coloured with many rainbows, his forehead had a mark of sandal on it which surpassed the moon in a cluster of clouds, his cheeks were adorned with enchanting ear rings of makaras made of jewels.

Gita Govinda 2.2-7

Krishna Shringar: Krishna of Love

ज्वलदमदनमनोरथपथिकवधूजनजनितविलापे । अलिकुलसंकुलकुसुमसमूहनिरा
॥ कुलबकुलकलापे ॥ विरहः ॥२॥

Radha pines for Krishna
Gita Govinda, Mewar, 1525–70
Collection:
Prince of Wales Museum, Mumbai

In one of the earlier representations of the *Gita Govinda* the artist uses the *Chaurapanchashika* idioms to portray the longing of Radha from the first canto. An important artistic difference is the lush landscape vibrant with stylized trees and creepers, singing blossoms and frolicking peacocks, for that is where Jayadeva's classic poem unfolds. After the eye has taken in the verdant and idyllic background we discover the sullen and downcast Radha, her mood in contrast to the forest which is alive with the whispers and songs of spring. She is dressed in the characteristic western Indian *gaghra* and *choli* with the triangular downward pointing *patka* and the red monochrome backdrop makes no secret of her burning passion. As we leave the painting we note the empty bower with the large lotus and wish with Radha for Krishna's speedy return to her, for without him there can be no joy for Radha, no life for the blossoms and the birds of Vrindavana.

lonely wives of travellers moan
from love's mad fantasies
bees swarm over flowers clustered
to fill bakula branches
when spring's mood is rich
it is a cruel time for deserted lovers.

Gita Govinda. 1.28

The Adoration of Krishna

Krishnakarnamrutam, Western India
c. 1500
Collection: Author

he has a kasturi tilak on his forehead
the kaustabha jewel on his chest
a fresh pearl on his nose
the flute in his palm and a bangle on
his hand
a pearl necklace around his neck
and is surrounded closely by gopis
this crest jewel of the Yadavas is
always victorious

This verse by Bilvamangala from
Krishnakarnamrutam was traditionally
sung and interpreted by dancers at the
end of a dance performance

Bilvamangala

The artist of this important 13th century Vaishnavite manuscript attributed to Bilvamangala, draws on the well-established idioms of the western Indian style to create a folio with both a rich visual and literary content. The cross-legged Krishna is the centre of our attention as he plays his flute and is flanked by three *gopis* who are ready to serve him. His floral *dhoti* matches the *odhnis* of the *gopis* and this establishes a visual connection between Krishna and the *gopis*. The floral pattern on their clothes takes our eyes to the tree with similar flowers, which in turn suggests that the *rasa* that animates Krishna and the *gopis* is not different from the sap that makes the trees blossom. The solid red backdrop and the wiry outlines are reminiscent of Jain manuscripts but the triangular *patka* and the farther eye are absent and the ambience is one of quiet adoration. The simple composition, without any aesthetic pretensions, is still not devoid of an earthy charm and emphasises that its strength is both textual and visual.

Raas Lila
Orissa, 20th century
Collection: Author

The *patachitra* from Orissa recreates the magic of *raas lila* in its folkish but pretty idioms.

Krishna through yoga maya became many so that he could give his love to all and he was like a sapphire in a necklace of gold, there was such harmony of ragas and raginis that hearing it water and wind no longer flowed
the moon together with the starry firmament being astonished rained down nectar with its rays,
the wives of gods gathered in the sky, meanwhile night advanced and six months had passed
the name of that night has been the night of Brahma.

Surdas *Premsagar*

Of all the *lilas* of Krishna the *raas lila* is the most pivotal. It was on a full moon night in the season of *sharada* that the flute of Krishna drew the *gopis* away from their homes and they held their hands and forming a circle danced around Krishna who played the flute at the centre. Sahibdin, the master artist of Mewar, reminds us that this dance is being performed in Vrindavana by depicting a foliated red and green background against which the dance occurs. The azure blue of Krishna is the focal point of this composition and the source of its energy and the chain of *gopis* in their splendourous attire try to contain this through their rhythm and movement. While the *gopis* look at each other as the dance proceeds, their heart is fixed on Krishna and their minds reel with ecstasy. Two *gopis* provide the beat with cymbals and *mridanga* and in the enchanted ambience of Vrindavana it creates a cosmic rhythm. Within the unbroken *mandala* there is the perfect security of love, within the sanctified space of the circle there is *madhurya*, the perfect circle shuts out the imperfections of *samsara*, but even within this charmed space of *raas lila* Krishna cannot be captured for ever. Sahibdin gives us a glimpse of this by showing two *gopis* in a grove, distraught when they learn that Krishna has left. There are countless artistic depictions of *raas lila* but this particular folio is uniquely striking because of the series of concentric circles which creates the all-pervading sense of circular, timeless, endless movement, a movement which does not leave us unmoved, a rhythm that cannot leave us unstirred and an event that does not leave us untouched, as we wonder at this *lila* of Krishna.

Cheer Harana
Isarda thikana of Rajasthan, c. 1710–20
Collection: Author

*C*heer harana, as this *lila* of Krishna is called, brings out at once the childish pranks and the erotic mysticism of Krishna. Krishna's persona of apparent contrasts is portrayed in this folio of conflicting images. It is a cloudy day in Vrindavana as the *gopis* bathe in the Yamuna river. It is a river from which lotuses grow and in which fishes frolic but it is also the home of fierce crocodiles. And from this arises the *kadamba* tree which stands prominently and captures our attention and in which Krishna, having stolen the *gopi's* clothes, rests and plays his flute. Their colourful clothes are a contrast to their partially uncovered bodies as they plead with Krishna. Meanwhile, against an amber background two birds and blossoms droop on the *gopis,* assuring us that this is just another *lila* of Krishna, and as we focus on the tree we realise that just as we cannot take away Krishna from the *kadamba* tree, neither can we separate the pranks from his love for the *gopis*.

Cheer Harana
Kashmir, 19th century
Collection: Author

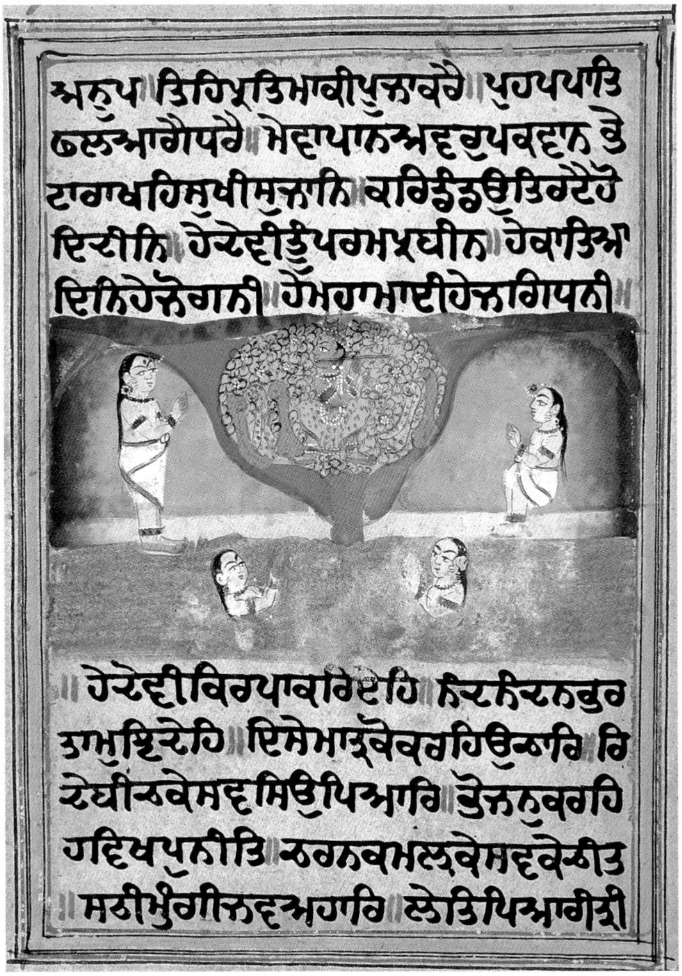

when the wind blows through the kadamba tree
and we hear the flute of Krishna, it whispers to us
that to love him is to lose ourselves our pride and our possessions.

*T*his 19th century page from a Kashmiri *Bhagavata Purana* written in Gurmukhi recreates the same episode in its simple but beautiful idiom.

Krishna appeases an offended Radha

Gita Govinda, Mewar, AD 1714
Collection: Author

It was Rana Sangram Singh (1710–1734) of Mewar who commissioned the painting of this *chitravali* of *Gita Govinda*, and the Mewari artist, probably Rupjit, brings a poignant moment from the ninth canto to life. We are led into a verdant and bucolic Vrindavana, of lush trees and the blossoming banks of the Yamuna. However, the eye is quickly led to an opening in the forest and then to the repentant Krishna who is led by a *sakhi* to the bower of a *manini* Radha where she sits in front of a green bolster. Radha's *mana* is quickly understood by the empty bower on our left where she, having her passion aroused by Kama, who is seen in the tree, waited with garlands and other paraphernalia of love but Krishna played truant. As our attention settles on the *sakhi* we almost hear her admonish Radha *madhave ma kuru manini manamaye,* don't turn your wounded pride on Madhava, and the waiting garlands on Radha's bower assure us that her pride will soon give way to love and that happy amorous moments will transpire.

See Hari on his cool couch of
moist lotuses
Reward your eyes with this fruit.
Your perverseness justly turns
your sandal balm to poison
cool moon rays to heat.

Gita Govinda. 9.6

Dana Lila
Chamba, c. 1740
Collection:
The British Museum, London

*Krishna, you asked us to gift you milk
and curd
but you stole our hearts.
Butter, curd and whatever else we have
are all yours
we have surrendered to you our lives
and souls.
Surdas says my Lord is such that he
cannot be attained by
yoga, sacrifices, austerities or meditation
but delights in asking cowherd girls for
gifts of milk.*

Surdas. Sursagar

It is a pastoral setting, the cows have been tended and the *gopis* have collected their milk. Holding a cup made of leaves and flanked by Balaram, who also wears a crown, along with other *gopas,* Krishna thirsts for milk which Radha gladly pours. But the energy of the composition is in the gaze of the *gopis*. Radha's gaze is coy as she looks downward, almost fearful of locking her gaze with that of Krishna, whose eyes clearly have mischief in them. It is that mischief that the two *gopis* standing behind Radha seem to be wondering about. Or are they concerned as to how they would account for the missing milk? For had they not complied with Krishna's request, would their milk pots be safe from his pranks? Suddenly the painting takes on a different turn, from a mere pastoral event it becomes a romantic moment as the *gopis* almost wish they had withheld the milk and given Krishna and the *gopas* the kiss they would have demanded as a toll. In setting the event within a pastoral ambience but yet not losing the romantic undertones, the Chamba artist with sure lines and skilful colouring shows his mastery as he makes this event from the *Bhagavata Purana* come alive. What at first glance was a pastoral activity becomes for us an intriguing romantic interlude, and with it the multiple nuances of the tenth chapter of the *Bhagavata* are clearly manifest in this image.

Radha and Krishna in a Grove

Gita Govinda, Guler, c. 1780
Collection:
Victoria and Albert Museum, London

It was our first meeting, I was shy
Krishna spoke tender and loving words
by the hundred
I responded with a soft smile and
sweet prattle.

Gita Govinda. 2.12

In the hands of the artist of the Kangra *kalam* the *Gita Govinda* reaches its lyrical and visual perfection, for he depicts like no other, the tender love of Radha and Krishna, a love that is at once human and divine, sensual and spiritual. The skill of the artist lies not only in portraying sensitively the lover and the beloved in their varying situations and nuances of love, whether it is the pleasure of belonging or the pathos of longing, but relating this love to the verdant and bucolic Vrindavana—its idyllic groves, its lush vegetation, blossoming trees around which wind delicate creepers, lotus flowers in the meandering Yamuna and birds that echo the sentiments of the lovers—a charming landscape that befits the love of Radha and Krishna, beautiful at one level and pointing to a higher reality at another. It is in such a grove, in the second canto of the *Gita Govinda* that we find ourselves when we look at this folio, as Radha and Krishna are together for the first time and share their love, he in a yellow *dhoti* affectionately embracing and she coy in her submission and pulsating with desire, he with his golden crown and she with her tresses strewn. The pleasures and the passions of this first meeting will long be remembered and poignantly recalled by Radha, particularly when Krishna is away from her, and Radha's nostalgic refrain *smarati mano mama krta parihasam* will ring throughout the *Gita Govinda*.

Raas Panchadhyayi
Kulu, style of Bhagwan, 1790–1800
Collection:
Victoria and Albert Museum, London

The gopis with their flashing
gold earrings,
their lustrous hair and the radiance of
their cheeks
looked at his radiant glance like the
nectar of the gods
were filled with joy
and sang in praise of his deeds.

      Bhagavata Purana. X.33.22

It is in the five chapters of the *Bhagavata Purana* that the *raas lila* of Krishna unfolds and it is here that the core of *shringara bhakti* is laid out. The enchanting forest of Vrindavana is where Krishna, for the first time, expresses his love for the *gopis*, a love that is as sweet as the waters of the Yamuna, as tender as the blossoms of the forest, as soft as the moonlight in *sharada* and as mellifluous as the notes of his flute. It is here that *bhakti* and *shringara*, religion and metaphysics blend into one fountainhead of Vaishnavism. It is such a moment in Vrindavana that the Kulu artist depicts. On the banks of the flowing Yamuna the *gopis* and the *gopas* have gathered to listen to Krishna. One *gopi* is in rapt attention with folded hands while the others listen with adoration and wonder. Krishna's flute is nowhere to be seen for it is a time when Krishna must explain and even admonish, teach and receive, for love, like the Yamuna, must flow, and like flowers must blossom and like the tree trunks be established. The artist with firm lines and strong colours gives a living presence to the people who inhabit this charmed and amorous space.

Krishna plays Holi

Nurpur, c. 1770–80
Collection:
Victoria and Albert Museum, London

There is a feast of colours, a frenzy of excitement, a fanfare of music and a fiesta of revelry as Krishna and Radha participate in the festival of Holi. While some squirt sprays of yellow from their syringe others fill their palms with *gulal* and scatter it in the air and Radha and Krishna add joy and mirth to the occasion. And as colours mingle so do minds, and as drums beat so do hearts, for this is a festival of love. These are not just pigments in the air but colours of romance, and not mere sounds of the drum but heart-throbs of passion. This is not a time of restraint but of release, not a time for words of love but for hues of the heart. As cowherds tend barrels full of *haldi* and *gulal* it seems as if the festivity will never end, and why should it, for unending is their love. The Nurpur artist leaves the landscape bare for this is the time and the place for a play of colours and nothing should distract our attention from indulging ourselves in the vibrant colours of love.

The festival of Holi in the Indian tradition is one of many rites of spring celebrating not only the end of winter and a time for growth but equally love and fertility. It is connected not only with Krishna and Radha but also with Shiva and Parvati, Kama and Rati and with the worship of trees. It is a time mainly for women to celebrate but ancient texts also describe the king participating in it, and in the spirit of festivity social divisions and caste barriers are dissolved. The coloured powders and liquids, derived from flowers, kumkum, gulal, musk and sandalwood have both a romantic and erotic connotation. The drenching of a woman with blood red colours not only sancitifies her fertility but is also an invitation for amorous pleasures. Sri Harsha's Ratnavali and Priyadarshika, Kalidasa's Malvikagnimitram and Madana's Parijata Manjari are some of many plays that extol spring festivals and are performed as part of the celebrations of Holi. In its ultimate analysis Holi is celebration of kama as desire and Kama as deity.

Theft of the Flute
Sikh Kangra, 19th century
Collection: Author

look at Shyam as he walks to the well
he laughed as he looked at me and
I wondered
today I will not let him go
instead I will make him a woman
and put ornaments on him from head
to toe
and even place a bindi on his head
Binda says what a spectacle it was.

a thumri by Birju Maharaj

This is a *lila* with a difference, for Krishna here is a victim not a victor. The flute, which is one of the three *shaktis* of Krishna, is a source of envy to the *gopis*, for Krishna holds it so close to him. So the *gopis* way lay Krishna and steal his flute and even more, dress him up as one of them. The victory is theirs and in the battle of love Krishna willingly submits. There is celebration in the air, joy in the wind, merriment in the charmed space as the *gopis* enjoy their moment of triumph. The artist renders the moment with measured grace. The Kangra artist depicts a landscape of rolling hills, temples and *havelis* and bathes the painting in a hue of blue, the colour of Krishna, for in the bevy of *gopis* he is after all the cynosure of our attention.

By the *Kadamba* Tree
Madhubani
20th century
Collection: Crafts Museum, New Delhi

what use do I have of the
parijataka tree
neither do I need the kalpavriksha
the mango and the ashoka bear no fruit
for me
but I shall wait under the
kadamba tree
for there I shall find my love.

a Maithili folk song

Madhubani, or the forest of honey, in the Mithila region of the present-day state of Bihar has seen the foot-prints of Vidyapati and when the wind blows through the trees of this area it brings with it the sounds of the flute of Krishna. In this mural from the recreated *kobhar ghar* where the newly-married couple spend the first few days of their marriage, the love of Radha and Krishna is given equal space as other mythic deities and fertility and auspicious symbols, emphasising that while marriage is a sacrament it should not be devoid of romance. The pride of place is given to the *kadamba* tree as it rises majestically from a stylised tortoise and its many branches provides a home to peacocks and parrots and under them Krishna plays his flute as Radha is drawn to him. That she is not the only one attracted to Krishna's flute is made amply clear by the Madhubani artist by the presence of a peacock who alights on the flute. Bold colours within strong outlines and prominent eyes make the figures almost iconic and the blue of Krishna resonates with Radha's azure attire and the plumes of the peacocks, as the *kadamba* tree comes to life with the sound of the flute. The border of female faces at the bottom of the mural is a reminder that this is a special time for the bride as she begins her married life, a life that will be filled with the joys of romance and the strength of the *samskaras* that will follow, and that in this life, she too like Radha, will be drawn to the love of her husband.

Moonlight Rendezvous
Kangra, c. 1820–30
Collection: Author

when my beloved returns to my house
I shall make my body a temple
of gladness
I shall make my body the altar of joy
and let down my hair to sweep it
My twisting necklace of pearls shall be
the intricate sprinkled design on
the altar
my full breasts the water jars, my
curved hips the plantain trees
the tinkling bells at my waist the
young shoots of the mango
I shall use the arcane arts of fair
women in all lands
to make my beauty outshine a
thousand moons.

Vidyapati

It is a starless moonlit night and under the crescent moon in the privacy of a courtyard between two *havelis* the moment is right for love's desires. Courtly life, though filled with regal and ceremonial dignity, leaves little room for intimate moments, moments when the passions and pleasures of love can be indulged in, for romance needs to be equally sensual as it is emotional. If amorous glances convey hidden thoughts, a loving touch can speak of tender feelings. For in a loving touch there is the assurance of love, the joy of togetherness, the magic of romance and the warmth of a romantic heart. For a loving touch is not just a sensation, it is a message, it is not just a contact but a commitment, it is not mere touching but a joining of the two hearts, not just a thrill, but a reaching out, it is speaking without words "I am yours". The Kangra artist skilfully renders the beauty of this amorous moment with a fine balance of the two figures and a beautiful harmony of shades of yellow and red, each in its place, along with the open doors of the *havelis* into which the lovers will return after their brief meeting. As Krishna leans forward towards Radha, she demurely accepts his touch, his gaze one of longing, hers that of bashfulness. The loving touch rubs off on us the joy of the moment and as the loving couple enter the open door of their *haveli* the memory of this will not only haunt them, but equally, us, till they meet again.

The Repentant Krishna
Sat Sai, Kangra, 1820–1830
Collection: Author

the tell tale ruby necklace on
your bosom
which you have forgotten to take off
shows you have exchanged clothes
with your mistress, making her play
the lover.
Its flashing redness which inflames
my eyes
is as though your deep love for her has
spilled out from your heart.

Bihari. *Sat Sai*

As dawn breaks and the sun rises above the rolling hills, a repentant Krishna, crestfallen and his left hand expressing guilt, stands at the door, remorse written all over his face. He has been truant before and has been able to save his honour with well-crafted excuses and ingenious alibis. He has been away all night and has not kept his rendezvous with Radha, but this time his truancy is for all the world to see, dressed as he is in female attire and a ruby necklace round his neck. His lower garment is not his usual *pitambar* but a *gaghra* and the upper garment is a red *odhni*, tell-tale signs of his passionate night with the other woman. A distraught and *khandita* Radha having waited all night, with the bed prepared in the upper chamber, is followed by her *sakhis* wondering how she would handle the situation and even the well-appointed lower chamber cannot hide their tension. And as the Kangra artist, who has deftly and gracefully portrayed this piquant romantic situation, leaves us involved in the drama, we can only hope that ultimately love will prevail and all will be forgiven.

Laur Chanda
Sultanate, probably Jaunpur, 1550–75
Collection: Prince of Wales Museum,
Mumbai

Even though many Persian features are seen in this manuscript, such as the ribbon-like clouds, blue and pink tile decoration and finely-drawn arabesques, the overall ethos in this pre-Mughal creation remains Indian. Both the male and female figures and their costumes are derived mainly from the western Indian style with the omission of the farther eye. The architecture is simple and the story is told in two or three registers. An ornamental hanging or *bandanwar* or wooden brackets is the usual decoration. The importance of this manuscript is the skill with which the artist blends Persian and Indian idioms but yet maintains an Indian ethos. This Laur Chanda which predates the Rylands manuscript by about 25 years remains a significant statement of pre-Mughal miniature painting and marks the emergence of a new style of painting in the subcontinent.

Laurak woos Chanda
Sultanate, probably Jaunpur, 1525–70
Collection: Rylands Library, Manchester

The Rylands manuscript, while sharing many features with the Prince of Wales documents, does have some unique features. The yellow and sandalwood tones have given way to a uniform reddish tone and both male and female figures approximate more to the Rajasthani type than the western Indian. Architecture is reduced to a minimum and a characteristic feature is wall brackets with tassels. Laurak wears the *chakdar jama* and Chanda a patterned *gaghra* and transparent *odhni*. Even though this manuscript probably demonstrates lesser artistic skill than other manuscripts of this popular Sufi romance, it still remains an important aesthetic treasure of the 16th century and is clearly a prelude to Rajput paintings of the 17th century.

Brishpat describing Laurak's beauty to Chanda
Sultant style, c. 1475
Bharat Kala Bhavan, Varanasi

The romance of Laurak and Chanda is an early Sufi romance and of the four manuscripts known so far the present one from Bharat Kala Bhavan is the earliest. The artist retains the western Indian style of Jain manuscripts with the three-quarter face and the farther eye, monochrome background and a two-tiered register. In the upper register, Chanda and her confidante Brihspat, who sits to her left, are in an animated conversation, probably about Chanda's attributes, alive with hand gestures. Chanda sports a head ornament and a stylised *odhni* while Brihspat is in a spotted *pyjama*. In the lower register Laurak triumphantly rides an elephant, who bears also his standard, testifying to his aristocracy and is preceded by an attendant wielding a spear. The strength of these manuscripts rested more on the narrative, written in Persian in two horizontal panels separated by borders decorated with brick-pattern and floral motifs, than on the illustrations.

Laurak meets Chanda
Sultanate style, c. 1525–75
Collection: Berlin Library

The Berlin Laur Chanda shares many of the artistic idioms of the Bharat Kala Bhavan manuscript, indicating that even though the two are separated by about a hundred years, the Sultanate style of the pre-Mughal period retained its Indianness and resilience in illustrating Sufi romances. Laurak seated on the edge of his seat, with his right hand held to his chest, offers a heart-throbbing welcome to Chanda with his left hand. Self-assured and poised, with her *odhni* almost like a halo, Chanda enters the room confident that Laurak will find her attractive and desirable and as she steps towards him she seems sure that their romance is on a sound footing. Sufi manuscripts were meant to be enjoyed in select company, with song and music and with the appropriate Sufi sensibility, and if we as enlightened aesthetes are to derive a sustained aesthetic experience we must, in our own mind, re-create that same courtly ambience. Only then will Mulla Daud's popular Avadhi poem reach the aesthetic and spiritual heights that it is meant to.

Two Folios from Mrigavat
Jaunpur, Uttar Pradesh, 1525–70
Collection:
Bharat Kala Bhavan, Varanasi

The provenance of this illustrated Sufi romance is more certain as the narrative is written, not in Persian, but in the Kaithi script, a variant of *Nagari*, which was popular in eastern Uttar Pradesh. This Sultanate manuscript also follows the western Indian idioms but is more folkish in its ambience. The costumes lack the refinement of the Laur Chanda manuscripts but amply make up for this in the vigor and animation of the subjects. The architecture is simple and consists of Lodi period domes and turrets. This manuscript is not the product of courtly patronage but probably of a bourgeois and cultivated clientele and shows that in the 16th century such patronage did exist and was responsible for creating illustrated manuscripts even outside the courts.

Padmavati

Bikaner, AD 1774
Collection: Berkeley Art Museum

Malik Muhammad Jayasi's Padmavati continues the rich ethos of Sufi romantic poetry inaugurated by Maulana Daud and through mystic resonances in the narrative brings out the muhabbat-al-ruh or love that comes from the soul. Jayasi uses the terminology, concepts and poetic imagery of the vernacular devotional poetry of the north to creative the distinctive prema rasa of the Sufis in Hindavi.

We join the narrative as Ratansen reaches the island of Singhaldeep with the help of the charmed parrot Hiraman and finds Padmavati in her home. Even as attendants stand by with whisks, platters of food and jars of drinks, all eyes are on Hiraman as he guides Ratansen. It is a romantic moment in gracious surroundings but even more so it is a moment of the fulfillment of love. The Bikaner artist prefers to render the event in shades of pink and green to emphasise the magical moment and, as we take our leave, the words of the parrot almost haunt us as we turn the pages of the manuscript to follow the narrative.

Raj Kunwar

Sultanate, AD 1600–1610
Collection:
Chester Beatty Library, Dublin

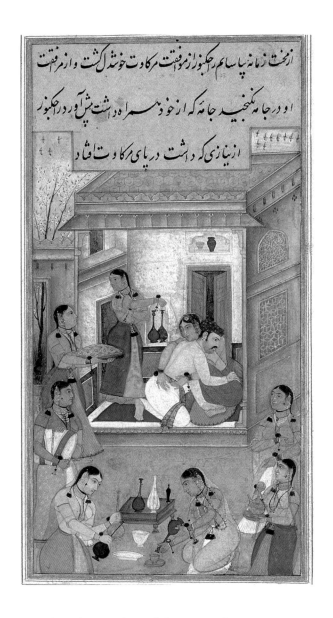

Qutban was one of several Muslim poets who adapted Hindu folklore to Sufi mysticism giving religious overtones to popular and secular romances. Sufi belief was that the love of beauty was linked to a love for God and became elevated through the trials of romantic quest. Raj Kunwar himself summarises this philosophy in the story when he says, "whoever gives his life for love buys both worlds."

This edition of a well-known Sufi romantic narrative goes by the regnal title of the hero, Raj Kunwar, rather than the heroine, Mrigavat. Composed by Qutban in 1503 in Jaunpur in present-day Uttar Pradesh, the tale had probably become obscure and was not in favour with Akbar. The Beatty manuscript was prepared in Allahabad a hundred years later for Prince Salim, and is similar in its stylistic features to *Yog Vasisht* and was painted mainly by Bishandas although this particular folio is attributed to Salim Quli. The composition shows the prince embracing Mrigavat, after the two were united when she emerged from the lake, while female attendants are busy preparing food and pouring drinks to celebrate the happy occasion. A blossoming tree and a flock of birds in the sky testify to the celebratory ambience. The strength of the Sultanate style, despite its rigid figures, are its well-chosen colours, princely attire which would change as the tale progresses, its courtly atmosphere and its attention to details of the architecture and in particular the *jali* work on the walls. The painting provides a restful pause in the manuscript before we take on the vivid, dramatic and not always happy occurrences in Qutban's tale.

Vasant Vilasa
Gujarat, 1451
Collection: Freer Gallery, Washington

O moon, you who are so full why do you inflict pain upon my body? Do not kill a woman sullied as you are already.

Old Gujarati

Your body is famed as the source of the ocean and the abode of nectar, your rays delicate as the young fibres of a lotus stalk rival a string of pearls, your beloved mistress is the white lotus and your close friend is Smara the essence of love. Why then are you a source of heat to burn me?

Sanskrit
Vasant Vilasa. 42

In one of the earliest scrolls of a secular romantic poem the Gujarati artist brings to life its sensuous lyrics with a vivid and animated portrayal. The separated *nayika* rests on a bed with bowls of fruits nearby as a *sakhi* offers her a goblet. Luxuriant foliage, a fruit-bearing plantain tree, blossoms and a deer invigorate the landscape. A moon hides within clouds. The characteristic farther eye, bright textiles, wiry lissom figures and earthy colours are typical of the early Gujarat style.

Vasant Vilasa
Gujarat, 1451
Collection: Freer Gallery, Washington

It is a special moment of adornment and romantic expectation for the *nayika* as a *sakhi* applies vermillion to the parting in her forehead. Erotically charged animals seem to foretell moments to come, while a parrot presages amorous words that will be spoken. The bright foliage, fruits and blossoms make up the idyllic landscape and the bright textiles once again speak of the Gujarati penchant for fabrics.

The part in her hair is filled with a
streak of vermillion and row of pearls.
The ruby studded rakhadi ornament in
her hair is just like a beauteous
snake gem.

Old Gujarati

The face of my beloved is fair as the
centre of a freshly opened lotus with the
lotuses of her eyes quivering in the
lassitude that follows sexual pleasure.

Sanskrit
Vasant Vilasa. 59

Chaurapanchashika
Jaunpur, Uttar Pradesh 1525–70
Collection:
N. C. Mehta Gallery, Ahmedabad

even now
my mind finds me idling with
her friends
embracing her lovely limbs
bantering and dancing
in elegant rooms alive with our play
if only my time could pass there.

Bilhana. *Chaurapanchashika*

The *Chaurapanchashika* is an important document of the Sultanate period which even though growing out of the western Indian style of Jain manuscript illustrations develops a uniquely Indian artistic style and illustrates a secular love story. The head, for the first time in the history of Indian miniature painting has turned and is in full profile and the farther eye is absent. The pointed nose and the double chin, and a two-dimensional space are a signature of this period of painting. Champavati as the lissome heroine in a transparent *odhni*, cutaway *choli*, checkered *gaghra* and triangular *patka* is a model of self-assured sensuality, while Bilhana with his sandalwood complexion, recurved moustache and whiskers and a *kulahdhar* turban, gesticulating with his hands, exudes a confident masculinity. Two *sakhis* occupy the second pavilion and provide music fit for romance. The intense red background within a simple pavilion shows a western Indian influence with its foliate eaves and tasselled fringes and is a beautiful re-creation of Bilhana's nostalgic poem. Within the two-dimensional monochrome background there is a sense of movement. Every feature of the folio is surcharged with emotional intensity and energy and the pictorial space seems to resound with the powerful and nostalgic *adyapi*, even now.

Sursagar

Mewar, 1700–1725

Collection: National Gallery, Ottawa

Radha says to Krishna: I would play the same notes on your flute that I have heard you play. I will put on your jewellery and I will put my own jewellery upon you. You will sit as if you were angry with me and I will assuage your anger by touching your feet. You go and hide in the forest bower, I will catch hold of the border of your garment and will pull you out. I will draw back the veil from the face of my beloved and then I shall embrace her in my arms. You become Radha and I will become Madhava, truly Madhava; this is the reversal which I shall produce. I will braid your hair and will put your crown upon my head. Sur Das says Thus the Lord becomes Radha and Radha the son of Nanda.

Surdas. *Sursagar*

In this emotionally compelling and graphically striking composition the Mewari artist converts a Surdas *doha* from *krishnalila* into a visually arresting narrative. Like the *bhanita* in his *dohas* the artist places the poet in the right-hand lower corner and we along with the poet identify with Radha as she entreats Krishna in the upper left corner to let her play on his flute. Wishing to reverse the roles between the loved and the beloved, for in this is the meaning and the reason for love, the artist leads us into a series of romantic encounters. Radha has taken the persona of Krishna seen clearly from her blue colour and Krishna, though retaining his crown has become Radha. Arranging his (her) coiffure, he (she) tending his feet, exchanging flutes, engaging in affectionate salutations and dallying in a grove, a passionate embrace and finally an animated conversation. As we take in this beautiful narrative our eye is confused even as our mind is enraptured by the sweet exchange of roles, *lilahava*, which highlights not just the intimacy but equally the intricacy of love. And as we leave them in the enchanted forest we are unsure where Radha ends and Krishna begins, but of one thing we are sure that in the depth and intensity of their love Radha and Krishna are truly one though different. The verdant green and white blossoms, enclosing spaces of passionate red provide the perfect visual backdrop for the enactment of this sweet affirmation of the love of Radha and Krishna, and as we reach Surdas himself at the bottom of the painting we have totally identified ourselves with Radha.

Shringara Kavya: The Poems of Love

Amarushataka
Malwa, c. 1680
Collection:
Prince of Wales Museum, Mumbai

It is appropriate that the richly sensuous secular love lyrics of Amarushataka be brought to life by a Malwa artist using the western Indian idioms of painting. The eyes feast upon a lavish landscape with blossoming trees and a pink gazebo with a palisade but quickly settle upon a *nayika* and her *sakhi* in animated conversation, she dressed in a red sari, yellow bodice and richly ornamented with pompoms sitting against a large bolster, and the *sakhi* in a blue-speckled *odhni*. It is an ideal setting to settle affairs of the heart, where the wind can whisper and the fragrance can linger, with a loyal confidante who can see through love's pretense.

Though frowning the eyes betray intense longing,
though the voice wavers the face lights up with a smile,
though the heart is hard the hair on the body bristle with joy.
Seeing such a person how can the pretense of anger be kept up?

Amarushataka. 26

Shringara Kavya: The Poems of Love

136

Amarushataka
Malwa, c. 1660
Collection: National Gallery, Ottawa

when her beloved had returned she
passed the day
with many day dreams, then entered
the pleasure house and saw
that the attendants were carrying on a
long conversation
the slender bodied one whose heart
grew impatient for enjoyment of love
cried out "Oh! Something has
bitten me"
and hurriedly tossing her silken scarf
and extinguished the lamp

Amarushataka. 86

Amaru's celebrated hundred verses on love found favour with the artists of Malwa who had in the 17th century been inspired by the *Rasikapriya* and *Ragamala* and produced a beautiful series of paintings. We are once again within the typical one room pavilion, with solid monochrome backgrounds. The *nayika*, dressed in dotted attire and her beloved, dressed in a striped *jama* and colourful *patka*, are in a spirited conversation, with large expressive eyes and animated hand gestures. However, even though this is a charmed moment for the lovers, the mundane world must go on and two attendants are in an equally animated conversation outside, which obviously is a source of nuisance to her. The Malwa artistic idiom excels in creating a living, pulsating presence of the characters, highlighting their adornments and their emotional state, while keeping the decor very minimal and the landscape limited.

*when deprived of the moon beams
a chakor eats embers instead*

Keshavdas. *Rasikapriya*

The earliest *Rasikapriya* was painted in the Mughal style of 1600, however the text became a favourite of the Rajput courts and in that ethos the Malwa patrons and artists of the early 17th century asserted their Hindu heritage and used their unique artistic idioms to create a unique *Rasikapriya* portfolio. The colophon page of this widely dispersed set is in the National Museum, Delhi. The Malwa artist recreates Keshavdas' *Rasikapriya* in the simple setting of the one room *haveli*, where the action is clearly outside the vacant chamber. The empty bed against the stark green background speaks eloquently of Krishna's emptiness and the solid red background and the peacock on the turret suggests his longing for Radha. As he tries to hide his pain the *sakhi*, says "what ails you Krishna, you look in a mirror and tie and untie your turban, you scratch your ears and twitch your fingers, you twist and turn, gaze vacantly, and yawn like a sick person." And as our eye turns from Krishna to the empty chamber the answer to us is obvious.

Rasikapriya
Kotah, c. 1725
Collection:
Jagdish and Kamla Mittal Museum
Hyderabad

Keshavdas in his Rasikapriya describes many sports of love where the nayaka and the nayika employ various tricks to meet each other. Once the maids of Vraja adorned Krishna as a maid and he playfully hid in mock pretense in their home and in this guise dallied with Radha. On another occasion a fire had broken out in Vrishabhanu's home and all of Vraja had poured in to help and Krishna saw this as an opportunity to enter the bed chamber of Radha, wake her up and steal a kiss. It was Balarama's birthday and there were festivities at Nandaji's home, with throngs of people and women sang and danced, when Radha spied Krishna's empty bed and slept in it and Krishna went to her as to a bride and slept by his beloved's side. Once when Radha was afflicted by an ailment and when despite religious oblations and medicinal cures she did not improve Krishna disguised himself as a physician and on the pretext of examining her stole some amorous embraces.

If there is one text that has inspired the patrons and painters of Rajasthan it is Keshavdas' *Rasikapriya*. Its encyclopedic taxonomies of lovers and love situations, their moods and methods has provided the ateliers of Rajasthan with an endless stream of images and they have done justice to this rich treasury of poetic images with their beautiful visual creations. It is an amorous meeting of Radha and Krishna on a starry night but it is a meeting with a difference for they have some business to conduct. Concerned about his many pranks, fearing deceit and unsure of his intentions Radha takes on the role of a palm reader and Krishna willingly submits. Her gaze is on his palms, his on her, as he wonders what his new-found palm reader will predict. There is no time for amorous pleasures or for the dalliances of love, as Radha is hard at work as her future, she feels, lies in the writing and the lines on his hands. Krishna resists a smile as he is sure that when this sportive moment is over Radha will be convinced of his love and in the well-appointed chamber with flickering lights in the splendidly domed *haveli,* her fears and anxiety will be assuaged, and that love's pleasures will flow like wine from the goblets. The Kotah artist chooses to depict this romantic moment in shades of rose and pink, appropriate hues, when depths of the heart are being examined by a self-styled palmist.

Rasikapriya
Bikaner, c. 1750–1770
Collection: Author

to exchange glances in person
to see a portrait
to meet him in fond dreams
to hear her sweet voice
these are the four ways of meeting
one's beloved.

Keshavdas. *Rasikapriya*

The Bikaneri artist in this folio from the *Rasikapriya* creates Radha's *chitradarshan* or meeting through a picture as he leads us through the agony of Radha's longing which starts in the *haveli* on the right, where within the bare and grey walls suggesting her state of mind, and in the light of a lamp, she smells food and then walks into another chamber to our left, where she looks at herself in a mirror, and then settles in the chamber above where she paints a portrait of her beloved and then finally feeling disappointed, sits under a tree, where she is addressed by her *sakhi,* "how can you destroy darkness by thinking of a lamp, end starvation by looking at food, quench your thirst by relating stories of water, expect wealth by seeing a picture of Lakshmi, and how can you have the pleasure of meeting your beloved by painting his portrait"? The monochrome green background with very little landscape keeps us focused on Radha and her valiant attempts to overcome the pangs of separation.

Shringara Kavya: The Poems of Love

Rasikapriya
Bikaner, c. 1750–1770
Collection: Author

when Krishna came she went to
meet him
and with love made him sit
then washed his feet and placed a box
of betel
then he caught her arm and teased
and asked who it was who taught her
the art of love.

Keshavdas. *Rasikapriya*

The Bikaner artist leads us though four phases of a romantic rendezvous. We begin at the top left corner where Krishna is received warmly and affectionately by the *nayika*, and as he catches a glimpse of her eyes he is enlivened. After this gracious welcome it is time for the *nayika* to serve him and this she does by washing his feet. There is love even in this servility. This is followed by games of love where romantic feelings are aroused and then finally she lovingly leads him to the bedchamber for the culmination of love. Appropriately, the couple ascend a flight of stairs suggesting that this is the height of their romantic dalliance. Moreover, the artist in choosing the monochrome background uses a burning red for the final passionate fruition of love. There is not only a sense of movement in this folio but equally a feeling of the fulfillment of love, a joyous coming together of the hero and the heroine, and above all the finesse in romance of a *praudha nayika*.

Rasikapriya
Bikaner, late 17th century
Collection: Author

The two praudha nayikas depicted in this and the previous folios show how the simple, naive and guileless gopis of the Bhagavata Purana have progressed to the scheming, mature and experienced nayika of the Rasikapriya. The innocent and spontaneous love pranks have given way to certain sophisticated and well-planned love situations, coyness has changed to seduction, heart-throbbing love has now been covered by layers of intrigue, the simple canopy of the blossoms and the trees of Vrindavana has been replaced by regal trappings and the charming love of Krishna and the gopis has moved to the courtly love of Radha and Krishna. The change in ethos from the Bhagavata to the Gita Govinda and then on to the Rasikapriya is quite evident. It is quite obvious that shringara and bhakti which were tandem rasas until the Gita Govinda get bifurcated and each goes its own way.

The previous *praudha nayika* is a *dhira*, or one who is skilled and experienced in love and artfully wins over her beloved. Yet another type of *praudha*, shown in this folio, is shrewd and scheming. The Usta artist of Bikaner recreates the dynamics of such a *praudha* as she presides in her chamber like a queen, exuding an air of regal confidence with a *sakhi* with a whisk in attendance, while another *sakhi* accosts Krishna as he approaches her. The *nayika* from the comfort and security of her *haveli*, which as the *doha* says is deeper than the ocean, has launched a scheme to ensnare Krishna and deploys a *sakhi* to carry out her plan. Krishna, innocent and guileless, devoid of any aristocratic airs, meets a *sakhi* under a cloudless sky and their gestures and expressions bespeak an animated encounter. The lotus pond, the fountain and the floral rug brighten an otherwise plain composition, not atypical of Usta artists.

Rasaveli
Malwa, c. 1660
Collection: National Museum, Delhi

*as the beautiful Radha made her way
to Vrindavana
branches with newly sprouted leaves
bent down
Krishna had spread lotus petals for her
to tread
and the cuckoo knew what treasure
awaited her
but the thousand headed serpent
could not tell the difference between
these petals
and foot prints of Radha, such was
her beauty*

Puhakar, *Rasaveli*

A verse from Puhakar's *Rasaveli* is brought to life by this artist from Malwa. It is a tender moment on a dark night in Vrindavana, the peacocks serenade and monkeys frolic and the trees have put out their white blossoms to welcome Radha and Krishna. Krishna's attention is on Radha's tender feet and he has collected lotus leaves which he arranges so that she can tread softly on them. Only he and the birds on the trees know what treasure awaits her. In the romantic ambience of Vrindavana these soft lotus leaves not only provide comfort to Radha's feet but speak to her about Krishna's delicate and sweet feelings and at the end of the walk she will probably gather them up and make a garland for him. Such romantic moments make Vrindavana an enchanted forest of love. The Malwa artistic style with its close affinities to the early western Indian tradition and the characteristic flower pond are very much in evidence in this folio.

केसवकूठिर हो तुमहीं सौं किधौ भय काहू की भीतु भयौ है वैनौ है काहू के हाथ कै नाथ
किधौ तुम काहू के साथ दरयौ है ॥ मेरी सौं मो सहुमा ने हु वे गि दिहा मनु नाहीं कहा पठ्यौ है सा
चीकही हरिहा रौहै काहू मौं कांहु ह यौ कै हिरा दि गयौ है ॥ ६

Rasikapriya
Mewar, c. 1650
Collection: Author

A folio from the same atelier of the same doha from *Rasikapriya*.

Keshavdas' nayikas, as we see in this folio, while possessing both grace and beauty, can tackle a difficult situation with confidence and finesse. Coy when wooed, resentful when offended, languid when met by truancy and positively assertive when she feels abandoned, the fulfillment and enjoyment of her romantic love is important to her and she is totally consumed by it.

The Mewari artist once again draws upon the countless situations in the *Rasikapriya* to portray a moment of interrogation for Krishna. The artist leads us into a room with a bright red monochrome background but the mood of the moment is not romantic. An assertive *nayika* dressed in a green *jama* clearly has the upper hand as Krishna sits meekly, looking toward but unable to gaze straight into her questioning eyes as she asks: you sulk as if you have sold yourself to someone, you appear as if you have gambled away your mind or have been robbed. It is a tense situation as a distraught Radha questions the sulkiness and indifference of Krishna. The room has been prepared for a romantic rendezvous with betel leaves and jars of wine, even as a *sakhi* is ready with a platter of flowers and as our eyes settle on the *sakhi* we hope that the red blossoms in her hands will be for a romantic celebration. There is a certain restraint, a subdued elegance; the use of strong chromatic backgrounds by the Mewari artist offsets the figures and brings out the piquancy of the moment.

Rasamanjari
Basohli, c. 1660–70
Collection:
Victoria and Albert Museum, London

In one of the finest series of the *Rasamanjari* the Basohli artist takes us to a moment of embarrassment for the *nayika* who has spent a romantic night with her lover and is shy to admit to the nail marks on her body. She tells her *sakhi*, "my mother-in-law may get angry, my friends may become hostile to me, and sisters-in-law may slander me, but I shall not sleep again in that house where the cat, suddenly pouncing in her attempt to attack a mouse, scratched my body with her sharp nails." The *sakhi* sees through this lame excuse, as do we, as what catches our eye is the bed of amorous pleasures and not so much the cat. The idyllic landscape outside the *haveli,* with birds and ducks in pairs and luxuriant trees, is further confirmation that this indeed is the abode of love, a place of romantic pleasures.

scratches and bites
the shattering of pearl necklaces
and the breaking of the garland of
bakula flowers
these are the marks of a nayika who
delights in love sports

Bhanudatta

श्रमत्

Rasamanjari
Basohli, 1660–1670
Collection:
Victoria and Albert Museum, London

let my mind not waver, let me not be
bashful
may my eyes be wide open
and Kama you will have to forgive me
for a moment
for my handsome Krishna approaches
with a peacock feather on his head
and lotuses and flute in his hands

Bhanudatta. *Rasamanjari.* 136

The strength of this celebrated series of the *Rasamanjari* from Basohli is in its iconic figures in full profile, against monochrome backgrounds, with large expressive eyes, bejewelled bodies and animated gestures. While rendering the single chamber of the *haveli* in minute detail the artist gives equal space to the environment outside which is equally expressive of the romantic situation. Krishna's mood is shown not only by the lotuses on his head and in his hand but equally by the creeper winding around the tree, while Radha's longing and expectation are equally revealed by the well-appointed chamber—flaming red carpet and alcoves with fruits and wine. It is a moment she has been waiting and preparing for and now the time has come to redeem that patient waiting with a *sakshat darshan*, a meeting in person, a romantic union not just of the mind but also of the body. The Basohli artist admirably catches the tension and expectation just moments before the long-awaited union of the two lovers, a moment in which the expectant heroine whispers a prayer.

Her dazzling splendour shining through her transparent dress is breathtaking, like a kalpa tree that plays in the waters of the placid ocean. Her bindi is like Mars, her face the Moon and the yellow tilak of saffron Jupiter and quench the thirst of my eyes, just as the planets the parched earth with life giving rain. The black mark her sakhi put on her cheek to guard her from the evil eye heightened her charm so greatly that men's gazes turned to her all the more. Seeing her put on the round black mark to keep off the evil eye he smiled and said "your moon like face now really looks like the spotted moon." Her eyebrows are as a bow, her bindi its bowstring of Kama's arrow which pierces the hearts of its youthful admirers. The pendant on her forehead is as though the sun had entered the moon's orbit and yet her moon like face does not pale but is even more radiant. Her ear ornament quivering in her white sari seems as the golden ripples of the rising sun reflected in the Ganga. Fascinating is the glimmer of the sapphire in her nose pin it seems as though a black bee alighting on a champa flower were sucking its nectar.

Bihari. *Sat Sai*

The Nurpur artist brings Bihari's *dohas* about Radha's beauty to life in this resplendent creation framed in an oval floral border characteristic of paintings from the *Sat Sai*. It is a charmed and charged moment that Radha, Krishna and a *sakhi* share under a tree. Their expressions are animated and so is the ambience shared equally by the cows in their pen. This is not a time for romantic dalliances but to be struck and possessed by Radha's beauty as is evidenced by Krishna's gaze and the *sakhi's* gestures. A demure but self-assured Radha is the centre of their attention and the energy of this composition, a Radha who is sweet as the blossoms that reach out to touch her and tender as the vine that creeps around the tree. Adorned with jewels around her neck and arms, dangling earrings, a crest jewel on her forehead and bangles on her wrists, wearing a red *gaghra* with golden imprints and wrapped by a diaphanous *odhni* which veils her body but reveals her radiant face, Radha is picture-perfect and romantically desirable. The arabesque in the borders bathes the entire composition in a rose-coloured hue and sets the mood for Krishna, and we along with him, to celebrate the beauty of Radha through the *dohas* of Bihari which a scribe has inscribed on the back of the painting.

Rasaraj
Datia, c. 1770–80
Collection: Author

A folio illustrating a verse from Matiram's *Alankara Utpreksha* is about precious treasures for a forthcoming journey by those in love. The Datia artist takes us to the moment when the *nayaka* prepares to leave for a distant land, and as the household gathers to bid him farewell, his attention is somewhere else and his eyes have a distant look as he conjures up the beauty of his beloved, an image that he shall take with him on his journey. Just as a newly-married woman, seen to our right, holding a flower in her hand, carries a glimpse of her childhood with her as she leaves her natal home. Tender moments, richly remembered, are precious possessions for a journey. The artist while providing details of the *haveli* and the fountain outside manages to keep our attention fixed on the uplifted gaze of the *nayaka* and the *nayika* as they embark on their respective journeys.

a farewell glance, treasured memories
this I shall take as provisions
for my voyage

In Anticipation of the Nayaka
Alwar, c. 1775
Collection: Author

Adornment is not only an act of self-expression, even more importantly, it is a self-offering. Step by measured step, and from one perfumed colour to another fragrant hue, the *nayika* thoughtfully adorns every part of herself and as the body reaches a certain perfection of beauty the mind soars to moments of excitement and anticipation. Even as her beauty has blossomed by the various adornments her mind can only find its fulfillment when the eyes of her beloved will fall on her. It is for that special moment that she has worked, it is for that charmed rendezvous that she has longed. In the midst of various activities there is a look of anticipation and longing in her eyes even as Krishna, hiding in a tree, steals a mischievous and loving look at her. If there is mischief in his eyes there is a hint of romance in hers and as we take our eyes from the painting we can be sure that amorous moments will follow.

*S*hangar or adornment is a very special moment in the depiction and enjoyment of *shringara rasa*. Not to be understood as mere decoration or ornamentation, adornment is a very special form of self–expression and self–offering. While not neglecting the adornment of the *nayaka* or the romantic hero the Indian artistic tradition has emphasised the adornment of the *nayika* or the romantic heroine. The literature is rich with descriptions of the *nayika* who adorns herself, temple sculpture is replete with sensuous *surasundaris* who are shown in every act of adornment, no classical dance repertoire is complete without the *abhinaya* of adornment and adornment has a very special place in miniature paintings. Traditionally, a *nayika* adorns herself with sixteen adornments which include *vastra* or clothes, *mahavar* or red dye to the cheeks, *keshbandhan* or coiffure, *pancha angarag* or the five colours to the body (vermillion on the parting, sandal on the forehead, a black mole on the cheek, saffron on the body and henna on the palms), *bhushan* or ornaments, *shauch* or a cleansing bath, *pushaphar* or flower garlands, *dantaranjan* or cleaning of teeth, *misi* or fragrant paste for the teeth, *lali* or red colour to the lips and or the mark on the forehead.

Nayika's Shangar
Jodhpur, mid-18th century
Collection: Author

*My beloved's clove shaped ear
ornament has pierced my heart like
Kama's arrow.*

*Her dazzling splendour shining
through her flimsy dress is breathtaking
as a kalpa tree reflected leaf and branch
in the waters of the placid ocean.*

*The black mark her friend put on her
cheek to guard her from the evil eye
heightened her charm so greatly that
men's gazes turned to her all the more.*

*As Mars, Jupiter and the Moon
combine to revive the parched earth
with life giving rain, her forehead
marks and red and yellow make
lovelier her moon like face and relieve
the thirst of my eyes.*

*All over her flame like body gleam the
gems of her ornaments. Their flashing
brilliance lights up her house even after
she puts out the oil lamp.*

*When she spreads out her naturally
glistening smooth unsullied fragrant
black tresses, my mind remains so
entangled in them that it cares not for
propriety.*

*Her eyebrows are as a bow, her
forehead's auspicious mark its bowstring
and the ornamental line extending to
her nose's bridge the shaft's pointed
barb, with which Kama, bow full
stretched pierces the hearts of her
youthful admirers, as a huntsman
shooting gazelles.*

*Say, who could have spotted her amidst
the yellow jasmine creepers if it wasn't
for the natural fragrance of her limbs?*

*Her gem studded toe ring shines so
brilliantly that it seems the sun*

*humbled by the splendour of her ear
ornament had fallen at her feet.*

*Her bosom resplendent with a garland
of lilies, a hemp flower dangling from
her braid upon her forehead and her
taut breasts jutting out, that charming
village girl stands looking after her field.*

*When she ties her long black glassy
hair whose heart does she not bind
with its loveliness? And when she
loosens it whose enraptured mind is not
lost to the world?*

Bihari, *Sat Sai*

Madanika Darpana
Kangra, early 19th century
Collection: Author

The *nayika* adorns herself thus with great excitement and expectation, for it is a happy moment for her as the various adornments will enhance her innate beauty and bring to life her tender emotions of love and romance. Helped by her *sakhis* she loses herself amidst the various bottles and jars, flowers and ornaments, boxes and accessories that contain all her unguents and pastes, oils and perfumes, colours and hues. In her adornment every colour brings a special meaning, every anointment a special feeling, every fragrance a remembrance, every ornament a glitter to her body. The *nayika* tarries as she prepares herself, pauses to make the right selection, changes her mind if she feels that something is not just right, adjusts her hair and looks at herself in the mirror. The mirror is a very special accessory in the *nayika's* adornment for it creates a duality essential for the *nayika's* self-awareness for without the mirror she has no visual realisation of her own beauty. In its reflection she sees herself as others would see her and finds confirmation of her beauty. It is through the mirror that she redeems her self-worth. When she holds the mirror in front of her it is as if she talks to herself and her mirror image talks back to her, conversations and whispers half-forgotten resound in her mind, moments of romance speak to her and in that dialogue there is both pride and vanity. It is while looking at herself in the mirror that she makes a final check and assures herself that she is picture-perfect and worthy of her beloved's gaze and it is while gazing in the mirror that she breaks into her first sweet smile, a smile of reassurance as well as invitation, as she waits longingly to be seen by him. It is in the mirror that she will catch the first glance of him and her gaze in the mirror is as much to find him as it is to assure her that her adornment is perfect. While still waters or polished stones served as ancient mirrors it was with the introduction of glass that mirrors took on various shapes and sizes. Contained within decorative frames or ornate handles mirrors also could be small enough to be placed on rings on fingers or as large as entire walls in palaces of glass.

Madanika Darpana
Garhwal c. 1800
Collection: Victoria and Albert Museum, London

The Adornment of Radha
Kangra, 1810–20
Collection: Cleveland Museum of Art

*I bent my head to stop my eyes from
stealing
yet still they ran to drink the face of
my sweet love
they ran like chakora birds soaring for
the moon
I forced them from his face and pulled
them to my feet
like bees drunk with honey my eyes
could scarcely fly
yet even then they spread their wings.*

Vidyapati

It is a moment of adornment but equally of adoration, of anticipation and also of expectation, as Radha makes a final check in the mirror after her toilette and there is a look of excitement in her eyes. Her *sakhis* have tried to guard her privacy even as they have helped her, but as we lift our eyes we see the tree which has provided a canopy for this special event, and we notice the two birds who have been silent witnesses, suggesting perhaps that what is to follow is a romantic union. And as we light upon Krishna's adoring but surreptitious eyes, stealing an unexpected glance from the window, we are led into the *jarokha* where amorous moments will be spent. When their glances meet we will be sure that it is for his eyes that she has adorned herself and it is for her beauty that his eyes have thirsted.

Adornment and Anticipation
Kangra, c. 1820–30
Collection: Author

There is certain ritual and a special joy when it comes to the adornment of a *nayika*. Water is carefully collected from a spring or a river, perfumes are thoughtfully selected, pastes and oils are lovingly prepared and every part of the body is treated with an artistic fervor, for adornment is not mere beautification, it is the outer expression of a cherished feeling and preparation for a romantic moment. It is not to be misunderstood as a statement of vanity but a *nayika's* self-assurance and dedication to her romantic feelings. It is that feeling that the Kangra artist conveys in this folio. The courtyard of the *haveli* has been transformed into an atelier and we are witness to a beautiful spectacle as each *sakhi* goes about her task with artistic dedication and the faraway look in the eyes of the *nayika* leaves no doubt that she prepares with anticipation for that magic moment when his eyes will behold her. Adornment played a very special part in the life of a *nayika* and as we participate in this special moment we cannot but share that anticipation and excitement written all over and specially in the eyes of the *nayika*.

Adorning Her Feet
Kangra, c. 1790
Collection:
The British Museum, London

*Her ruby red feet seem to shed red dust
as she goes along, as though a
dhupariya flower had blossomed at each
step she takes.*

*Her feet are so tender that the barber's
wife can't touch them for fear of causing
blisters, and even when she rubs them
clean with roses for a brush she does it
with a faltering heart.*

*This is not the rosiness of her tender
feet, dear lad! It seems to me it's the
lacquer dye being squeezed out by the
weight of the toe ornament.*

*Her gem studded toe ring shines so
brilliantly that it seems the sun
humbled by the splendour of ear
ornament had fallen at her feet.*

*When the barber's wife came to dye her
heels with the lacquer dye she found
their ruddiness matching the red gourd;
perplexed she stayed her hands not
knowing what to do.*

Bihari, *Sat Sai*

It is usually the barber's wife who tends to the *nayika's* feet even while her *sakhis* offer to help. In the adornment of the *nayika* her tender feet were never neglected. Decorative foot scrubbers, foot baths, henna and lac to colour them red were pre-requisites for the *nayika's* toilette. Bihari in his *Sat Sai* does not exclude the *nayika's* feet as he evokes her beauty.

A Nayika in a Jarokha
Jaipur, c. 1800
Collection: Author

when two jarokhas face each other
and eyes meet and glances are
exchanged
it is as if there is a silken thread
that connects the two

A *jarokha,* whether in the house or overlooking the outside, is the most romantic part of a *haveli.* It is a window from where one sees and is seen, observes and is observed, it is at the junction of the world of intrigue and the security of the home, it is a spot from where one can participate in the world outside and yet be within the comfort of one's home, it is public yet private, it is the threshold from where one allows the world outside to gaze at you but at the same time retain much of your privacy, it allows the light from outside to come in but protects the inside from the heat, it is a statement of availability yet is not an invitation, it is a place where one can let one's thoughts wander afar and yet return home, from where one can dream of romantic moments and come back to reality, for after all it is a window and not a door. Decorated with drapes or carpets, marble or wooden trellis and adorned with *chajjas* or canopies, it gives a distinctive character whether it is a modest *haveli* or a regal palace. The Jaipur artist, familiar as he was with Mughal architecture and sensibilities and Nihal Chand's Bani Thani, places this adorned *nayika* in such a *jarokha* and the look in her eyes and the gesture of her right hand leaves little doubt where her thoughts are.

Head Studies
Kishangarh, 18th century
Collection: Author

The love of Savant Singh and Bani Thani, their refinement and good looks, their poetic sensibilities and above all their devotion to Krishna inspired Nihal Chand to convert their likeness in painting to that of Krishna and Radha. The Kishangarh *kalam* in thus immortalising their love created an artistic idiom that was not done in any other atelier.

Bani Thani
Kishangarh, c. 1735–50
Collection:
National Museum, New Delhi

Her face is gleaming like the brightness of the sun
High arched twin pencilled eyebrows hover on her brow like black bees over a lily pond
And her dark tresses fall here and there like the curving tendrils of a creeper
Bejewelled is her nose curved and sharp like the thrusting saru plant
And her lips have formed a gracious bow parting in a queenly smile.

Savant Singh

It was Nihal Chand in the Kishangarh atelier who immortalised Savant Singh's consort in an artistic creation that not only captured the beauty of Bani Thani but idealised her as a romantic heroine creating a model for others to follow. Her bejewelled body ornamented with pearls on her forehead, wrists, fingers, neck and arms, large doe-shaped eyes and aquiline nose came to life with the demure gesture of touching her chin. The blue diaphanous *odhni* caressing her long black flowing tresses has the appearance of a starry sky on a black night, a kind of romantic night that she would have shared with Savant Singh in amorous pleasures, and it is the anticipation of that pleasure that her nascent smile seems to reveal. The marble balustrade is just enough to give her a sense of privacy but not enough to hide her charm. Bani Thani was not only the embodiment of sensual beauty but the paragon of romantic love and it was Nihal Chand's genius that he was able to bring both together in this stunningly expressive portrait.

A Nayika in a Palace

Kangra, c. 1790
Collection:
Victoria and Albert Museum, London

There is an atmosphere of unhurried grace, poetic charm, regal splendour and cultured sensitivity in this *zenana* inside a palace. Within the open courtyard there is still a sense of privacy. The centre of our attention is the *nayika* who is being adorned by three *sakhis* and an older companion in attendance, each ensuring that no effort is spared in preparing the queen. In the chamber of mirrors on the left the queen presides regally while the mirrors reflect various aspects of her face, a face that gazes distantly, with eyes that reveal what she does not speak. It is a charmed moment for the women, as two musicians fill the air with melody and rhythm to create a romantic ambience. It is a sensual feast and cuisine is an important part of the ethos of regal living as spices are delicately made, food carefully prepared and drink lovingly poured. There is magic in the air but yet the moment is incomplete without the *nayaka*. Will he enter soon and charge the atmosphere with his romantic presence?

Rajput palaces were designed so that matters of state and those of the heart could be conducted, each in its proper ambience. While there were public assembly halls where the king would meet loyal confidantes and subjects of his court and where complaints were heard and justice meted out, there were also private chambers and mysterious passages where political schemes and secret matters of the kingdom could be whispered. The zenana, which had open courtyards and which usually opened into the garden, was where the women spent their lives raising children and supervising the regal household but it was not devoid of political intrigue for this is where the queen would have the king's ear. It was also a place where the nayika waited in anticipation of romantic moments and amorous pleasures.

Reflections of Love
Garhwal, c. 1790–95
Collection:
National Museum, New Delhi

*a mirror that offers self-assurance, a
confirmation of beauty
is the madanika darpana, the mirror of
a sensuous nayika
but a mirror in which you see him and
he sees you
a mirror that is a testament of the
togetherness of lovers
is the shringara darpana, the mirror
of love*

It is a moment of quiet contemplation and reverie as Radha and Krishna reaffirm their love in their own reflection in the mirror. It is Radha who holds the mirror for it is she who nurtures and holds their love together, and it is in her persona that their love grows and finally rests. They gaze at the mirror and the mirror in turn gazes back at them in mute testimony, and in that exchange of their own glances through the reflection in the mirror is the truth of their love. Nothing need be spoken, no words need to intervene in this quiet and reflective confirmation of love. Even the *sakhis* rejoice in the loving togetherness of the lovers. In the landscape beyond, as birds have gathered for evening prayer and lotuses seem to meditate, it is as if the sanctity of the love of Radha and Krishna resonates with them as well. The Garhwal artist renders the moment with admirable skill and grace.

A Nayaka Returns
Bundi drawing, late 18th century
Collection: Author

victory for the Rajput
is not only on the battlefield
but is even more when he returns
and rests his eyes
on his nayika,
and when their glances meet
they shall speak
not of adventure, but of longing

The Bundi artist of this drawing takes us to a moment of romantic drama as it unfolds within a *haveli*. The *nayaka* has returned, probably sooner than expected from an expedition, and hands his bow and shield to his courtiers and goes to a balcony overlooking the courtyard where to his delight he finds that his *nayika* is adorning herself. After the weariness of the battle, where he would have longed for her, this is a restful and reassuring sight, he will drink her beauty and fill his thirsty eyes. With his right hand he extends an invitation to her. The pair of peacocks on the turret are a sure confirmation that this will be a cherished and romantic moment. The drawing provides a glimpse of Rajasthani artists and their ateliers, and we are privy to methods of composition and colouring. Just as a rehearsal is sometimes more artistic and interesting than the actual performance, a drawing is often more revealing than a completed masterpiece.

A Nayika watching Pigeons
Bundi, c. 1725–50
Collection:
National Gallery of Canada, Ottawa

It is a moment of anticipation and of longing for the *nayika* who has just completed her toilette and is being helped by her *sakhis* in the final process of adornment. While one looks after her ornaments for the feet another is ready with a decanter and a goblet for a drink and a third stands in attendance. The *nayika* herself is attending to her coiffure. However, the cynosure of attention for the ladies and therefore for us are the pigeons, three on the rack, one on the balustrade and a pair on the carpet. There is a certain life and vitality and even romantic activity with these pigeons, they play and frolic, chatter and even dally and this is not just a source of entertainment to the *nayika* but even more importantly very comforting. Her eyes are fixed on them and she looks longingly at them as if to say how she wishes she would be doing the same. Perhaps the play of the pigeons presages that happy times will soon be here when her beloved will return and she like the pigeons will spend amorous moments full of romantic play. The pigeons though peripherally placed are the source of energy and attention in this beautifully executed Bundi painting.

in the cooing of the pigeons
there is a song of love
and in the flutter of their wings
there is a dance of love

A Fond Welcome
Kotah, c. 1760
Collection: Author

the Rajput's rich reward
for his courage and sacrifice
is honour in battle
but even more
a passionate welcome from his beloved.

A lavish *haveli* is the scene of this fond welcome to a returning Rajput by his beloved on a hot summer day. The brilliantly colourful Kotah *kalam* portrays a *nayika* who has waited long and patiently while her beloved was away, and has adorned herself, and prepared with excitement and anticipation the courtyard where she will greet him with fruits and flowers, the cool inner chamber where there will be sweet conversation and the tastefully appointed terrace where the evening hours will be spent in amorous pleasure. The Rajput who has also longed for her during his absence is impatient upon seeing her and quickly discards his sword and gives her a passionate embrace, while she, eager to look into his eyes, seems to ask, "how much did you miss me?" There is lot of catching up to do for the two of them, the world can wait, and so should we, while the two share richly deserved private and romantic moments.

Nayikas and Nayakas: The Heroines and Heros of Love

The Embrace of Love
Bikaner, c. 1810
Collection: Author

Stalwart as a tree his deep embrace
squeezes the vine with branch like arms
when I want sleep Krishna makes love
the whole night through
like a bee that lingers on the fragrant
malati
he sucks my lips.
The forest has burst open
with white kunda blooms
but the bee is enraptured by
malati and her honey.

Vidyapati

It is a moment of quiet togetherness, of silent embraces, of unspoken feelings, of tender thoughts being conveyed by the warmth of a loving touch. It is a sweet embrace, an *alingan* of commitment, an assurance of abiding love, a promise that their precious love will forever be protected, a coming together of two who feel like one. It is an altar of an abiding romantic love that the Bikaner artist creates, a lotus pad in the centre of a hillock, a flowing river with lotuses, two plantain trees on the sides and a cow and *hamsa* as companions in this charming moment. There is a certain earthiness in this artistic creation for when the earth is witness there is no need for trappings of nobility and opulence. Their gazes have a faraway but a satisfied look, for in this loving embrace there is a security, an assurance, that no storms of life can separate their loving relationship. It is refreshing to see this touching and idyllic creation of the Bikaneri artist, reminiscent of romantic moments in Vrindavana, despite the popularity of an ethos of courtly love in 19th century Rajasthan.

The gathering of women at the well in the morning is the theme of this painting. While most are engaged in the filling and carrying of water in pots, and an elderly lady drinks with her hands, the arrival of an equestrian prince, from the *haveli* in the background, evokes a subdued romantic response. He is served water but the bevy of girls remain preoccupied with their chores, while the two who are walking away are in an animated conversation.

A Prince at a Well
Deccan, Hyderabad, c. 1725
Collection: The British Library

The theme of a thirsty prince receiving water from a village belle was popular during the Mughal period, probably inspired by the story of Mohna Rani and Chel Batao. It is an otherwise quiet day and as deer rest by the river's edge a group of women have gathered at the well. Their morning chore is interrupted by a pleasant surprise as a prince stops by. He is indeed a prince charming dressed in a green *jama*, a sword in his *patka* and a quiver of arrows on his saddle and riding a well-groomed horse. While one woman offers him a small pot of water which the prince readily accepts, the other looks on vacantly, the third is coy and the fourth is busy drawing water from the well, the fifth sitting on the steps is clearly frozen in a romantic moment as she stares at the prince. And as each of them wonder what the real reason would be for the prince to come there we are sure that as the bevy of women walk back to their homes and get busy with their day the morning's incident would be on their minds. And what of the prince, where would be his thoughts be? The artist in creating this folio charged with emotion starts us on our own romantic quest to complete the story that he has just begun.

the body marches forward
but the restless heart flies back
like the silken cloth of a banner
that is borne against the wind

Kalidasa

It is a special moment for the self-assured *nayika* for she has not only the complete attention of her beloved upon her but has enlisted him for her adornment as well. On an otherwise bare terrace, overlooking a garden of tall cypress trees and blossoms, Krishna lovingly attends to Radha's hair while a *sakhi* holds a mirror. The bareness of the terrace focuses our eyes on the two lovers as they share their romance. The mirror seems to have momentarily stolen their attention away from their activity for as they both look into it they have perhaps caught a glimpse of their two faces, and in that togetherness in the mirror they have discovered their love all over again.

My waist is not slim, my bosom is not youthful
my body is not lustrous, my gait is without langour
my gaze is not artful, my dancing is immature
my speech is without wit and my laughter is not vivid
How then, O sakhi does he dote on me alone?

Bhanudatta. *Rasamanjari*

Svadhinapatika Nayika
Kalighat, late 19th century
Collection: Author

The Kalighat artist in his typical artistic idiom and iconic figures presents a similar situation as Krishna rubs Radha's feet.

Mugdhasvakiya Nayika

Kangra, late 18th century
Collection:
The British Museum, London

It is an opulent court setting and the ambience is distinctly romantic. While our eyes feast on the manicured garden with pools and fountains, blossoming trees, frolicking ducks and birds engaged in sweet whispers, a bevy of *sakhis* ensure that nothing is overlooked and that every need of the romantic couple is met. One *sakhi* feeds the parrot, others bring platters of food while a group provide music suitable for a charming soiree. Having taken in the beautiful surroundings we turn our attention to the two lovers and the two bolsters, one empty, which is where she sat as the evening began, till he drew her close for a passionate embrace. Her coy withdrawal from his embrace and her hesitation in not letting their gaze meet is appropriate for a young and inexperienced *nayika*, whose shy behaviour is only a veneer for her hidden passion and her secret desire to love and be loved. There is every indication that as the music flows and the evening unfolds her sweet protestations will cease and it will be a romantic evening after all, much to the delight of the *sakhis*.

although no is ever on her lips
from her laughter filled eyebrows she
sends another message
while denial lies in her uncertain words
her eyes consent

Bihari. *Sat Sai*

Abhisarika Nayika
Mandi, 1810–1820
Collection:
Victoria and Albert Museum, London

back from meeting my lover on a dark
night
I was unnerved to see the moon come
out
when I was only halfway
but my good fortune, friend
drawn by my body's fragrance
black bees so swarmed around me
as I went along, that I remained hid
from prying eyes

Bihari. *Sat Sai*

It is a starry night, the day's work is over and peace has descended on this delightful town, many people are asleep, some chat in their *havelis* and some others are exchanging gossip in the courtyard even at this late hour. The *nayika*, tastefully dressed in a pink attire, who is the centre of the composition and of our attention, is however torn by her desire to steal an amorous meeting with Krishna, who lies awake in an adjacent *haveli* and the fear of being detected by the gossipmongers of the town. As she emerges from her bedchamber, where she lay restlessly, the *nayika's* dilemma is clearly seen as she holds the door open with her left hand and with her right ponders the wisdom of her romantic desire. And as we share her predicament the look on her face tells us that ultimately her heart will triumph over her head and that before the night is over she will have shared amorous moments with her beloved and before the day breaks she will be safely home.

Abhisarika Nayika

Kangra c. 1850
Collection:
Victoria and Albert Museum, London

*Keshavdas in his Rasikapriya describes
three types of abhisarika nayikas. The
premabhisarika who is sure of her love
and impelled by this sets out to meet her
beloved. The garvabhisarika is self
assured of her beauty and sets out to
meet her beloved confident that she will
be able to draw him towards her. The
kamabhisarika who is so driven by her
love that she sets out in the middle of
the night notwithstanding any dangers
that lie on her way. Then there is the
krishnabhisarika who sets out on her
love mission at night and
shuklabhisarika who does so during the
day. Although the term abhisarika does
not appear in the Bhagavata Purana the
gopis when they leave everything and
are drawn to Krishna's flute are a type
of abhisarika nayika. Bhanudatta in his
Rasamanjari classifies the abhisarika
into mugdha, madhya and praudha.*

*O my young friend, lightning like a
messenger brings an invitation for you
the night like a companion is your
guide
the cloud like an astrologer predicts
with its thunder the auspicious moment
of departure
the engulfing darkness of the night
recites benedictions through the chirping
of the crickets
Give up your bashfulness for this is the
proper time for you to go out and meet
your beloved.*

Bhanudatta. *Rasamanjari*

Of all the *nayikas* in *vipralambha shringara,* love in longing, the *abhisarika
nayika* is the most striking. Driven by her relentless love and her
overwhelming desire to meet her beloved, the *abhisarika* will not be deterred
by anything, not the raging storm, nor the dark night, neither ghosts and
goblins or snakes that thwart her path. Her mind is resolute, her
determination is adamantine, her commitment is unshakeable, her love
abiding. Nothing will stop her, no hazard will deter her, no danger will
frighten her, no obstacle will obstruct her, no difficulty will weaken her
desire to be with her beloved. The Kangra artist uses the wellworn idioms of
his atelier to depict a love-driven *nayika* who is rushing against all odds to
meet her beloved. Adorned and bedecked she looks back only momentarily
at the snake but will not be deterred by it. Birds of the night, chirping
crickets and lightning complete the foreboding darkness of the night, but
even as she flirts with danger, night blossoms reach out to touch her,
wishing her godspeed in her courageous journey, as do we.

*where the sandalwood tree stands
with tender bright leaves entwined by
clove creepers
there she ran and hid herself and
glanced with startled eyes
at every sound of the breeze and leaves
and birds
as she yearned for her beloved*

Keshavdas. *Rasikapriya*

To adorn and prepare for his arrival and to wait with anticipation is the *dharma* of the *nayika*. She picks out with great care the clothes that she will wear for she knows what his favourite colours are, and then selects the appropriate jewellery, beautifies and anoints her body, has on hand betel and condiments and then waits for that special moment when his eyes will behold her. Her adornment is her offering for his eyes, her beauty is for him to enjoy, her pleasure is to see that glint of excitement in his eyes when he sees her. It is an occasion that she has waited for, in this is the fulfilment of her love. Such is the *nayika* in this folio rendered by the Kangra artist with his usual flourish. Even though the artist gives her almost an iconic presence in this single chamber of her *haveli* we are sure that she will wait for him longingly at the door, when the waiting seems too long.

Shankhini Nayika
Isarda thikana of Jaipur
late 18th century
Collection: Author

ॐश्वसंपिनीलछिनादोदाकायमालंकाविदंकपटा॥सजलसामसरगाप्याछारा॥
गांधउतमारुजल्ला॥तहचलपिलंगाढेहु॥सुरतारतत्रअतिसंधानो॥वरनकेकविंगा॥
नलादेहुपया॥सर्वदेश्यो॥ज्ञाठनवाकदलाकिगलानिनिलविधिलेवदलामुदना॥
ते॥आदरसोंअतिआदरकेयातमोंदुवदेकवतिकौउपुजावेा॥जाकाउकेसेझनाग
॥वंगलतालवली॥अवलानचरावेाषारिकदाघषवाईसरेंकोईईंरटि॥॥रुटकटा॥
॥ोईंसावे॥॥धा॥

While mainstream Rajasthani painting took place in the major courts such as Mewar, Marwar, Jaipur, Kishangarh, Kotah and Bundi, the thikanas or outposts, patronised by chieftains and lesser royalty, maintained their own ateliers. Many artists of these thikanas had received their early training from the master artists of the courts, but once on their own, they ventured into bold experiments and less sophisticated themes such as this folio of the shankhini nayika. The subject of shringara rasa was so rich that it had room for both the classical and not so classical styles, for romantic moments were celebrated by the raja and the praja alike.

O f the four types of *nayikas* in the taxonomies of Keshavdas' *Rasikapriya* namely *padmini, chitrini, shankhini* and *hastini* we are here in the company of the *shankhini nayika* in this folio. The *shankhini* delights in wearing red clothes and the artist captures this by casting an ochre glow in the entire composition. Her *sakhis* advance in a formation towards the *nayaka* suggesting that she would use every guile in her love games. Not shy of showing her passion she welcomes nail marks. Keshavdas compares her to a camel who prefers prickly leaves to lotus leaves or the clove creeper and chews thorny bushes rather than the *champa* flower or the plantain tree. And as the *shankhini* and the life-size camel both share our attention, we ponder the fate of the nayaka holding a flower, as he looks expectantly at the *nayika*. The folkish composition which avoids artistic sophistication does justice to the persona of this type of *nayika*.

How can I help looking at him, my friend?
His eyes trick away all prudence
Who can remain unmoved
by their bewitching glance?

Bihari. *Sat Sai*

The Kangra artist takes us on an amorous journey as our eyes settle on two *havelis*, of different architectural styles and decor, adjacent but independent, as between them we are led to a distant landscape of a mosque and rolling hills. But we quickly return and note Krishna, in his yellow *pitambar*, his gaze directed toward the opposite *haveli,* his left hand holding a betel, leaving no doubt that he waits expectantly for Radha. A tastefully adorned Radha in the other *haveli* also gazes distantly with anticipation, and then we follow her to the lower chamber where her *sakhi* cautions her about the treacherous eyes of Krishna. Radha listens, but her gaze is still steadfast, as is her desire. Radha says that his attractive eyes are enough to forget all prudence and wisdom. And as we see the open door to Krishna's *haveli* with its curtain rolled up, we have no doubt that despite the advice of the *sakhi* Radha will fall victim to Krishna's inviting gaze. The red carpet on which Krishna waits, and the decanter of wine, is a reflection of the desire in Krishna's eyes, and is an assurance that the inviting gaze is for sweet dalliances, and we can almost imagine Radha coyly entering that open door into the open arms of Krishna as their gazes melt into one another.

Ukta Nayika
Kangra, 1820–1830
Collection: Colonel R.K. Tandan

It is an atmospheric moment, there is a certain excitement in the air, a magical brightness in the light, trees are in blossom and a pair of birds create a romantic setting. The Kangra artist provides a perspective with distant evergreens but our sight quickly returns to Radha, adorned and expectant, as she waits in the upper chamber while her *sakhi* has engaged Krishna in an animated conversation. Radha's demeanour suggests that she has sent a message to Krishna and she waits anxiously for an answer. Krishna lets the *sakhi* look into his eyes which can only speak of his love and longing for Radha and this surely is the answer the *sakhi* will carry with her, and what follows can only be an amorous rendezvous. We, who identify with the *sakhi,* can only be charmed at the role she has played in this transaction of love. The Kangra artists renders this composition with mellifluous line and evocative colours.

I swore I would unite you to this
precious girl
and I have redeemed my promise
Now keep her twined to your bosom
as you would a champa garland

Bihari. *Sat Sai*

Baisakha
Kotah, 1810–1820
Collection: Author

The month of *Baisakh* has ushered in an exuberance in the world around. Spring has touched the hearts and minds of everyone and the flag atop the *haveli* flutters in fragrant breezes as trees blossom in joyous abundance, hunters have embarked on their hunt, fish frolic and even the fountains throw up coloured water. It is an amorous and aromatic spring morning and the *nayika* with her *sakhi* having completed their morning *puja* are making flower garlands as an ascetic sitting near by is obviously distracted by their presence and the fragrance of lotuses in the river. Having taken in the verdant and delightful atmosphere, which the Kotah painter has executed with finesse, our eyes settle on the upper chamber of the *haveli* where the *nayika* offers a sip of wine from her goblet and the *nayaka* drinks instead her intoxicating gaze. Despite the amorousness of the situation there is a certain pain in her heart for she fears that she might lose him if he leaves her in this season of love, and we, along with the *nayika*, leave the painting with a fond hope that the charm of *Baisakh* would not be lost for her.

the earth and sky are filled with
fragrance
the gentle aromatic breeze intoxicates
the bees
do not talk of going away in baisakh
as the arrows of Kama are hard to bear
in this month of amorous pleasures.

Keshavdas. *Kavipriya*

Jyestha
Bikaner, c. 1830
Collection: Author

the sun is so bright and scorching that the five elements have become one. The roads are deserted and the tanks are parched dry seeing which the elephants do not go out. Even the cobra and lions stay indoors. Keshavdas says that the elders are of the opinion that one should not leave one's beloved in this month.

Keshavdas. *Kavipriya*

The Bikaner artist portrays the month of *Jyestha* with unusual delicacy and gives us a glimpse of a dozen people engaged in the activities of summer. The lower register is a window on the lives of the everyday people: tilling their field, selling their produce, women helping in the chores, a courtier attending to his horse, an itinerant singer and a listener who draws on his hookah under the shade of a tree, even as a deer drinks water on this hot summer's day. There is a sense of order and purpose. But as our eyes turn upward we are led into the intimacy of a *haveli* as a romantic couple are exchanging betel leaves as an attendant with a whisk provides a gentle breeze to mitigate the heat of the summer. Summer months are meant for the comfort of one's home and it is a time to stay with one's beloved. The Bikaneri artist has skilfully conveyed the ambience of summer and has inhabited a dozen people in the small pictorial space with a a lot of space to spare, an artistic feat that only comes from consummate brush work.

Pausha
Malwa, late 18th century
Collection: Author

चित्र के देवनागरी शिलालेख

learning from her friends in the month of Paus
her lover was to go abroad next morning
that girl expert on the vina played malhar raga
causing such a downpour that he could not go.

Bihari. *Sat Sai*

The chill of the winter months of December and January has set in and a fire has been lit and as the romantic couple warm themselves, the artist by painting their chamber red, suggests that the fire of their hearts has also been lit. It is the season when the earth and the sky are cold, people like the pleasure of oil and the comfort of cotton around their bodies. The *nayika* is secure in the company of her beloved who has settled with a sash around his legs, eating betel. She has adorned herself and the upper chamber of the *haveli* has been prepared for amorous pleasures. The *nayika's* security is short-lived, for the *nayaka*, having equipped himself with his bow and arrow, is ready to embark on an expedition, when we quickly notice the red hands of the *nayika*, hands that have been specially adorned, asking him not to leave her in this month of love-making, and as she confronts him thus, their eyes seem to engage in a dialogue. The Malwa style shows a close affinity to the Jain and early Hindu pictorial traditions.

अथ अ्साढा॥ पवनचक्रप्रचंरुचलंतिनिच्वार्वपलगति भवनभामिनीतर्जति
व्रमातिमानञ्रतिनिकिसिति संस्यासीइदमासहोतरक्र्श्रामनवासी वुरिषिनि
काकोकहेनरपंछीयो निवासी इहसमयसजनसोवनलियो सियासहितश्रीना
थहं करिकेरावदासस्त्र्शचलमंमेनसयोश्रनिगाथर्ु॥

With this month come strong winds; birds do not leave their nests and even ascetics go on only one daily round to collect alms. Even Vishnu and Lakshmi retreat to their chamber and even the scriptures suggest that one not leave one's home during this month. This is the gist of the protest that the distraught *nayika* makes to her beloved who prepares to leave. The Malwa artist renders this sentiment beautifully in this folio.

Shravana
Kangra, 1820–1830
Collection: Author

the sight of the river rushing towards
the ocean pleases the mind
the creepers like young damsels cling
to trees
clouds shine as lightning touches them
peacocks make happy sounds as earth
and sky meet
the lover and the loved delight in each
other's company
in this month of shravana even the talk
of leaving should not be heard.

Keshavdas. *Kavipriya*

The rainy months have special associations with romantic love. If the sight of dark clouds and the sounds of thunder and lightning makes a peacock sing a paean of love, the heart of the *nayika* who waits for her beloved trembles with longing. Kalidasa likens the arrival of the rainy season to a king with flashes of lightning like flags and the sound of thunder as drums. Other poets describe rain as the mating of the sky and the earth and some others regard it as a blessing from Indra. It is a season of blossoms like *bakula* and *malati, kakubha* and *kadamba,* flowers which women wear to adorn themselves. Fragrant winds, trumpeting elephants, confused bees, frightened deer and the aroma of the wet earth intoxicate the young at heart. Wandering ascetics refrain from their travels and the pious undertake special fasts. It is such a rainy night in *shravana* that the Kangra artist depicts with his usual artistic finesse. Krishna asks Radha to let him leave while Radha pleads with him not to, while two *sakhis* await anxiously and cranes fly away in the cloud laden sky.

Bhadrapad
Deccan, c. 1880
Collection:
The British Museum, London

अथ भाद्रपद मासि सिषा घोरत घनविद्युतवोरघोषनिघोषनिमंडहि धारधरधा
रिधरसिघगुंजरतिघुंजरतिघुंजरतुंतारहि निसिदिनबेसेषनि रोषमिरिजाता
सुबोलीबोडिये देसपियुषविदेशाविष भादोंनवनननछोंदिये

*dark clouds gather and there is thunder
everywhere
rain pours in torrents
tigers and lions roar and elephants
break trees
birds chirp continuously and a fierce
wind blows
the day is as dark as the night
a storm rages outside but there is
comfort within the home
no one should leave one's home this
month.*

Keshavdas. *Kavipriya*

The Deccani artist brings the month of *bhadrapad* to life in this animated creation of the rains. The rains which started the previous month have now intensified, as lightning streaks the dark and foreboding sky, peacocks are seen in a variety of activities, some dance, some are frightened, others seek shelter in trees, while elephants swimming in the restless river go into a rage. The artist convincingly captures the turbulent environment of the rainy month, but within the comfort of the home leads us into another tumult as Radha urges Krishna not to leave her in this month, as two *sakhis* wait in attendance, even as they are distracted by a monkey. In placing the anxious *nayika* between two registers where dark hues and agitated birds portray the stormy rain, the artist eloquently suggests the nervous state of her mind, a mind that rages like the storm outside even as she negotiates with her beloved not to leave her.

Phalgun
Kangra, 1830
Collection: Author

*in the month of phalgun the rich and
poor are given to merry making
young men and women play holi with
great abandon
and smear each other with gulal
the fragrance of the scented powders fills
the air
in such a festive season the lover should
not leave the beloved.*

Keshavdas. *Kavipriya*

It is romantic moment in the month of *phalguna* but with a tinge of pathos. The festival of Holi will soon be here and the empty courtyard will be full of the riot of colour and the sound of merrymaking, knots will be tied and new alliances will be made. There will be frivolity and men and women will steal romantic moments with each other. It is a time to light bonfires and the fire of love in every heart. The demure Kangra *nayika* in a pink *gaghra*, which speaks of her desire, looks forward with anticipation and excitement to moments of romantic pleasures and urges her beloved, dressed in a yellow *jama* appropriate to the colours of spring, not to leave her in this festive month. The deserted *haveli* in the midday sun with the temple in the distance seem to reflect the forlorn state of the *nayika's* mind. The Kangra artist renders the moment with restraint and encloses the space in an oval floral border, quite commonly seen in *barahmasa* paintings.

Ragini Megh Malhar
Malwa, c. 1675
Collection: Author

of blue splendour
attached to the roar of the rain cloud
of tender body and lovely form
proud and playful
the god of love
is said to be Megha.

Ragmala Text

The rainy season has strong romantic associations, for it is a time for the pleasures of love as well as the pathos of longing. Dark clouds, the sound of rain, the cry of the peacock, the aroma of freshly soaked earth send ripples of excitement through the heart of the lover and a flood of amorous feelings in the beloved. It is a time to celebrate, to recreate sounds of the season with drums and cymbals, dance to its rhythm, sway in the wind and let the mind be drenched with the pleasures of love. It is this special moment that the Malwa artist renders with his usual earthy motifs and a monochrome green. As the eye takes in the joyous romantic pair, surrounded by adoring drummers, the ecstatic peacock underneath the rain that comes down as a string of pearls arrests our attention and completes the iconography for this *ragini*. Mallar, a *raga* in early compilations such as Narada's becomes later known as *Megha Malhar* and finally as *Megha*.

Raga Dipak
Malwa, c. 1640
Collection:
The British Museum, London

when the nayika bashfully returned
all she had to show
was a burn on her hand
and her sakhis were satisfied

lines from a Maithili song

*R*aga Dipak has engaged and inspired musicians and painters alike and there are a number of legends about this melody. It is said that Tansen, the court musician for Akbar, started a palace fire when he was asked to sing *raga* Dipak. The basic iconography of this *raga* is a pair of lovers and a lamp. It is left to the imagination of the artists how they choose to depict the lamp. The commonest is a clay lamp but a number of other types of lamps are also shown and some artists show a flame on the head of the *nayaka* or *nayika*. An Amber *Ragamala* text has this description: *Dipak* is born out of the sun's eye, his body is like the blossom of the pomegranate flower, he rides an elephant in rut and many women accompany him on the ride, his *raginis* are five Des, Kamod, Nat, Kedaro and Kanara. Harivallabha's *Sangita Darpana* describes Dipak thus: he went to the apartment of his beloved under cover of darkness looking forward to the dalliances of love. The dazzling rays of his jewels appeared there as a second sun. The Malwa folio, executed with finesse of central Indian ateliers, shows the lovers in a romantic embrace, attended by musicians, as the *nayika* tries to extinguish the lamp. The use of red in the *patka* of the *nayaka*, the *gaghra* of the *nayika* and in the windows of the *haveli* creates a mood of heightened passion and romantic excitement, as the anticipation of amorous pleasures after the lamp has been extinguished fills the air.

*R*agini Gauri is a *nayika* who is separated from her beloved and finds comfort and solace from collecting blossoms. Traditionally, she holds branches of the *Kalpa vriksha* and wears mango blossoms in her ears. Her complexion is said to be shining and she possesses a sweet voice. The Sirohi artist adheres to the traditional description of this *ragini*, as she skirts between luxuriant trees and fragrant blossoms and holds two clusters of flowers. Two pairs of peacocks are witness to her lonesome state as she turns around as if to speak to one of them and share her pain.

Ragini Bangali
Sirohi, c. 1675
Collection: Author

in a shiny white temple
she sits on a rug of deer skin
and contemplates Lord Shiva
leaving the hermitage she sits in
the wilderness
surrounded by trees of various forms
on which some monkeys gambol
clouds come thick and fast
below the shrine of Shiva sits a lion
beyond is a lake in which are lotuses
and birds
Bangali is a separated heroine with
her heart
fixed on her Lord
she cannot brook the presence of
her companions
for she is anxious to meet her beloved.

Ragamala Text

This folio of *Ragini* Bangali from the same Sirohi series features a *nayika* who occupies a *jarokha* in an opulent dwelling amidst verdant trees. The traditional description of this *Ragini* is on the left.

Ragini Gunakali
Sirohi, c. 1675
Collection: Author

*Sitting in great expectation to meet
her beloved
she has a lotus flower in each hand
she is seated in a beautiful palace,
surrounded by a pond
a fountain and fruit trees.
Suddenly her confidante brings
the news
that her lover is coming and she is
very happy.*

Ragamala Text

*R**agini* Gunkali is a *vipralambha nayika*, waiting anxiously for the return of her beloved. She holds a lotus bud in her right hand which suggests the loveless and forlorn state of her mind. The *sakhis* outside the pavilion however show her a fully open lotus indicating that her love will bloom again. Two empty vases along with two arabesques at the bottom are very suggestive that it takes two to share love. In some *ragamala* paintings the *nayika* is shown placing flowers in the two vases. The typical Sirohi touch is seen in the treatment of the trees. While anxiety is writ on the faces of the *nayika* and her *sakhis* there is promise in the air as we enjoy this well-executed *ragini* and are reminded of the music which is sung at dawn.

Ragini Khambavati
Amber, c. 1710
Collection: Author

In this early *ragamala* set from Amber *ragini* Khambavati of Raga Malkaus is portrayed as a music loving *nayika* being entertained by two female musicians, sitting next to an empty bed by the light of an oil lamp. The Amber artist departs from the traditional iconography of this *ragini* which is a *nayika* worshiping the four-headed Brahma.

Ragini Deshavarari
Malwa, c. 1675
Collection: Author

*to find music in her movements and
poetry in her lips
a message in her mudras, a mantra in
her whisper
a longing when she turns away, a
yearning when she looks askance
a rhythm in the dance of her bangles, a
melody in the sound of her ankle bells
to find shravan in her tears and the
aroma of jasmine in her smile
is to transform shringara rasa to a raga
and a raga to ragamala.*

In a Rajasthani *ragamala* text attributed to a poet Kashyapa this *ragini* is described thus: at ease and in silence, her body twisted as the creeper, arms up-stretched and rolling eyes—such shall be Deshavarari the fair one. A Malwa text by Lachhiman Das describes this *ragini* as a fair-complexioned woman who is angry or offended and whose beloved tries to win her over. Deshavarari as a music mode became extinct sometime in the 17th or 18th century and painters in several Rajasthani schools replaced its iconography with popular *ragas* such as Behag and Purvi. In the Deccan its iconography was taken over by Shyam Kalyan. A special feature of this *ragini* is the twisting of her body away from her beloved and raising of her arms, an iconography that denotes anger. However, in this Malwa folio we know that this is only a lover's resentment as she looks longingly at the empty bed while her *nayaka* tries to appease her. This *Ragamala* uses the characteristic Malwa artistic idioms, idioms that have been used so successfully in illustrating *Rasikapriya*, to create a mood of romantic tension within the familiar architectural setting. The use of a monochrome background of red for the lovers and a grey green for the empty bedchamber but a bright red bed cover and bolster are evocative. Shown in vertical perspective, the lotus pond is quite striking.

Ragini Bilaval
Bundi, c. 1610–1700
Collection: Art of the Past, New York

having arranged a tryst
blue complexioned and with red clothes
of beautiful limbs
with sixteen adornments
she awaits the beloved
with sweet thoughts of him

Ragamala Text

It is a charmed moment in an opulent *haveli* as *ragini* Bilaval adorns herself and waits with anticipation and excitement for her beloved. She has put on eight ornaments and sixteen adornments and turns away from the incense being blown toward her by her *sakhi*. The empty bedchamber has an inviting air with a red bedcover, a garland of flowers and two wine jars. More aromatic than the incense, and more beautiful than the ornaments are her thoughts of that magic moment when he will arrive, her waiting will be over and she will lead him to the bedchamber. Her uplifted arms and blue *choli* which reveals her inviting and sensuous form is an indication of her expectation and desire. The Bundi artist renders the *ragini* and her *sakhi* with consummate grace and rare artistic skill. The predominance of the red and yellow are in keeping with the mood of restrained passion. The tall evergreen tree between two blossoming trees is very suggestive.

Ragini Dhanashri of Raga Dipak

Radhanpur, Gujarat, c. 1810
Collection: Author

*R*agini Dhanashri is a *nayika* overcome by the pangs of separation. An Amber *Ragamala* text describes her as seated under the *Bakula* tree, red with grief, she weeps and heaves deep sighs, her *odhni* and bodice are coloured red, it is difficult to find a lady of such slim grace, by the heat of her separation her body withers. Another text describes her as a great beauty with the loveliness of a blue lotus who takes a drawing board and draws his picture in many forms. Mesakarna in his treatise gives the iconography of this as a woman in black holding pomegranates with a voice that *ragini* resembles that of a hare. Her confidantes are Jatishri and Bhimpalashri. The present folio, possibly painted in Gujarat, departs slightly from the texts, but maintains an ambience of longing on the one hand and a restrained rejoicing on the other at having seen her beloved at least by proxy. It shows the *nayika* in a gold sari holding a drawing board on which she has drawn her beloved dressed in a green *jama*. The paraphernalia of painting have been spread out and her *sakhi* is not only her helper in her artistic endeavour but also assuages her feelings. A bright red awning and bolster enlivens an otherwise simple setting and as we take in a mango tree we return to the *nayika* and share her longing.

O my friend how can darkness flee
without a lamp
by thinking on a flame?
O princess how can thirst be quenched
by tales of water?
How can wealth descend by gazing
on a picture of Lakshmi?

Keshavdas. *Rasikapriya*

Ragini Madhu Madhavi
Alwar, c. 1830
Collection: Colonel R.K. Tandan

in the sounds of thunder there is a
desire
in the flash of lightning a wish
to wind around my beloved
like the madhavi creeper around a tree

It is a stormy night, there are dark and ominous clouds and streaks of lightning are in the air and a *nayika*, dressed in a blue bodice, rushes towards the ornately decorated *haveli*. A *sakhi* waits to see her safely home and out of danger. While the *nayika* shelters herself with her sari she looks backward at the approaching storm and the leaves of the *tamala* tree, and there is in her gait a certain hesitation. On the one hand she wants to be indoors and protected from the storm, but then on the other the clouds and the lighting create in her a desire to be with her beloved and she has half a mind go out in the storm looking for him in the fashion of an *abhisarika nayika*. The artist follows the *Ragamala* texts and in particular in the use of blue which is the prescribed colour of her clothes but which seems to overflow into the walls of the courtyard as well. However, frightened and thirsty peacocks which are a feature of this *Ragini* are absent in this folio.

Ragini Kakubha
Central India (Rewa) c. 1750
Collection: Author

Rewa in Madhya Pradesh under its cultured patron Raja Ram Chand was a great centre of music during the second half of the 16th century. It was from here that the noted musician Tansen was sent to the Imperial court in 1562. Also from Rewa came the rhetorician Kshemakarna who compiled his well-known treatise on Ragamala in 1570.

The *Ragamala* texts describe Ragini Kakubha as a *nayika* who is accomplished in love, and after a night of having enjoyed erotic pleasures is tortured by her separation and is frightened and weeps as she walks through the woods; she carries the marks of love's union on her body but is startled by the voice of the cuckoo. Moon-faced and with long tresses, she wears yellow silk and is said to carry a garland of *chamapaka* flowers in her hands and every part of her body is fashioned after Kama the god of love, such is her beauty. She sits on a mound playing the *vina* and the peacocks are attracted by the sound of the music. The Bundi artist renders the *ragini* very close to the traditional description incorporating blossoming trees, a flowing river with lotuses, a number of peacocks and a distant temple with frolicking monkeys and a romantic couple in the background, all washed in exquisite colours which adds a special relish to this *ragini*.

Raga Vasanta
Deccan, Hyderabad, c. 1725
Collection: The British Library

Vasanta *raga* is the incarnation of Kama, the god of love and his persona is best brought about by the festivities of Holi, the spring festival of love. It is a colourful moment of celebration in the courtyard, and *Vasanta's* ethos is evoked by the graceful *jarokhas* in the background, a fish pond surrounded by blossoms, a landscape of suggestive plantain trees and erect evergreens and a distant sky, mute symbols of passion and desire. *Vasanta* embraces *Rati* and to the rhythm of a *mridanga*, the beat of *duff* and the notes of an *ektara*, he dances. A syringe of yellow liquid is prepared and a platter of *gulal* is at the centre and very soon these colours will speak of love and passion, and amorous feelings will be exchanged through animated glances and movements during the festival of colours. Nothing need be spoken, no words are needed, no rituals performed and no vows exchanged, for it is a time when love is freed from restraints and inhibitions as *Vasanta raga* reigns. The Deccani artist renders this *raga* with a perfect blend of colour, specially yellow and red, and line and is able to capture the ebullient spirit of the occasion.

Kama
Orcha, c. 1680
Collection: Victoria and Albert Museum, London

Raga Vasanta in the genre of ragamala paintings is the visual celebration of vasantotsava, the spring festival of love and equally of Kama, the god of love. As early as the Atharva Veda Kama is mentioned as the god of sexual desires. Kama is armed with a bow made of sugar cane, its string made of bees and the tips of his arrows made of flowers. His vehicle is a parrot and the sign on his insignia is a fish, his crest is made of ashoka and mango leaves, his headpiece is made of jasmine, his messenger is the cuckoo. Humans and animals alike are touched by Kama's arrows and none other than Shiva was hit by his arrow and this led to Shiva's arousal and attraction towards Parvati. Shiva was angered and destroyed Kama to ashes but then revived him to life. The death and rebirth of Kama at the hands of Shiva becomes the motif of regeneration and transformation and therefore of spring and of romantic love. The mango tree is especially associated with Kama and many rituals associated with the vasantotsava prescribe the eating of mango blossoms by young women, while another ritual requires the queen to kick the ashoka tree with her left foot and make it blossom. The joy of romantic love and the vernal beauty of vasanta can only arise from the arrows of Kama.

Ragini Patamanjiri
Sirohi, 18th century
Collection: Author

*P*atamanjiri etymologically comes from *prathama manjiri* or the first blossoms which evokes longing in those who are in love. *Patamanjiri* is a lonely *nayika* longing for her beloved as she spends her time with two *sakhis*. One attends to her with a peacock whisk while the other consoles her with an account, most probably of her beloved. An important part of the composition is the cat who seems to listen attentively. The Sirohi style is particularly evident in the depiction of the trees outside the *haveli*. The costumes are simple and the *haveli* plain in keeping with the mood of painful longing.

*she wears a flower garland around
her neck
the separated one is extremely stricken
one moment she revives
the other moment her life fades
she does not relish food or her
living quarters
she does not sleep and sits alone
and bends into two due to pangs
of separation*

Ragamala Text

Ragamala: The Music of Love

Ragini Pancham

Bikaner, early 18th century
Collection: Author

Various sets of ragamala paintings that were so popular in Rajasthani courts reflect not only the ambience of the courts but equally the courtly love that was so much a part of the Rajasthani tradition. Many ragamalas are set within courts and havelis and show the romantic couple in a number of different romantic situations in idioms and motifs that reflect courtly love. By the time ragamala paintings had become popular Hindustani classical music and dance was also a court activity.

Pancham *ragini* of Sri Raga is said to be immersed in the joy and colour of melodies. Accompanied by her lord, who listens to two female musicians, one on each side, and pleased with the music rewards the musicians, but the beauty of the fifth note is such that the romantic couple are enchanted more by each other than the music. The Bikaner artist renders this *ragini* in an opulent *haveli* replete with musicians and dancers, blossoms and fountains and convincingly conveys the sense of joy that pervades everyone, especially the romantic couple who celebrate the music with a delightful embrace. This *ragini* in particular demonstrates how the various performing arts were an integral part of courtly activity but also woven into the romantic life of the nobility.

Raga Ramakali

Deccan, early 18th century
Collection: Author

Golden in hue and with shining jewels
arrayed in a garment of blue
though besought by her prostrate lover
she remains adamant

Ragamala Text

Among the contribution of the Deccan the genre of *ragamala* painting is particularly evocative. The Deccani artist in this folio picks up on the theme of the *khandita nayika*, the offended heroine, from the poetry of *raga* Ramakali. In the verandah overlooking a manicured garden complete with fountains, flirting fish and a pair of ducks, the obdurate nayika expresses her resentment in many different ways. She turns her face away from her repentant lover and almost covering her face with her *odhni*, pushes him away with her left hand and even lifts her left foot remonstratively not letting him express his admission of guilt. She makes sure that he does not catch even a glimpse of her face lest her inner feelings of love be seen. Two *sakhis* stand in readiness should her mood change and the event calls for an amorous celebration. The repentant *nayaka* fixes his gaze on her feet remorse writ on his face for not having kept his tryst perhaps because of another dalliance. The shut door of the room on the terrace is further indication that she would not be giving in so easily but in the dynamics of romantic love it is entirely possible that her displeasure is only feigned. The Deccani artist with his usual penchant for colourful flowers and blossoms renders the *ragamala* with appropriate sensitivity. The artist of this *ragamala* seems to derive his iconography from a Rajasthani text, probably *Sanita Sara Samgraha*, which was used in several early schools of Rajasthan, Malwa and Deccan.

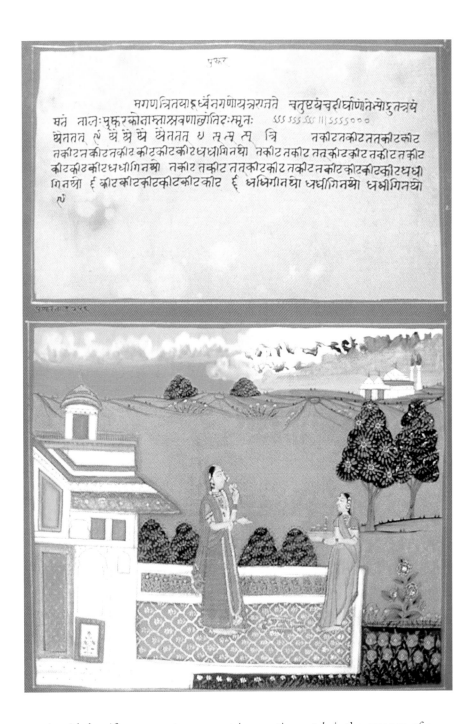

*the changing of the seasons and the
phases of the moon
the tides of the ocean and patterns in
the sky
the whisper of the trees and the
movements of the birds
suggest to those who see and hear the
rhythms of the earth
and it is to the beat of those rhythms
that our lives must resonate*

It is said that if a *raga* captures a certain emotion a *tala* is the essence of a cosmic rhythm. The *talamala* artist deftly uses the various rhythms of music to express human emotions. In this folio the Maharashtra artist takes our attention to a bejeweled *nayika* being met by her *sakhi* in a colourful garden, as she holds a lotus in her left hand and accepts the accessories for an amorous tryst from the *sakhi*. The multiple perspectives in the composition only enhance the romantic tension of anticipation as one almost hears the footfalls of the arriving paramour and the eyes are led away to a distant *haveli*, one is captured by the rhythms of love. *Talamala* paintings seem to be the speciality of Maharashtrian artists. In this and other folios of this genre of painting a Deccani influence is clearly seen suggesting possibly a southern Maharashtra atelier.

If the *sakhi* is the perfect confidant of the *nayika* the *nayaka* needs a friend as well, for many are the needs of one in love. Two folios from this celebrated series of the *Rasamanjari* from Basohli, with its characteristic picturisation of the tastefully appointed room with a prominent and empty bed, leads us into the role of the confidant. As Krishna sits by the empty bed longing for his beloved, he laments to his friend that there is no remedy for the fever in his heart as he yearns for her whose thighs are like plantains, eyes like lotus, locks of hair like *saivala*, face like the moon, speech like nectar, waist like a lotus stalk, navel like a pit, fold in the belly like a stream and hands like leaves. In this folio Krishna has a success story to relate to his friend for he says that he coaxed his beloved to the bed and while she was removing her ornaments, his other friend who was a jester made crowing

पुँधउपतीरॅटक

sounds like that of a rooster heralding the dawn. Both folios while emphasising the empty bed convey beautifully the role that confidants play for the romantic hero in the many twists and turns that love can take. The Basohli artist renders the situation with a rare finess and as we sense the vulnerability of Krishna as the romantic hero he seems all the more human and no less adorable.

Bhanudatta in his Rasamanjari describes three more types of sakhas. The first is pathamarda sakha who appeases an indignant nayika with words such as, speak with sweet words so that the whole earth may feel joyous as if with fragrant nectar. Then there is vita sakha who is adept in lovelore and he tells the nayika: the moon has arisen, bees are humming, Kamadeva is here, how can your pride stay in the presence of such sure remedies? The third is cheta sakha who cleverly brings about the meeting of the lovers and then disappears on some pretense.

A Nayika and a Bird
Guler, c. 1775
Collection:
Victoria and Albert Museum, London

Painters and poets alike show a close affinity between *nayikas* and birds as does this Guler artist. It is a pensive moment for the *nayika*, dressed in a diaphanous attire, as she affectionately holds a hawk on her left hand which has been protected by a silver amulet. While she seems lost in her thoughts, surely of her beloved, she ruminates and draws on the *hukkah*, the bird looks attentively towards her. Any minute now she would utter his name and want the bird to repeat it and that would break the deafening silence and the painful estrangement. The strong monochrome red background with the two cypress trees highlights the bird and deftly heightens the passion of the moment, a moment of intimacy and friendship that belongs only to the *nayika* and her avian friend, as the *sakhi* holding the *hukkah* is reduced to a mere profile in the background.

Talking to a Peacock
Kangra, late 18th century
Collection: Author

Sometimes dismissed as acts of lonely women cloistered in harems and thirsting for love and companionship there is another, more poetic, level of understanding the close association of birds and romantic heroines. In sharing her feelings with birds and drawing strength and succor Indian poets emphasise that the love that surges through the breast of the nayika is not different from the life that animates these birds, in sharing her love with them she entrusts them with her intimate feelings. For her love is too precious, too beautiful to ignore, too fragile to scatter it to the winds, it is a love that can only be understood by a sensitive heart as that of a bird and as she entrusts this love to the bird she lets her thoughts soar heavenward with the bird.

Peacocks are special to a *nayika*. They herald the rain and create a longing in her for the return of her beloved. When she is frightened she seeks the comfort of the peacock. And at other times the mere sight of it creates joy and reinforces her pride and self-assurance of her own beauty. The Guler artist captures one such moment in the life of a *nayika* and a peacock.

The Message of the Crow
Chamba, c. 1800
Collection:
Victoria and Albert Museum

there was no news of his coming
yet her longing made her bosom heave
her left eye lid flicker
the doe-eyed girl adorned herself to
receive him

Bihari. *Sat Sai*

A door is a special part of the home. It is at the junction of the enclosed and protected space inside and the vast and unknown space outside, and is specially important to a *nayika*. It is through the door that her beloved will enter and be warmly received and it is at the same door that she will stand anxiously to see if he is anywhere to be seen. It is at a door that we see the *nayika,* her feet firmly inside but her gaze directed into the distance where her beloved has gone, a gaze that is yearning for a sight of him, for the separation from him has been too intense, the longing for a glance of him too painful. Just then both she and her *sakhi* spot the crow that seems to have brought a message. Women believe that when a crow comes to one's home it tells of a visitor who is coming. Looking at the adornment and the anticipation of the *nayika* and the *sakhi* we should have no doubt who that visitor will be. If the two ducks in the courtyard are any indication the *sakhi* is sure that the *nayika* and the *nayaka* will soon be united and that her longing and waiting will soon be over.

A Sakhi and a Nayika
Guler, late 18th century
Collection: Author

Keshavdas in his Rasikapriya lists two types of sakhis, those who work for the love of the nayika and others who will perform a service for a fee. In the first group are a neighbour, a dancer, female ascetic and faithful servant. In the second are a barber's wife, a gardener's wife, a bangle seller, a beetle seller, goldsmith's daughter, a girl of mixed caste, a clever wife of one who works in ornaments with silk and gold threads. Vatsyaayana in his Kama Sutra lists eight types of sakhis: one who performs the entire job, who does only part of it, who carries letters, who acts on her own account and gets involved with the lover herself, who acts for an innocent young woman, a wife who serves as a go-between, a sakhi who is mute and one who carries a message with a double meaning. Bhanudatta in the Rasamanjari gives this list of sakhis: mandana, one who decorates; upalambha, one who carries a complaint to the nayaka; shiksha, one who instructs the nayika; sakhikrita, one who jests with the nayika; sanghattana, one who unites; virahanivedana, one who describes the plight of the lonely nayika.

Sakhis, play an important role in the romantic life of a *nayika*. Friend, confidant, go-between, she plays a number of varied roles depending on the situation, now comforting, now admonishing, at times jesting and at others carrying messages, but always keeping the welfare of the *nayika* uppermost in her mind. It is such a moment that the Guler artist renders. An expectant *nayika* rests on a blue bolster and welcomes with open arms the arrival of her *sakhi*. The *sakhi* rushes toward her pointing with her left hand, announcing to the *nayika* probably that her beloved is about to come. There is on the face of the *nayika* the excitement of the fulfillment of an anticipated moment, while on that of the *sakhi* the joy of seeing her mistress united with the *nayaka*. The pale architecture provides a contrast to the vivid carpets in this otherwise plain *haveli*.

Patralekha, a love letter
Kulu, late 18th century
Collection: Author

what if we are apart dear girl
you are ever in my thoughts
wherever a kite may fly
the string always remains
in the flier's hands

Bihari. *Sat Sai*

To receive a love letter is a moment well worth waiting for, for it will bring news of his well-being, but even more there will be sweet words of love, perchance a petal or a love token, but most of all his handwriting. For the love-starved *nayika* a love letter is more precious than food, more comforting than *mantras*, more to be treasured than jewels. In his absence she will tuck it inside her clothes and its presence will remind her of his touch. The *nayika* in this folio from Kulu touches a branch of the willow, and like the *salabhanjika*, shares her *rasa* with that of the tree. The presence of the *sakhi* with the *tanpura* suggests that it a celebratory moment and that the letter has carried glad tidings. The simple composition is enlivened by the garland of white flowers that the *nayika* wears, her jewellery that includes a hair ornament, diaphanous *jama* and striped pyjama. Adding their own melodious notes to the music of the *tanpura* are birds on the willow that makes the reading of this love letter a memorable event.

Patralekha, a love letter
Kangra, c. 1790
Collection: Author

what message can I send you?
you are dear to me, I am yours
without you I cannot live

Banabhatta. *Kadambari*

Various are the methods that the *nayika* uses to convey a message and many are its messengers. For there are moments of love that can no longer be contained within oneself, there are certain feelings that must be conveyed, there are emotions that must be expressed, there are times when one needs to touch one's beloved with tender thoughts. This is one such moment in the life of a *nayika* as she writes a love letter. As she occupies the space between two bolsters, with her writing instruments close by, the expression of longing on her face leaves no doubt as to what the contents of the letter will be, a letter that is being written on paper and which will be speedily taken by the waiting *sakhi, patrahari duti,* to her beloved. And as we share this special moment of the *patralekha*, in this painting which is incompletely painted, we think of the tradition of love letters in the tradition, letters on *bhurja* bark, petals of flowers, leaves or on fabric, scratched with a nail or a stylus, letters that have taken unspoken thoughts, unexpressed feelings, desires too intense to be left in the heart, to the beloved.

Patralekha, a love letter
Mughal c. 1750
Collection: Author

Standing spellbound, almost with an iconic presence, between two trees in a lonely forest, unaccompanied by *sakhis*, the *nayika* reads a love letter. Clothed in a cloak of velvety darkness and illuminated within a pool of light, probably from the moon, while the world sleeps the romantic heroine is anxiously awake and has her eyes transfixed on a letter, lovingly held close to her. It is an intensely private moment, a muted moment where only the letter speaks, it is a moment not to be publicly shared but experienced and savoured in romantic isolation, a moment so secret that she dare not even whisper lest the winds may hear, for it is a moment that is to be treasured within the beating of her heart. The artist draws our attention to the *nayika* and her romantic tension by placing her in a dark forest where in spite of its many dangers she, like the *abhisarika nayika,* seeks fulfillment of her love.

Madhavanala Kamakandala
Bilaspur, c. 1700
Collection: Art of the Past, New York

The story of Madhavanala and Kamakandala was written in 1583 by Jodh a court poet of Akbar. Indignant husbands and fathers, residents of Pushpavati, complained to their ruler Gobind Chand about the irresistibly amorous effect on their women of the vina played by Madhavanala. The king put their complaint to test and sent for sixteen girls and shut them up in a room and ordered Madhavanala to play. Under its effect the girls were wildly excited and the king banished Madhavanala from his kingdom. Madhavanala arrived at Kamavati, capital of the kingdom of Kamsen on a day when the sensuous Kamakandala was dancing in court. Madhavanala

In this illustration of this love story the mendicant *vina* player Madhavanala is brought before the king Vikramaditya of Ujjain by two women who had found him in a Shiva temple. The dark appearance and simple clothes mark him as a commoner but he holds his *vina* proudly. The king on the other hand is royally attired with two attendants behind him. The iconic figures in this otherwise bare room are striking and show a turning point in the life and fortune of Madhavanala.

who was not allowed inside, detected a flaw in the music and surmised that one of the musicians had a defective thumb and sent a message to the king. Kamsen was impressed and invited him and gave him gifts. Kamakandala performed and when a bee alighted on her breast she was able to force the bee away by making her breasts move with her breath. Madhavanala was the only one who noticed it and fell in love with Kamakandala and gave her all his

gifts, much to the annoyance of Kamsen who banished him. Madhavanala decided to seek favour with King Vikramaditya of Ujjain and when he could not get an audience with him expressed his grief in a Sanskrit couplet which he wrote on the walls of a Shiva temple. Vikramaditya chanced to read the couplet and summoned Madhavanala, heard his plight and waged a war with Kamsen and united Madhavanala and Kamakandala.

Prem Katha: Stories of Love

213

Nala Damayanti
Kangra, 1820–30
Collection: Author

२७.

It is a happy moment in the lives of Nala and Damayanti as Nala approaches Damayanti in a two-horse open chariot. Dressed in a saffron *jama*, bejewelled and with a plumed turban and wearing his sword under his *patka*, Nala sitting in the open chariot looks distinctly regal. Not to be outdone are the two bluish-white steeds, smart and well-groomed, graciously moving forward. Two *sakhis* receive the groom while an expectant Damayanti with an uplifted hand waits in a *jarokha* inside. The excitement of the moment is shared by women of the town who cannot contain their curiosity and peek outside their windows to catch a glimpse of this royal procession and the handsome prince in particular. The Kangra artist captures this very special moment with his usual finesse and in positioning the procession within rows of homes includes the viewer and gives us a unique vista.

It is in the Aranyaka Parvan of the Mahabharata that rishi Brihadashva relates to Yudhishthira and Bhima the story of Nala and Damayanti. Sri Harsha's Naishadhacharita of the 12th century recreates the same story. The handsome and accomplished Nala was the ruler of Nishadha. The neighbouring kingdom of Vidharbha was ruled by Bhima whose daughter Damayanti was renowned for her beauty. Nala hearing about her virtues fell in love and spent many sleepless nights. Seeking solace in his pleasure garden he saw a golden hamsa. Nala held the bird at which point the bird requested that he not be killed and in return it promised that it would get the prince married to his love. The golden hamsa flew to Kundina the capital of Vidarbha and found Damayanti and described to her the virtues of Nala. Damayanti confessed her love for Nala as well but then fell into a swoon. Her father rushed to her side with the royal physician and his minister. The physician prescribed nalada, a fragrant herb which the minister interpreted as Nala the prince. Hearing this the king organised a swayamvara for his daughter. While preparations were going on for Damayanti's swayamvara Narada went to meet Indra and gave him the news of the event. Indra abandoned the heavenly apsaras and along with the gods Agni, Yama and Varuna decided to go to the swayamvara. As they were approaching the capital Indra met Nala and asked for a favour. Nala was to tell Damayanti that she should choose the gods over anyone else. Nala reluctantly agreed and in turn was given a boon by Indra that he could become invisible. Nala became invisible and entered the chamber of Damayanti and conveyed the message of Indra but Damayanti in turn professed her love for Nala at which time Nala revealed his identity. At Damayanti's swayamvara kings and gods came to ask for her hand. The gods took the form of Nala but Damayanti quickly recognised the true Nala, as being a mortal he blinked when she approached him, but the gods did not. Damayanti's father accepted Nala and arranged her marriage. Kundina took on a festive appearance, houses were decorated and there was music everywhere as Nala rode in his chariot through the city. The women of Kundina rushed to their windows and were so overcome by his beauty that they did not realise that their pearl strings were broken while another put a lotus leaf in her mouth instead of betel.

Nala Damayanti
Bilaspur, 1760–1770
Collection:
Victoria and Albert Museum, London

In these two folios from the same series the Bilaspur artist takes us into a royal wedding. In this folio, amidst a gathering of women of the court, where the priests are conspicuous by their absence, Nala and Damayanti go around the sacred fire. It is a coy Damayanti dressed in the traditional red bridal attire and a regal Nala, and as the two circumambulate tied with the sacred knot, the women show their joy and excitement. Some hold platters of flowers, others containers of vermillion and others express through their hands the joyousness of the event. As musicians outside the pavilion play *shehnais* and the marriage is solemnised a heart-throbbing love story comes to fruition.

In the above folio we are privy to a very special moment. The wedding vows have been exchanged, the celebrations are over, the guests have returned and Damayanti is being led to Nala for the bridal night. While Damayanti herself carries the ritual lamp, her *sakhis* hold a torch, incense and perfumed water. Nala waits with dignity and anticipation.

The Bilaspur artist renders both the scenes with grace and restraint and despite the large number of people in the composition ensures that our eyes stay with the central figures of Nala and Damayanti for, after all, it is their special day. Nala and Damayanti were so happy in each other's company that they did not feel the time go by, much to the annoyance of the gods. Kali contrived to enter the person of Nala and instigated Pushkara to play dice with him. Damayanti dissuaded Nala from engaging in this sport but Nala persisted and lost his entire kingdom and was banished to the forest. Nala discouraged Damayanti from joining him but she insisted. One day Nala was so moved by her state that he decided to desert her so that she could return to her father's home. Finding

herself alone Damayanti was distressed and decided to search for Nala and wandered alone in the forest disregarding snakes and wild animals. She met a caravan and with their help reached the Chedi country and eventually returned to her father's home. In the meantime Nala joined the service of King Rituparna as his charioteer. When Damayanti heard of this she asked her father to arrange another swayamvara and invited Rituparna with his charioteer. It did not take long for Damayanti to recognise Nala and they were united. Nala had a rematch with Pushkara and won his kingdom back.

Sohini Mahinwal
Jaipur, late 18th century
Collection: The British Library

The romance of Sohini and Mahinwal captivated the north in the 18th and 19th centuries and several versions of their story were written in Punjabi and Persian, but it was the ballad written by the poet Fazal Shah of Lahore in the mid-19th century that caught the imagination of the people and led to a number of paintings. According to legend, Mahinwal, whose real name was Mirza Izzat Beg, was the son of a wealthy merchant in Turkey, and came to India during the reign of Shah Jahan. On his return journey he stopped at a small town on the river Chenab and wandered into a potter's shop where he beheld Sohini. Her beauty captivated him and he abandoned the caravan and decided to stay behind so that he could be with Sohini. Eventually he found a job in the potter's shop. Their clandestine love affair soon came to light and Mahinwal was removed from the household. Sohini would cross the river every night with the help of an earthen pot to meet him but her treacherous sister-in-law replaced it with an unbaked pot which dissolved in the river and as Sohini was drowning in the river Mahinwal jumped in to save her, but he drowned too and the next morning their bodies were found in their final embrace.

It is a dark and starry night and the river Chenab that separates Sohini from Mahinwal shimmers in the moonlight. She has reached halfway across, swimming with the aid of an earthen pot. If the flute of Mahinwal from the yonder shore is inviting, the presence of the *fakir* who prays to the river god Khwaja Khizar for protection, is reassuring to her. There is a look of courage in her eyes, and an expression of determination on her face, a willingness to meet any obstacle that comes in her way, such is her love for him. Sitting under a tree, with his red *patka* tied tightly round him, Mahinwal plays on his flute which draws not only Sohini but also the buffaloes which he has tended during the day, and as he will turn his gaze, we are sure that it will light up with the sight of the approaching Sohini. We rejoice, along with the stars, at the meeting of the lovers, but within the velvety folds of the dark night is there a sense of foreboding: could this be their last meeting?

Rupamati and Bazbahadur
Bikaner, late 18th century
Collection: Author

Bazbahadur, the prince of Malwa met the beautiful Rupamati by accident and fell in love with her. Rupamati was not only sensually charming but a talented singer and legend has it that the couple would ride through the hills and valleys of Mandu searching for the secret and miraculous spring of Rewa kund. Baz built a palace by this kund and the couple would hold nocturnal soirees at this place. The songs of Rupamati and Bazbahadur were sung by the itinerant bards of Malwa and were heard even in the court of emperor Akbar. Suleman, the confidant and friend of Baz, disapproved of this romance and through the intervention of her family had Rupamati locked in her room, but Baz rescued her and brought her to his palace in Mandu. Baz's father, the king of Malwa in order to break up this romance ordered Baz to leave Mandu and tour the kingdom. Unable to bear the separation Rupamati sent a message to him through a pigeon and even though Suleman once again tried to intervene, Baz and Rupamati were united and enjoyed romantic bliss. This however was not to last long. Adhamkhan, Akbar's general, waged war against Mandu and Baz died valiantly at the Delhi darwaza defending his kingdom. Adhamkhan asked Rupamati to marry him. Rupamati gave him wine, sang a song and then sucked poison from her hath phool and killed herself. It is said that even today when the wind blows through the deserted palaces of Mandu it whispers of the love of Bazbahadur and Rupamati.

It is a starry night in Mandu and Rupamati and Bazbahadur are on their nocturnal soiree, as was their wont. While the city seen in the distance sleeps, the two faithful steeds keep a watch as Rupamati, having removed her slippers, falls asleep on the knee of Bazbahadur. Dressed in royal regalia, a goblet and a flask by his side, Bazbahadur rests his sword and keeps vigil over his sleeping beloved. In a composition that is dominated by the green of the trees and the bushes, the bluish white horses in the starry black night have a special presence. The Bikaner artist through the choice of colours, fine brush work and the judicious use of perspective has captured the ethos of this celebrated and legendary love of Mandu that would unfold night after night.

Madhu Malati
Kulu AD 1799
Collection:
Jagdish and Kamala Mittal Museum,
Hyderabad

The love story of Madhu Malati is
attributed to Chaturbhujdas Naigam.
The story revolves around a beautiful
girl called Malati who was the daughter
of Raja Chandrasena of Lalitnagar.
Malati loved Madhu who was the son
of her father's minister Tanan Shah.
When Malati expressed her love to
Madhu he did not accept her love as he
was a kayastha and a commoner and
she a brahmin of royal blood. Malati
employed special incantations with the
help of her favourite maid Jaitmala and
finally succeeded in winning over
Madhu. When her father heard of their
marriage he was enraged and sent his
army to kill Madhu. Madhu defeated
the king's army whereupon the king
realised his mistake and learnt that in
his previous life Madhu was none other
than Kama and Malati was Rati. He
then gave his blessings to the marriage.

The colophon of this illustrated manuscript of this popular love story states that it was painted by Bhagvandas in the state of Kulu during the reign of Raja Pritam Singh. The love story of *Madhu Malati* was popular not only in the hill states of the Himalayas but also in Rajasthan. Kulu artists took their inspiration from the murals in their palaces and created iconic figures with strong lines against solid backgrounds, set with a minimum of landscape and without a sky. They were particularly adept in using two shades of red, *singrafi* (cinnabar red) and *mahavari* (carmine) which they deployed not only for skin tones abut also for borders, both of which are seen in this folio. The hero in this folio is seen wearing a *chaubandhi jama* with a *patka* of the same fabric and a *kulahdhar* turban. A shy and reticent Malati at the extreme left of the folio is being led by her *sakhis,* while a kneeling *sakhi* announces their arrival to a waiting Madhu who has lowered his bow and has set his glance on his heroine and there is no doubt that happy times will follow.

Madhu Malati
Jodhpur, c. 1875
Collection:
Prince of Wales Museum, Mumbai

The inset which is a folio from a 19th century Malwa folk manuscript shows Malati at her toilette in the company of her *sakhi*.

Rukmini Haran
Kangra, c. 1820–30
Collection: Author

*Rukmini was the only daughter of
Bhishmaka the king of Vidarbha. Of
matchless beauty Rukmini had an
abiding love for Krishna, the king of
Dwarka and wished to be married to
him. Her brother Rukma had other
plans and wanted her to marry
Sishupala the king of Chedi. Rukmini
fearing this deputed a brahmin to
Krishna with a message and her love
letter to Krishna is one of the most
moving in romantic literature. In it she
writes: my heart has already accepted
you as lord and master. I ask you
therefore to come and rescue me before
Sishupala carries me away. The matter
cannot brook any delay and you must
come here tomorrow. I will be going to
the Parvati temple to offer worship and
that would be the time for you to come.
Sishupala's forces as well as
Jarasindha's will oppose you and will
have to be overcome before you can
have me. If you do not come I will end
my life so that I may at least join you
in my next birth. Krishna lost no time
and mounted his chariot and arrived in
Kundinipura even as the wedding
preparations for Rukmini's marriage to
Sishupala were on. Balarama hearing
of Krishna's sudden departure went to
his side. When Rukmini emerged from
the temple she saw Krishna in his
chariot and without losing any time she
fled towards him and sat in his chariot.*

The Kangra artist leads us right away into the pitched battle that is being
waged between Rukma and Krishna. As the horses charge towards each
other and the charioteers engage each other with their gazes, as flags flutter, the
battle is on and Rukma loses no time in discharging his arrows while he keeps
his sword in readiness. Krishna is also battle-ready and his arrows are not meant
to destroy but only to nullify; a demure Rukmini sits by her side assured that
her lord would win and that her love would be fulfilled. In restricting the
composition to the battle scene we are allowed to concentrate fully on the fury
of the action and even then we cannot but be touched by the glint of love in
Rukmini's eyes, a love so strong that it has led to this conflict.

Dhola Maru
Jodhpur, late 18th century
Collection: Author

It is a triumphant moment, a moment of celebration for all three, Dhola the valiant Rajput, Maru his beloved and the faithful camel and joy is written on all the three faces. And the artist recognises all the three participants in this love story. The sprightly camel, adorned with *ghorbunds*, whisks the lovers away and holds his head high, sure of his path that will take them back where they belong. Dhola holds a spray of flowers and looks lovingly at Maru who in turn returns his affection and offers him a drink even as she carries a flask in her left hand. In keeping the landscape sparse the artist ensures that we enjoy the threesome on their victorious march home.

The story of Dhola Maru is one of the most popular ballads in Rajasthan and is kept alive not only through paintings but by itinerant singers as well. Composed originally by a poet of Jaisalmer by the name of Kallol, Dhola is a young prince of Narwar, near present day Ujjain and is married in his childhood in the town of Pushkar to Maru who was a princess of Pungal which was a state between Bikaner and Jaisalmer. Dhola grew into a valiant young prince and his father, in order to strengthen his political alliance, got him married a second time to the daughter of the king of Malwa. Meanwhile Maru grew up to be a beautiful young woman and desired to be united with Dhola and urged her father to send bards to Narwar to sing of her love for Dhola. When Dhola heard of this he decided to go to Pungal to bring Maru back but was thwarted in his attempts by his scheming and clever wife. Dhola, carried by his faithful camel which was given to him as a dowry when he was married to Maru, managed to reach Pungal after a hazardous desert crossing. When he arrived at Pungal Dhola led the camel to a well as he was thirsty and the rebranas at the well recognised the camel that was given to Dhola as dowry. Word was quickly sent to the king of Pungal and Dhola was warmly received. Dhola and Maru were happy to be reunited and the faithful camel took them back to Narwar.

Dhola Maru
From a 20th century folk manuscript
Collection: Author

Gulshan-i-Ishq
Deccan, 1770
Collection: Author

In a folio from this Deccani romance, we are led into the secluded quarters of Manohar, where despite elegant fountains, opulent canopies, beautiful but empty terraces and an indoor garden replete with blossoming trees, a sombre Manohar dressed in white sits in isolation without any attendants. There is a sense of muted grandeur and an air of starkness is felt both in the ambience of the palace and in the mood of Manohar. This is soon to change as he is approached by a winged angel who promises a romantic rendezvous and Manohar's eyes light up in expectation. The Deccani artist, normally given as he is to a colourful palette, restrains himself as he renders this scene from the story.

The Gulshan-i-Ishq or the Rose Garden of Love is a romance written in Deccani Urdu incorporating words in Persian, Arabic and Marathi. The author Mian Nusrati was a poet at the court of Sultan Sadi Adil Shah II (reigned 1656–1672) to whom he dedicated this work. Nusrati took as his source the Avadhi romance Madhu Malati written by Sheikh Manjhan. Nurati converted this Hindu text to fit the Indo-Persian ambience of the Deccan. The story begins with king Birbal asking angels to carry him to the noted dervish Roshan-e-dil to ask a boon for progeny. The dervish gives him a magic fruit and Manohar is born. Because of an astrological prediction the king tries to save his son from the sufferings of love and builds for him a shining palace with an artificial garden and keeps him in seclusion. One night angels see the prince and carry him in his bed over the seven seas to Dharamnagar and set him down in Madhu Malati's bedroom. In the course of this night both fall in love and exchange promises. When Manohar wakes up he yearns for Madhu Malati and sets out with a large fleet. In the ocean a huge sea snake destroys all his ships but Manohar escapes. He crosses deserts and forests and in the middle of the darkness he meets a dervish who gives him a magic belt. Manohar meets the demon who had abducted Champavati the princess of Maharas. Manohar kills the demon and restores Champavati to her father king Surbal. Surbal arranges for Manohar to meet Madhu Malati secretly but Madhu Malati's mother transforms her daughter into a parrot. The parrot is caught by Chandrasena who brings it back to king Subal. The parrot is transformed into Madhu Malati and Manohar is found and the two lovers are finally united.

Bookcover, *Gita Govinda*, Rajasthan, late 18th century. Collection: Author

BIBLIOGRAPHY

Ambalal, Amit. *Krishna As Shrinathji.* Mapin Publishing Pvt. Ltd. Ahmedabad, 1987

Andhare, Shridhar. *Chronology of Mewar Painting.* Agamkala Prakashan. New Delhi, 1987

Archer, W. G. *Indian Miniatures.* New York Graphic Society. Greenwich, Connecticut, 1960

————. *Pahadi Painting.* Thames and Hudson. London, 1968

————. *Love Songs of Vidyapati.* Motilal Banarsidass. New Delhi, 1963

Ashvaghosa. *Buddhacharita.*

Bahadur, K. P. *Bihari, The Sat Sai.* Penguin (UNESCO). New Delhi, 1990

————. *Love Poems of Ghanananda.* Motilal Banarsidass. New Delhi, 1977

————. *Rasikapriya of Keshavdas.* Motilal Banarsidass. New Delhi, 1972

————. *Poems of Surdas.* Abhinava Publications. New Delhi, 1999

Barrett, Douglas and Gray, Basil. *Indian Painting.* Rizzoli International Publications. New York, 1978

Brown, Norman W. *The Vasant Vilasa.* American Oriental Society. New Haven. Connecticut, 1962

Crill, Rosemary. *Arts of India (1550–1900).* Victoria and Albert Museum, London, 1990

————. *Marwar Painting.* India Book House Limited. Mumbai, 2000

Desai, Vishakha N. *Life At Court. Art For India's Rulers, 16th–19th Centuries.* Museum of Fine Arts. Boston, 1985

Devdhar, Chintaman Ramachandra. *Amarusatakam.* Oriental Book Agency. Poona, 1959

Dwivedi, V. P. *Barahmasa.* Agamkala Prakashan. New Delhi, 1980

Ebeling, Kllaus. *Ragamala Painting.* Ravi Kumar. New Delhi, 1973

Goswamy, B. N. *Essence of Indian Art.* Asian Art Museum. San Francisco, 1986

————. *Krishna The Divine Lover.* B. I. Publications. New Delhi, 1982

Hawley, John Stratton and Wulff, Donna Marie (eds.) *The Divine Consort. Radha And The Goddesses of India.* Beacon Press. Boston, 1982. See "Where Have All The Radhas Gone" by Karine Schomer

Kale, M. R. *The Meghaduta of Kalidasa.* Motilal Banarsidass, New Delhi, 1969

————. *The Ritusamhara of Kalidasa.* Motilal Banarsidass. New Delhi, 1967

Kossak, Steven. *Indian Court Painting, 16th–19th Century.* The Metropolitan Museum of Art. New York, 1997

Krishna, Anand. *Chhavi 2.* Rai Krishnadas Felicitation Volume. Bharat Kala Bhavan. Varanasi, 1981

Losty, Jeremiah P. *Art of the Book.* The British Library. London, 1982

Markel, Stephen. *Pleasure Gardens of the Mind.* Los Angeles County Museum of Art. Los Angeles, 1993

Miller, Barbara Stoller. *Gitagovinda.* Motilal Banarsidass. New Delhi, 1977

Miller, Barbara Stoller. *Phantasies of a Love Thief.* Columbia University Press. New York, 1971

Mittal, Jagdish. *Lalit Kala Journal. An Illustrated Manuscript of Madhu-Malati and Other Paintings From Kulu.* Numbers 3 and 4, March 1957

Pal, Pratapaditya. *Indian Painting. Volume 1.* Los Angeles County Museum of Art. Los Angeles, 1993

————. *The Classical Tradition in Rajput Painting.* The Pierpoint Morgan Library. New York, 1978

Ramanujan, A. K. *Poems of Love And War.* Columbia University Press. New York, 1985

Randhawa, M. S. and Galbriath, J. K. *Indian Painting. The Scene, Themes and Legends.* Houghton Miflin Co. Boston, 1968

Randhawa, M. S. and Bhambri, S. D. *Basohli Paintings Of The Rasamanjari.* Abhinava Publications. New Delhi, 1981

Saigal, Bimal. *Radha Kishangarh. Indian Perspectives.* Ministry of External Affairs. New Delhi, March 2000

Spink, Walter M. *Krishnamandala.* Centre for South Asian Studies. The University of Michigan. Ann Arbor. Michigan, 1971

Srinivasan, K. R. *The Ethos of Indian Literature. A Study of its Romantic Tradition.* Chanakya Publications. New Delhi, 1985

Vaudeville, Charlotte. *Barahmasa in Indian Literatures.* Motilal Banarsidass. New Delhi, 1986

Bibliography

Mithila painting, Madhuban, 20th century. Collection: Author

GLOSSARY

A

abala, a weaker woman

abhisarika, one of the eight heroines

abhinaya, outward expression of emotion

adishilpi, primal artist

adhyatmika, spiritual

advaita, non-dual, monism

adyapi, even now

agama, ancient scripture

aham, a form of Tamil love poetry

ahamkara, ego

alingan, embrace of love

ananda, bliss

anitya, eternal

apabrahmsha, corrupted language

apaureshya, non man-made

apsara, heavenly damsel

ashatchap kavis, eight poets of the Nathadwara tradition

B

bahuvrihi, adjective compound

bandish, poetry for music

barahmasa, twelve months

bhakta, devotee

bhakti, devotion

bhakti shringara, ecstatic devotion

bhandara, store house

bhanita, signature line

bhasha, vernacular language

bhava, emotion

bheda abheda, different yet not different

bhuja patra, bark of birch tree

bidas, betel leaf

braj, part of present day Mathura

brajbhasha, language of *braj*

brahman, cosmic reality

brajbhasha, a dialect of Hindi spoken in *braj*, the land of Krishna

brhat, vast

C

chakravaka, a bird that cries for its mate at sunset on the banks of the Ganga

chataka, a bird that drinks only rain water

chitra, painting

chitravali, a string of paintings

choli, upper garment of women

churidar, lower garment with many folds

D

dampatya, married

darpana, mirror

devamaya, deified form

devata, god

devbhasha, language of the gods

devi, goddess

dharma, moral order

dhoti, lower garment of men

dharmashastra, treatise of ethics

dhoti, lower wrap for men

dhvani, resonance, extended metaphor

dhyana, concentration

diksha, initiation

doha, couplet

dutakavya, messenger poetry

E

ektara, one stringed instrument

G

gaghra, skirt, lower garment of women

ganika, courtesan

gatha, story

geet, song

gokul, land of the cowherds

golaka, mythic abode of the cows

gopa, cowherds

gopi, cowherdess, milk maid

gulal, pink powder

H

haldi, turmeric

hamsa, mythic swan

haveli, mansion

J

jama, lower garment

jarokha, balcony

jivatman, individual soul

jnana, knowledge

K

kadamba, tree sacred to Krishna

kalpavriksha, wish fulfilling tree

kalam, pen, artistic style

Kama, god of love

kama, passion, desire

kamini, desirable woman

karma, volitional action

kathak, a type of classical dance

kavi, poet

kavya, poetry
khandakavya, fragmentary, lyrical poetry
khayal, a form of classical music
kirtan, religious chanting
kobar ghar, home for the newly weds
kulah, conical cap
kshatriya, the warrior caste

L

lata, a creeper
lila, cosmic play, divine sport
lilahava, play with exchange of clothes

M

madhava, name of Krishna
madanika, sensuous woman
madarsa, an Islamic school
madhurya, sweetness
mahakavya, epic poem
manini, offended heroine
mandala, cosmic circular diagram
mantra, ritual formula
mehfil, gathering of poets
mithuna, intercourse
mridanga, double sided drum
muktaka, miniature poem

N

nagarika, urban elite
nari, woman
natya, dance drama
navadha, nine-fold
nayaka, romantic hero
nayika, romantic heroine
nayikabheda, different types of romantic heroines
nigama, Vedic texts
nirguna, devoid of attributes
nirvikalpa, non-ratiocinative

O

odhni, scarf worn over upper garment by women

P

padma, lotus
parakiya, another's (wife)
paratman, cosmic soul
pata, scroll
patka, sash
patli, book cover
patracarca, epistolary art
patrahariduti, love messenger that carries letters
patrakavya, a letter in the form of a poem
patua, scroll painter

phagu, type of ancient Gujarati literature
pichwai, painted fabric at the back of an icon
pitambar, yellow dhoti
pothi, hand written manuscript
praja, people
prakriti, primordial matter
pratibha, inspiration
praudha, mature
prema rasa, Sufi romantic emotion
priyatama, beloved
puram, Tamil heroic poetry
purana, ancient stories
purnatva, wholeness
purusha, man
Purusha, cosmic Man, primal subject
pushtimarga, sect of Vaishnavism
pustaka khana, library

R

raas, circular dance
raja, king
raja rasa, the supreme emotion
raga, musical mode
ragamala, garland of ragas
ragaputra, son of a raga
ragini, wife of raga
ramani, pleasing woman
rasa, aesthetic emotion
rasakavya, poetry of emotion
rasananda, bliss of rasa
rasika, aesthete
rati, source of love
rishi, realised person
ritikala, the time when *ritikavya* was popular
ritikavya, mannered poetry
rta, cosmic order

S

sabda, word
sadhu, acetic, mendicant, godman
sahradaya, one of the same sensibility
saguna, with attributes
sakhi, friend, messenger
sakshat darshan, meeting in person
salabhanjika, tree nymph
samkalpa, intention
sampradaya, religious sect
samsara, phenomenal world
samakara, latent psychic impressions
samyoga, love in union
savikalpa, ratiocinative
sarai, stopping place for caravans
saulabhya, easily available
shanta, peace, serenity

shastra, treatise
shastradan, gift of *shastras*
shehnai, oboe like instrument
shilpa, artist, sculpture
shangar, adornment
shataka, centenary
shyam, another name of Krishna
siksha, training
shringara, romantic
smriti, remembered texts
stupa, funerary mound
sundari, beautiful woman
surasundari, sensuous woman
sutra, pithy couplet
svakiya, one's wife
svayambhu, spontaneous

T

tantra, branch of philosophy
tapas, austerity
thikana, outpost
tilkayat, priests at the Nathadwara temple
torana, festoon

U

upanayana, opening of eyes

V

vairagya, detachment
vasanta, spring
virahini, the lonely heroine
vina, stringed musical instrument
viraha, longing
virahini, a heroine in longing
viyoga, love in separation
vriksha, tree
vrindavana, mythic forest of Krishna lore
vyakarana, grammar

Y

yajamana, one who presides at a yajna
yajna, ritual fire sacrifice
yakshi, celestial damsel who is also the spirit of trees
yatra, pilgrimage
yogi, ascetic, seer